KAY ROSE-HATTRICK

Becoming me
A fairytale THE BEGINNING

ODONATA

2014

Published by Odonata

ISBN: 978-1-78222-296-5

Design, typesetting and ebook creation by Paul Jackson: www.othila.com
Print on demand management by Into Print: www.intoprint.net

www.becomingme.co.uk

EDICATIONS

We never know the love of a parent
till we become parents ourselves.
– Henry Ward Beecher

This book is dedicated to my husband, Tony Rose-Hattrick, for being there for me through thick and thin, despite all odds and judgement from others. It is also dedicated to my daughter, Freya Gabriella Rose-Hattrick, for being the best thing that has ever happened to me, and the catalyst for *Becoming Me*.

This book is also dedicated to my father, Gordon Hattersley (RIP), who never really believed in me, and my mum, Sheila Hattersley, who always believed in me. But I thank them both, for making me who I am today. And I do hope that that's a good person, and the best that I can be.

CONTENTS

Introduction

To be a punk you must not follow a role model,
You must be a role model
And not care what everyone thinks!
– Siouxsie Sioux

Writing and completing this book has been the most life-changing experience ever; that is, after the birth of my beautiful daughter Freya Gabriella in November 2011, which was definitely the most far-reaching. I suppose by writing this book I've laid many old ghosts to rest and undergone a spiritual cleansing. Giving birth to my daughter, whom I gave life to and carried for nine months, gave me new hope for the future and this book became her legacy. I had no other way of making enough money to follow our dream and live a self-sustaining, simple life with chickens and goats in sunny Portugal, and to give Freya some chance of survival in this crazy world. I'm not capable of rejoining the corporate world. I can't; my head would surely explode! Holding Freya in my arms, skin to skin, for the first time, I knew that I could no longer talk about this book – I'd better get it written and sold.

Freya was born, intentionally, on the bathroom floor in a flat above the National News in Sheffield, England. But I like to think Freya's birth made *international news* that night! She certainly came from very humble beginnings, and can only go up in the world now. Thankfully, Ahmed, the newsagent and our landlord, had shut up shop only sixteen minutes earlier as I made the final heave, with my husband by my side. Freya was delivered by Sarah, my wonderful midwife from the home birth team, which sadly no longer exists in Sheffield. Also, a big thanks to Helen, and to Ella, the trainee midwife: it was her first day on the job, and her first ever birth. That's enough of that for now though, as this book covers my life from birth to 40, when they say life begins. It sure did for me.

I started writing the book and set off on this particular journey in January 2009, when I left my employer, NHS Sheffield, with work-related stress. I started writing it for my father so he could finally see the real me, and not the parts he wanted to see. I also needed to write it for myself. I have spent my whole career in communications, so have always been writing something: either an article for my internal newsletter, a staff bulletin, the dreaded *Team Brief* or the dull annual report. I think I always wrote them to make them fun, so that they didn't have the usual boredom factor normally associated with achingly corporate documents. In fact, my annual report won a national award for being just that: not boring.

The tough writing challenge for me was always the press release, as for a number of years I was the sole press officer for an NHS primary care trust (PCT). I was definitely in the hotseat and my heart would always miss a beat if, when I picked up the phone, it was a press enquiry. In those early days, when my confidence was non-existent and my experiences of dealing with national press enquiries were only sporadic, I was anxious, and it showed. You have to be so careful when dealing with journalists because they can quote you as the 'spokesperson'. You can say too much, especially before you've found out the facts. I found many journalists quite intimidating and rude, but once I had gained confidence and I knew more about the PCT's wider remit, I learned how to play their game too.

I am not trained in communications: my degree was in social science. I think this is a much more important skill for a communications manager to learn, in terms of understanding people and how they tick, than how to write a good press release. I didn't find the writing style hard, but I did find the content difficult and I sometimes had to compromise my beliefs. So when internal communications became my sole remit, I was glad to be free of the pressure of the press phone at long last. I loved my job, because I loved the people, and we were one big NHS 'family'.

I wanted people to feel valued by their organisation and did whatever I could to achieve this. I became a UNISON shop steward when I personally became disillusioned with the organisation and the government that controlled us. As you'll see, the two hats that I wore worked in symbiosis at first, but the pressure became too much for me and I had to give priority to my primary post. In fact, the pressure became so much that I had to leave that post too and, in January 2009, I was signed off sick for the second time by my GP, who couldn't believe I'd gone back again. Ironically, the NHS had made me ill.

So why would you want to read my story? I'm not a celebrity, nor indeed rich or successful, and I certainly wouldn't warrant a place in the jungle. But I am real, and I think I speak for many. I worked for the fourth largest employer in the world and currently live in the fourth largest city in England, so statistically I'm just average. But it could easily have been the top three, with this story being written by someone who worked for Asda, and living in Leeds. They say that everyone has a book in them, and we all have our story to tell. In the following pages you will read how I became myself, then lost my identity, then found myself again. *Becoming Me* is my journey, as I did, in fact, write the book!

I think you will be able to empathise with my story. I'm billing it as a fairytale, which is at times ironic, but should surely ensure a happy ending? If you've ever worked for the NHS, lived in Sheffield, London, Hull or Sydney, been a student, taken drugs, been divorced, drank far more than recommended, practised reiki, backpacked, rebelled against your father, lost a cat, had a miscarriage, been bullied, been anorexic or overweight, had friends and family get cancer or Alzheimer's or die, been lied to and shafted by your employers, then I think you'll know what I'm talking about. For I think this is your story too and a story well worth telling.

For this is a journey we should all make once in our lives, a journey into ourselves, as the Buddhist teachings tell us. Because if we are not truly happy with ourselves, then how can we expect others to be happy around us? We just make ourselves miserable that way, and it's a perpetual never-ending misery. I'm naturally a positive person, but still have my dark days, especially with the weather being so utterly wrist-slittingly bad lately, with spring delayed as a result. And I, like most of you, suffer from seasonal adjustment disorder (SAD) to some degree. We all need Vitamin D to function and remain disease-free. Thankfully, the weather seems to be improving, and I'm sitting on my step (my preferred place of writing – ask Margaret, my 84-year old neighbour) writing this on a gloriously sunny day.

It's been so hard writing this book: delving into the dark, dusty recesses of my mind to get it all down in black and white, *fettle* (Sheffield term for clean thoroughly) and be free of emotion I had kept as clutter, or a keepsake for too long; finally expelling it for good. Over the past few months, as I've sat at my kitchen table, or on the back step, listening to Radio 6, my preferred radio station, there have been times when I've burst into tears. Finally letting go, as if it were being sucked out of me by an industrial grade vacuum cleaner. *Becoming Me* is no longer about me; I've become a voyeur, like you, to someone else's life. That person was me, but is definitely not me now, because now I have the fight and the confidence to move my life forward and realise my true potential for the first time this lifetime.

It's taken me four and a half years to get to this point in my life, for me to be finally free of it. I now hand it over to you, the reader. In my defence, I have had a small baby to deal with, and those with kids know how hard that is. Tony, my husband, and I have had countless arguments, to the point of potential breakup. After each chapter I wrote, and then edited, I couldn't help but relive the memory still lodged deep within. This, in turn, understandably brought up the emotion that was still attached. This has, of course, had a massive impact on my energy. It is Tony who has had to deal with my deep, long, untapped emotions being unleashed on him, behind closed doors.

I know I feel so much lighter now that it's finally completed (I know that Tony's relieved!) and my life is in black and white, but it's been the most strenuous self-therapy I could have ever done. The first printed copy (as you can't burn a Kindle, right?) will be thrown onto a ceremonial fire; the second goes to my dad and the third to Tony. I can finally send all my former life into the ether and let it go once and for all. Then I will have a blank canvas on which to be as expressive as I like, so as not to pass on any of my baggage to Freya. Unfortunately, a lot of us pass on our baggage to our children, until we break the cycle.

I had conformed all my life, and as my father had always insisted that we "get a degree, get a job, get a mortgage", it was instilled into me from an early age to be part of the programme. Of course, I did rebel on occasions, as you'll see, but all in all I knuckled down and did my best. But I didn't like the programme; it just wasn't fair and I had to shout about it. I wasn't going to put up and shut up, but I was forced into a corner and I knew I was up against a much stronger opponent and couldn't win, as the tarot cards had foretold. I had to admit defeat and run scared from a system that had ultimately made me ill.

Fear is our worst enemy. To be truly free is to not fear anything but fear itself, and to love unconditionally instead. I finally shook fear into touch when I jumped off that proverbial cliff, like doing a bungee jump without the cord, into the complete unknown, to start a new life in Portugal with my husband, as my dream had foretold. It didn't quite work out as expected and we were forced by God, for want of a better word, back to the society we had fled only six months earlier. But with time outside the UK, as a tourist in a foreign land, we were able to piece ourselves back together again, take a deep breath, and explore other, more preferred ways of living.

We were living free for a while, and we were truly living again. Being on the road does give you that freedom and you become almost undercover when travelling overseas, despite the GB indicators making no secret of your nationality. If truth be known, I'm always slightly embarrassed to say that I'm British, with all its connotations. I'm immensely proud of our music, comedy, art, *Doctor Who* and our achingly dry sense of humour, which not all nations fully grasp. But I am NOT PROUD of our royal heritage, or government these days. That's even before even mentioning the other 'thugs', who at least have an excuse, of being pissed up and incapable. When we travelled abroad we dutifully displayed our fluorescent jackets ('in case of breakdown') for the authorities to see, and we were not stopped by anyone. We even picked up a few locals thumbing lifts along the way.

When we were forced back to Britain in sub-zero temperatures, just before Christmas 2010, with only a van to call our sanctuary and the streets of Sheffield to call our home, it was a different story, and we were met with some hostility. But with the kindness of strangers, empathy of friends and the support of our families, we started to build our life again. God had something else planned for us too, and on Valentine's night 2011 (as we had no money for anything else that night) our beautiful daughter Freya was conceived. She had not been planned by us. I was in the worst financial position I had ever been in in my life, and living in a shared house. But this fairytale had to have a happy ending now: a child was about to be born.

Although my resolve was at rock bottom and confidence blown beyond belief, her birth has been the catalyst to finally become me again. I'm afraid you'll have to read *Becoming Free*, book two, to find out what happened on our adventures through Europe, about the characters we met, what brought us back so soon and our re-entry back into the society we had fled, thinking we would never return. *Becoming Free* picks up where this book ends, and is a diarised account covering one year.

Throughout my life I've had people tell me I'm not intelligent enough, not good enough, not articulate enough, not spiritual enough, and I'm sick of it. How *very dare* they! For a long time, employers, politicians, bankers, lawyers, even peers suppressed me with a language I didn't understand, leaving me feeling stupid and ignorant. But over my forty-something years, I have come to realise that it's all just bravado (bullshit) and that they are actually telling us nothing but lies, to keep us all trapped under their regime. They don't want us to question, because if we do, then they have to justify their actions. I don't like the world I live in and I don't suppose you do too, because, let's face it, who are the winners in this world? It's certainly not the mass population, who are increasingly being bled dry by our government and the higher echelons of society. We all know this.

Not long ago, I was told by a Shelter employee who knocked on our door, and who was promptly invited in, that the homeless charity is now advising people how to remain in their homes. He told us that their message was to pay the council tax, as otherwise you can be sent to prison, and offered advice about the payment of other utility bills. He said that people were opting to go back to the street, because when living in normal society they couldn't afford to pay the rent, utility bills and council tax etc. By staying on the street, where you only have to find money for food, they were under less stress.

Before you can even feed yourself in this society, you've spent most of your hard-earned cash on bills and other unnecessary stuff, keeping you in a perpetual consumerist's dream that doesn't ease the pain, anyway. You're left with very little, if any, to have some fun with or to be spontaneous. A close friend of mine is paying almost exactly the amount in childcare as she's earning from her job. Where is the incentive? She's trapped and she knows it, but thankfully there is another income coming in, and they can afford some luxuries to make it worthwhile – but not many.

Prices are soaring and it's a constant battle trying to keep finances afloat, as wages no longer even cover living costs. This is an incredible stress and worry for us all, before even taking into consideration the other stresses: children, jobs, mortgages etc. The prices of even the staples continue to increase every day, so that the bosses at the top can still make their millions. The rich are getting richer, at the expense of us. But they don't care. Sheffield people still talk about when the bus fare was just 2p and 10p to travel anywhere in town, but privatisation put paid to that. This equates to 6p and 30p now, and not the £1.50 or more that they charge for a one-way journey these days. Bus travel is a luxury, and walking your only option, if you're on a very tight budget. I could go on, and on, about how difficult it is living in this country, but you know the truth anyway.

Although I consider myself to be spiritual, I am not a Christian. I believe Jesus taught us great lessons, in simple terms, for us all to understand. And it couldn't be any simpler: it's all about love. LOVE – LOVE – LOVE. Go on, say it out loud: LOVE – LOVE – LOVE. Now shout it (who cares who can hear you!) and finally sing it, with the Beatles tune playing in the MP3 player in your head: LOVE – LOVE – LOVE. I won't stop you there – feel free to finish the song now and at least next door won't think you're mad; just singing along to an actual radio! Right, by repeating this three times you've made a wish/cast a spell/said a prayer and this has already had a positive effect on the universe. Check out Dr Masaru Emoto, who has done an interesting experiment with ice crystals, giving them positive vibration and then ceasing this vibration. The results are amazing. Remember, over half the human body is water.

The Mayans predicted the 'End of the World' as we know it for 21st December 2012, something that had been on every spiritual person's lips for many years as they discussed with others what they thought was going to happen. Despite what a lot of people feared, I knew the outcome would be positive. I invited close friends over to a group meditation to start at exactly 11:11 GMT and, as they continued for the next hour, I could feel the energy rise from below, reaching me in Freya's room in the attic as it rose ever further into the ether. I had to take her upstairs in the end, as I didn't want her to disturb the deep meditation of the group, but she was understandably overexcited by all our guests.

I had read that if 10 million people across the planet had done a similar thing, sending much-needed positive love energy up to the universe/ether/divine, our planet would move to a higher vibratory level. It is estimated that there were nearer 40 million people participating that day. Where love brings harmony. I could definitely feel that things had shifted, and as we huddled round the fire on that grey but dry day, drinking homemade hot ginger wine, we all agreed that it did feel different somehow. I'm sure that most people would say that it's just bollocks! But what you can see isn't necessarily all there is. What you can feel as instinct/inner understanding is often more real.

One single person cannot initiate change, but collectively, we can achieve anything. If you're still reading, perhaps you'll continue, and if you like the book, then perhaps you could do me a favour? Could you please tell three of your mates about it as well? Word of mouth communication is the most effective way of publicising anything. For although my story has finally been written, I have to get it published and sold and cannot do that without your help. I'm not daunted by the task ahead of me because I know that I can't stop now, even if I wanted to. You may laugh in my face, Dad, but I don't care any more!

My intention has always been to self-publish: not such a daunting task, in our social networking-crazed society, and it is becoming the norm these days. I want to keep the integrity of my story, which I fear a publishing editor would interfere heavily with. And of course, I fear the inevitable rejection from them too! Who knows what the future truly holds, and whether my dreams will come true, but, inspired by Robert Tressell's *The Ragged Trousered Philanthropist*, I go forward with the ethos of philanthropy (love of humanity).

I do have a personal wishlist, or you could call it a manifestation list, which includes Leeloo mark 2, a home in Portugal and my own writing shed! How I'm going to achieve this is a potential Channel 4 documentary, but details will certainly be on my website, www.becomingme.co.uk.

Some names have been changed to protect identities. Some people decided to make up a name for themselves, some weren't given a choice, and some people decided to play themselves in this fairytale. Some people may not like what they hear and what I have to say, but I have to tell the truth, and the truth cannot be libellous. However, I do hope that I don't offend anyone, for that was certainly not my intention. I thank **everyone** in my life, even those characters who have caused me the greatest challenges. Without them, I wouldn't be the person I am today and this story would never have been written. These challenges have come to test me and give me the knowledge and skills to be able to venture further on my quest for the truth. Don't judge me for what I have chosen to experience, but celebrate the lessons I have learned.

I feel like I'm starting to go on a bit now, so I'll let you read on. I hope that you enjoy my life story and its ups and downs – for I have, mostly. We all have the capacity for unconditional love, despite the fear and pain we have to endure every day in this world that we live in. A world where the poor get poorer, and the rich get richer, as inflation and pay rises won't ever balance again. A society in which pensioners die of hypothermia because they are scared of turning on the heating, while the energy companies make millions out of the population. A place where child services and benefits have been cut from people who are already on the breadline. A Britain where the NHS and schools are being privatised in front of our very eyes. The list goes on as to why this country isn't a great place to be at the moment. I'm sure you have your own personal gripes. But you will have to wait until *Becoming We*, book three, for that. I will be asking for contributions in book two.

"So hold on to your hats, for the rollercoaster is about to depart..." And don't forget that tune on your internal MP3 player. One last thing, and I promise I won't ask you to do

anything else, but please, if you've got time, watch the *'Greatest speech of all time'* on YouTube. It's taken from the film *The Great Dictator*, which features Charlie Chaplin as Hitler. It ironically says everything we should aspire to, which is also possible, if we want it to happen. And my special childhood book, *Little Gems of Wisdom* by Fredric Fewings, always taught me that *with hope and faith, we can achieve anything we want to, each day at a time!*

I just hope my father actually reads this bloody book now...

CONVERSATIONS WITH DAD

"Respect is something to be earned, not demanded.
I demand only to respect this."
– Kay Rose-Hattrick

I buried my father this time last week on a cold, rainy day at St Swithin's church in Holmesfield, north-east Derbyshire. Discovering his skin cancer to his ultimate death took only a matter of months, and during this short period it spread rapidly everywhere (even behind his eyes), until we kids had to prepare for the worst. He was desperate to return to Berry Hill to die, but he was just too poorly to leave hospital. I went to see him in Chesterfield Royal Hospital the day before he died and I held his hand, knowing his time was coming to an end.

I only had two hours to spend with him before I caught the bus back to Sheffield to pick up my daughter from nursery; the bus journey had eaten all the other precious time. I knew deep down this would be the last time I saw him and the last opportunity to ask him anything. He told me he didn't want me to talk, but just hold his hand. I did as I was told. The tears started as I held his hand, resting my head on the pillow that the kind patient next to me, who also provided the tissues, had given me to rest on.

Dad looked up twice in the first quiet hour. Holding on to his oxygen mask he asked, almost with annoyance in his tone, "Are you sleeping?" "No," I replied, looking up into his eyes, nose streaming. "Just reflecting."

I joked, "You'll never read my book now." He looked at me and laughed with a wry smile and an obvious sense of relief on his face! I think he was a bit worried about what

I'd written about him, to be honest, but perhaps he was just scared of the truth. I'd just had a meeting with a printer, to talk about potential design, paper, format and typefaces, and I'd felt obliged to mention this. He didn't seem impressed. When I had finally completed the manuscript, Dad had said that he was proud of my achievement in actually writing a book, but that I should set my sights lower, as failure, he said, would hurt.

I was itching to say so many things and ask those final questions of a parent on their deathbed, and although I didn't want to upset him, I knew I would regret it if I didn't and *I* would have to *live* with that.

"Are you proud of me?" I asked him. And he snapped, "I'm proud of all three of you," as if it was a stupid question.

If you're proud of someone, but never let them know, how is that person ever going to know? Surely a wasted opportunity on both sides? I knew that Mum was always proud of us; she told us often enough. And I will always let my own daughter know how proud I am of her, otherwise this could cause some serious damage in later life. Because it did to me. Thank heavens for my mum.

I also asked him, "What are we going to do without you, Dad?" He snapped again: "You'll have to cope without me one day." This was chosen to almost 'big him up' and show him that we cared.

Before I left I asked him one final question: "Is there anything you want to say to me, Dad?"

"No," he snapped again.

I left it at that, but selfishly wanted something: a little gem of wisdom perhaps; some encouragement, or even that there's a letter in the desk drawer. Nothing. I kissed his head and said for the last time, "I love you, Dad," trying desperately to keep my wailing at bay and smiling at the older gentleman in the bed to one side, and thanking the kind gentleman at the other side. They both knew this was the end and they had heard everything; it showed in their understanding eyes.

I came away from the hospital and got on the bus back to the city centre, saying repeatedly, just under my breath, "I hate you, Dad." Then, "I don't hate you; I love you, because you are my father." I didn't understand why he had been the way he had in his last hour; emotionless and without empathy. But that was him through and through. You'd never change him and I guess I should respect that to some extent. I certainly needed to accept it, but he refused to see the real me right to the end, and that made me sad.

I gave the eulogy in church last week (my brother and sister were happy to let me) and was told on numerous occasions afterwards that he would have been proud. I think I truly celebrated his life and achievements, but also gently said the things everyone knew about him anyway. It was, incidentally, my Mayan Kin day, White Spectral Worldbridger, which is all about death and liberation. In my address, I read out an extract from the book about him growing up, which was my first public reading. Afterwards I was approached by many people wanting to read the book when it's out. The church and the wake at the George and Dragon afterwards were full to capacity, which reinforced that he was well-loved and respected, although many people had known him as Grumpy Gordon.

My mum, bless her, didn't have a clue where she was, but she was protected by her sisters and family and kept saying, "Gordon's picking me up soon." She is riddled with Alzheimer's, and was cocooned by her disease in her own little world. She talked about Mr Hitler continuously all afternoon and detailed stories from her childhood, confirmed by Auntie Aileen and Auntie Sue. Death puts the lives of those of the living into an abrupt perspective for a short while, until we forget again why we're truly here. That is *living* and *LOVING* in every moment, as we are all unsure when it will end.

Dad gave us all the best start in life and I thank him wholeheartedly for that. His determination and his success in life have made me even more determined to show him my true potential, wherever he is now. And to show me how not to deal with my own daughter, when I am on my deathbed!

Gordon Hattersley (RIP), I will always love you, for you are my father, but I have to walk without you now and you will *now* walk in *my* shadow. In death, you know everything now, anyway.

Freedom is More
Than a Seven Letter Word

I am not what I ought to be, I am not what I want to be,
I am not what I hope to be in another world;
but still I am not what I once used to be,
and by the grace of God I am what I am.
– John Newton

Typical Sunday morning: Freya dictates the time we get up and, after a change, we go downstairs for breakfast. Mum puts Freya into her playpen, as she has to go to the toilet in a hurry. Freya is unhappy that she's left alone and starts to cry. Daddy gets up grumpy and promptly falls down the stairs. They're a bit of a hazard at the best of times. Too late, and here we go – he lays into me, the full critique of Kay, and it's barely 9am! A short respite while I write this on the step, until I go in again and he continues to tell me I'm not free!

"You see, Kay, you have to be free from within, and you still worry about how people perceive you," says Tony.

"It's true," I declare: "I **am** living a lie!"

The Formative Years – Becoming Me

My childhood was a fairytale, cocooned in innocence and wonder,
only for me to be then catapulted out into the world,
with little real understanding of the true dangers of adulthood.
– Kay Rose-Hattrick

 nce upon a time in a land not very far away, a baby girl was born, on 25th March 1970. This is where this story begins, for in the beginning, it was a fairytale.

I was born at home in a bungalow in Dronfield Woodhouse, the village where John Shuttleworth keeps his caravan. This makes me a Derbyshire lass. My brother, who was born in Nether Edge hospital, was proud to have been born in Sheffield, making him eligible to play cricket for Yorkshire. Up until fairly recently, you couldn't play for Yorkshire County Cricket Club if you weren't born in Yorkshire, and he made me and my sister know that he was special.

My family are made up of me, the youngest, an Aries; Trace, a Scorpio, who is three years older than me, and Mike, a Virgo, who is five years older than me. My mum, Sheila, is a Gemini and my father Gordon a Capricorn; both were born in 1933. The significance of this year will become apparent later. That makes me half-Shiregreen, half-Rotherham; hardly exotic, but at least made famous by the Arctic Monkeys' songs. And the Chuckle Brothers certainly put Rotherham on the map!

My dad, hailing from the Shiregreen area of Sheffield, came from a less privileged background than Mum, as her father, Stanley, had his own bread round. When they were of age, the children joined the family business too. My father's mother, Amy, left her

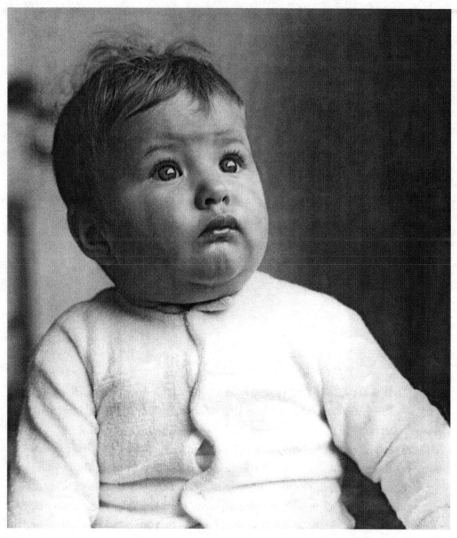

Me, 1970

confinement to attend her husband Cyril's funeral when Dad was only a few days old. It was tough for Nan being a single parent with two children to look after on a buffer's wage. Buffers were the women who polished the cutlery for Sheffield's vast steel plants and it was the lowest-paid part of the production line as they always paid the women less in those days. Dad talks about the hardship she experienced on her own, until she married my grandad when Dad was aged about five. But they only had a few months of married life before Lionel was called up as soon as war was declared by Churchill, as he had been an army man before. The war was tough on everyone but Dad remembered the

KAY ROSE-HATTRICK

tin of precious salmon Grandad would bring with him when he came home on leave. Dad said he wasn't scared during the war, with the sirens and bombing; it was more like an 'adventure', especially when they found a timebomb in the road outside their house.

Mum had been evacuated to the grand Thurcroft Hall in the countryside on the outskirts of Rotherham and stayed with the housekeepers in a separate dwelling, with her siblings and her mum, who had refused to leave them. They wanted for nothing as they grew their own vegetables and had chickens and my mum even had bananas, which were quite a rarity during the war.

My mum and dad met in the Sheffield Ballroom, under the City Hall, and were married in 1960. Four years later, Mike was born. I think it was the hardship that Dad had experienced during his childhood that pushed him to become a successful self-made man. He went to grammar school and then got his articles (accountancy qualifications, paid for by Nan) and joined an accountancy firm. In 1973, he became the senior partner, when he bought out the previous senior partner on his retirement. It was a financial gamble, and a massive strain on Dad at that time, although he made sure it didn't affect us children. I'm told that things were touch and go for a while as he rebuilt the business.

My earliest memories must have been from the age of two, when I remember looking out of the bungalow window at my dad, brother and sister getting into the car and going to work/school, and being desperate to join them. Another early memory is of my siblings tripping me up by pulling a string between opposite doors as I toddled up the corridor. I can remember getting up and dusting myself down and wondering why were they doing that to me and why it was so funny for them. I was told recently that your first memories are always traumatic!

When I was three, we moved to Berry Hill, a detached house in Millthorpe in Derbyshire, which boasts breathtaking views of the scenery across the Cordwell Valley. I found out years later that Millthorpe is also where Edward Carpenter, the English socialist poet, socialist philosopher, anthologist and gay activist lived in the 1800s.

> As a philosopher, he is particularly known for his publication of *Civilisation, its Cause and Cure*, in which he proposes that civilisation is a form of disease that human societies pass through. Civilisations, he says, rarely last more than a thousand years before collapsing, and no society has ever passed through civilisation successfully. His 'cure' is a closer association with the land and greater development of our inner nature.
>
> **– Wikipedia**

Edward Carpenter's 'cure' would become my way of thinking as I grew up unaware of the energy from such a revolutionary that still existed in my small hamlet. EM Forster was said to have been inspired to write *Maurice* following a visit to Millthorpe, where Edward lived openly with his lover, George Merrill. He lived opposite the village pub, grew his own vegetables and made sandals. Although his sexuality was tolerated by the locals, I believe that the police had investigated claims of homosexuality, which was then illegal, on a number of occasions.

Berry Hill was special too, and had been specifically written about in Betty Bunker's *All Their Yesterdays*, self-published in the year that we moved to Millthorpe.

I'm not sure of the exact year in which she died, but she spent the best part of her life in this village. She lived at the top of Millthorpe Lane and I remember her small bungalow in the middle of a field; her envious view available for all to see. Today, two large and very expensive new builds stand there, totally obliterating the scenery. Throughout her life she was an author, researcher and keen archaeologist, and wrote many books about the surrounding area.

I had read about our plot in my mum's copy of her book and was fascinated by the lives of those who went many, many years before Dad had bought the property for £20,000 in 1973. (This equates to £208,000 in today's money, but in this economic madness, is worth much more.)

Her book reads:

> In a garden (formerly a field) some fifty yards to the north of the destroyed hut-sites a smaller hut-circle can still be seen; and in the same garden about forty yards south of the site a remarkable discovery was made in 1952. In clearing a hummock covered with the weed growth of years, it was found that it consisted of a heap of stones of many sizes, and below the stones (which were just dug away haphazardly) several large bones were unearthed, and thrown away without thought. The writer then found a beautifully chipped flint tool, which had obviously been shaped as a borer and scraper. This was saved, and so were several pieces of dark grey, gritty pottery, one piece being from the base of a vessel. Flint flakes were found nearby and several loom-weights. The significance of the site was now apparent, and although no official excavation has been made, the story of 'Bury Hill' and the work of those distant, earliest 'parishioners' was revealed.

I was living on a spot where people had been living since the Neolithic era, thousands of years before the current Berry Hill was built. Those original dwellers shared the same viewpoint, but led such different lives to us. Their energy remained, still inhabiting the places where I would hide as a kid. I used to lie down in the long grass in the middle of a field just down from our house, so that my presence there would not be detected by passers-by or my brother.

My mind was full of thoughts and plans for the future, when I could realise my dreams of being an actress. My mum always referred to me as Sarah Bernhard, the famous actress of the 1920s, because of my over-dramatic portrayal of life's events. Many little girls dream of being an actress when they grow up and I also toyed with being a nun after seeing *The Sound of Music*. But my other career preference was definitely a vet; not a veterinary surgeon, "just a plain vet," I told my Auntie Margaret one day. She told me I would have to concentrate on the sciences to realise that dream. It would never come to pass due to my totally unscientific mind!

I was a sensitive and emotional child, which was understandable with my Cancer ascendant. Water elements are very emotional, and, as you get older, your ascendant becomes as important as your sun sign – some say more. You can go online to get a free chart but to get an accurate one, you have to provide the date, exact time and place of birth. If you don't know already, you can work out your element from the list below:

Fire	Aries	Leo	Sagittarius
Air	Libra	Gemini	Aquarius
Earth	Capricorn	Virgo	Taurus
Water	Cancer	Pisces	Scorpio

If you're an Aquarian, don't forget that although you carry the water, you are very definitely an air sign! I was initiated into the world of astrology by Katrina, one of our close family friends and a client of Dad's. She had settled in Sheffield from her native Germany, along with her dear, late husband Sydney Fowler (RIP). She also gave us German lessons as well as doing our astrological chart. She got me hooked on astrology for life, although I am aware there should be 13 signs, not 12, according to our 13 moon cycle.

Lying in the long grass during those quiet moments away from Mike's bouts of aggression towards his youngest little sister, I started to realise how life was not fair, even in my cushioned world. I didn't realise how much so until my life unfolded. I felt as though I didn't fit in; my head asking all those questions that my parents just couldn't answer. Did I really belong to this family when they had such a different way of thinking to me?

As a kid, I knew we were very privileged in having a swimming pool, installed when I was ten, the same age that we earned the privilege of having ponies. None of us were spoiled though; my father made sure of it. As a self-made man, he wanted to instil the 'work hard/play hard' ethic in us at an early age. Asking for new shoes, or anything really, was pointlessly drawn out by my father, who often reduced us to tears, questioning whether we had cleaned them regularly and had not played out in them. My mother would eventually just shout, "Gordon, for God's sake, they *need* new shoes!"

We didn't get the ponies until every bit of grooming equipment had been bought from our well-earned pocket money, and we didn't get paid until our daily list of chores was completed. We didn't get regular pocket money and it took us over a year until Dad finally honoured his promise and relented to our horse-mad pleas of getting our own. Gentle Fella was first: a 14-hand dark bay gelding, and not long after came Scampi, another dark bay gelding, standing at 13 hands, who was bought from a neighbour with me in mind. Years later, Pat, the neighbour, directed me on my spiritual path when she introduced me to the books of Betty Shine (RIP), a well-known spiritual healer.

Having your own pony is a massive responsibility: they require more looking after than your average pet and you are not in a warm, comfortable house. If you've trained your dog or cat well it will pee outside, or in litter trays, while ponies have no choice but to do it in their stables. And you think cat shit is big! Every morning, Dad would wake us at around 6.30am and we'd pull on our stinking horse clothes and go down to the stables, which were a short distance from the house. I always wore a hat after I'd smelled the strong smell of urine still lingering in my hair in school assembly one morning. We'd only have to muck them out in the winter months but they were long and cold, which didn't help the task ahead.

Me and Scampi, Trace and Fella

Depending on the weather, we would either muck out, feed them and then leave them for the day in the dry stables, or turn them out, having changed their rugs to New Zealands (waterproof rugs) to protect them from the elements, as both Fella and Scampi had their long winter coats clipped. On returning home from school, we had just enough light to repeat the process, so no TV for us. Sometimes Mum would have mucked them out already and on those days we adored our mum even more, as she had saved us at least an hour and a half's work and we had the freedom to do other things. We always managed to finish or take a break for *Grange Hill*, our favourite kids' programme of the time. We got a view of what happened in a real comprehensive, though I'm told it wasn't very truthful. It was still alien to us though, as we went to private schools.

I was never very good at mornings, just as some people can be more nocturnal than others. I remember clearly being dragged out of my slumber by Dad's bellowing cry of "Get up!" being shouted down my lughole. I was blissfully unaware that it was late and that Trace had once again got up for the ponies on her own. But in my dreams, I'd mucked them out and was feeding them when Dad's wake up call rudely yanked me back to the 'reality state'. It was a responsible job for anyone, let alone a ten year old, so I guess I should have had some leeway. I hated leaving my dreams, as those vivid movies I viewed in REM showed a bright future, where I had control of my own life.

I had a very happy childhood, clouded only by Dad getting us to tidy up every Saturday morning while we were trying to watch TV, when Mum had escaped to the hairdresser's. I preferred the sensible BBC, while my brother and sister dominated the TV with their enthusiasm for custard pies instead. This was back when there were still only three channels to choose from, not the hundreds there are today. This must cause many more arguments among siblings, although many kids now have TV in their rooms anyway. It was unheard of back then!

I remember endless summers of riding, swimming, riding, swimming and enjoying life, totally unaware that my life was generally not the 'norm' in this country. All of us were sent to private schools. My sister and I went to Sheffield High School, an all girls' school, and my brother was sent away to Repton; a private school previously attended by Roald Dahl. He shared a dorm with the sons of David Bellamy, Stuart Hall and Tom Baker. I remember going to his very posh open days and having afternoon tea, watching cricket and meeting his masters and classmates; all extremely well spoken and many with half a pound of plums in their mouths. We used to rag him about his accent and for pronouncing the non-existent 'r' in master or bath: certainly not the northern way! He just had to fit in, I guess, but he learned to adjust his accent according to his company after our continuous "You're so posh!" comments.

At least twice a year Mum would pack the caravan, make a picnic for the journey, bundle us into the car and we would set off on an adventure, always asking whether we could eat the picnic as we pulled out of the drive, as all kids do. We would rarely go to the same place twice, as Dad driving with Mike as navigator took us all around England, Scotland and Wales. My love of being on the road and travelling must have started here. We usually went to sites on farmers' fields, where we would immediately make friends with the farmer and his wife and help milk the cows, collect the eggs or just be a patient observer of life on the farm. I even drove a tractor at ten, my greatest achievement of liberation back then, as my brother had missed out as he'd found a girlfriend that day.

That year, I fell for my first boy, Danny. He was lovely, but clearly didn't fall for my first attempts at flirting. However, I recall my brother and his sister coming back with smiles; it was obvious they'd just been in the hayloft. It was all so innocent; like a scene from *Tess of the d'Urbervilles*, but with with Angel, not d'Urberville, although the landscape was Hardy's, that's for sure.

On another caravanning holiday, we went to Laugharne in South Wales, where Dylan Thomas lived and wrote *Under Milk Wood*, something that Dad played on our tape player in the car on long journeys. I remember this trip vividly and can still picture walking to his writing shed in the garden of his family home overlooking the bay, and which he used as the inspiration for his fictitious town of Llaregubb (bugger all backwards), which he describes in the beginning of this classic radio drama. His shed also gave me inspiration as I peered through the window, with Dylan's pen and writing tranklements (small precious objects) still on the desk as though he was only away from his desk for a short time, perhaps to get a cuppa. As I turned round to see his perspective, I became an *Under Milk Wood* fan straight away, and started reading the printed copy that Dad had bought at the shop. That day I acquired my own inspiration to be a writer, mainly because I wanted that shed! I'd love a shed of my own some day.

We were taught to respect the countryside, and with our responsibility for so many animals at an early age, I became at one with nature and its beauty. One year we couldn't go on our usual summer caravanning holiday as Berry Hill was at full capacity and it would have been quite a favour to ask of anyone to pet sit for a full two weeks. We had two ponies, one dog, four puppies, one cat, twelve rabbits and a goldfish called Fin.

Fin killed himself by jumping out of his tank. I saw him quite dead and unmoving on my bedroom floor, so I threw myself down beside him in floods of tears. This is where I was found by my sister and Mum, who had run up the stairs to attend to the screams. He'd had a good innings and lived for about two years, so much longer than most fairground fish. He was the only animal allowed in my room, so I used to chat away with him about all sorts.

With Brandy

We always had ginger toms, starting with Sandy, then Brandy, who would scarper when he saw me as a very young tot. If I caught him though, he would nap for hours in my pram with a bonnet on his head, until he could stand it no more and make a swift and understandable exit. Next came Bouli, a nickname for a baby boy in Greek. He was named after my first love, Bobby Bacopoulos from Boston, whom I had met on holiday in Crete when I was fifteen. Bouli went from being a very scared farm kitten to a cat who spent hours curled on your knee. Connie was a black female, breaking the tradition of ginger toms when I brought her back from Hull in around 1990. She became Mum's little darling and followed her everywhere.

We buried all our pets in the 'graveyard' above the paddock. It was a dark, sunless area covered by a canopy of trees, but was brightened up by the flowers that we put on their graves and little notes. There must have been a couple of hamsters and several cats and rabbits who ended up there over the years, but not Fin. His ceremony took place next to the loo as he had a watery grave, obviously. I suppose we learned about death and the cycle of life at an early age. When I was twelve, my grandad died, and as he lay in the front room on the day of his funeral my mum encouraged us all to go and say goodbye to him and even kiss him. I refused, telling her that the shell in the front room was not my grandad and that he had already left his body.

Trace and I with Sandy (Little Boy), Peanuts, Sandy and Elsa

Elsa, one of Kelty's puppies, lived until she was about twelve and she died in Mum's arms. I remember that unique smell after her passing, which stayed up your nose and was death itself. She was a dear thing and much loved. Elsa was the lovechild of Harvey, the 'Holmesfield stud' who must have got to Kelty while she was tied up one day when in heat. Three months later, she was acting quite strangely so Mum threw a towel on the floor for her to sleep on, as an alternative to her usual chair. The next morning, we heard Dad open the door of the porch to let the dog out, and then the scream: "Sheila!" Overnight, Kelty had given birth to four beautiful puppies. We kept Elsa and the other three all went to loving homes with Auntie Sue, my friend Rachel from school and the bread woman.

Kelty's end was inevitable. Every time she heard horses come up the road, which was often, she would rush out, barking loudly, and would nip the horses' ankles just as her instincts told her to. There were no sheep in the neighbouring fields, just dairy cows. When the family were outside, we would all be on alert, but once she'd got the scent, before we had even heard the clippety-clop of the horses' shoes on tarmac, no amount of calling would deter her from her mission in rounding them up. It was amazing that she lasted until the age of six before nipping her final ankle. On that sad day, a car had been overtaking the horses and the driver didn't see the barking dog run into the road. She died in Mum's arms too.

We had several rabbits as Godley Gardens (which is now a car park), who sold us our first two, were unable to sex them properly. They clearly weren't two males, as bought, as there was always a litter due. The litters, depending on their size, were called either Flip and Flop or Snap, Crackle and Pop. At one time, we had a small runt called Handful, not because of his boisterous nature, but because he could fit in my small hand. Mum left Handful in the porch where the puppies lived one night as she really didn't think he would make it through the night. But during the night, Handful had jumped out of his box and was found by my sister suckling on Kelty's teets, as an accepted adoptee. That little rabbit was fine after that and grew up to be as healthy as his siblings.

During the holidays, my brother was responsible for my musical education so that, unlike my peers, who were mainly 'Durannies', I listened to the Undertones, X-Ray Spex, Siouxsie and the Banshees and

With either a Flip or a Flop

Pink Floyd. The first single I ever bought was the dear late Ian Dury's 'Hit Me With Your Rhythm Stick'. I cried at my brother's party when, against my blushing protests, he played the B side, 'There Ain't Half Been Some Clever Bastards'. I was ten and very pure. The first album I bought was by the Bay City Rollers and I fell in love with Leslie, the lead singer, like most other girls of my age did in the 70s. I also continuously listened to Mike's copy of *Stairway to Heaven* by Led Zeppelin on the record player, and learned every word. When the Police started out, back in the late 70s, my brother was a fan, until my sister saw them on *Top of the Pops* and that was it: she was hooked big time. Maybe it was Sting's sex appeal, but after that, my brother didn't want to know that particular trio any more, as Trace liked them now! We always watched *Top of the Pops* and were avid listeners to the Sunday night radio chart show, recording our favourite songs every week.

Mike played guitar and would practise for hours. Whenever he'd learned a new tune he'd call me into his room and wouldn't let me leave until I'd heard his latest rendition, performed with a distant look on his face, while I protested that I'd heard it enough! He was in a band at school and then in several bands with my cousin Sean, a bassist. The late, great John Peel (RIP) even saw the potential in one lineup, when he played their single on his radio show several times. Sean and Mike were inseparable; only months apart in age and at every opportunity during holidays and weekends they would get together, alternating between my Auntie Aileen and Uncle Tony's house in the Bawtry area, or at our house. Sean and Mike liked to torment me when I was a kid and I had to fight back, which of course made me stronger. One day, they tied me to a lamp post in the garden and left me trying to wriggle out of the restraints as I claimed I could. I was finally rescued by Trace after about an hour, and had quite severe rope burns. Trace and I loved Sean and he was always our favourite cousin, despite his joint antics with Mike, as he stuck up for us in front of our brother.

My father was an amateur photographer and never missed his Thursday night camera club. As kids, we'd have to pose for hours while he got the lighting just right, and our photos would be entered into many competitions. We'd watch as he developed the film in his darkroom, and the image would magically appear on the paper in front of us. He produced some wonderful shots of us as children. My brother followed suit and is also an excellent photographer. He inherited Dad's ability to calculate shutter speed over aperture size with ease. Although I love photography, the technical side has always hurt my head and left me baffled, so I generally just concentrate on composition myself and let the camera do the rest.

At thirteen, I became moderately anorexic, which I believe prevented me from starting my periods until the fairly late age of fifteen. My lifelong battle with food started at puberty, when Dad used to catch us opening the fridge other than at meal times and shout, "You'll get fat, you know!" You've got to be so very careful with comments to adolescents about their weight. The final straw for me was when I saw the photos from our first foreign holiday, in Austria when I was twelve. In every shot, I'm eating some wonderful Austrian ice-cream dessert and my double chin is in shot in every one. Dad said to me, "Well, do something about it then. I bet you can't!" I remember leaving the Kit-Kat I had next to me for my pudding in defiance and then becoming food-obsessed for the next two years.

I went on the scales at every opportunity and if I went over six stones I was horrified, often sticking my fingers down my throat to get rid of unwanted calories. The next year's holiday photos, in Austria again, showed a very different me. I looked gaunt and there are no shots of me with ice-cream. I thankfully got to a weight which I was happy with and had a fairly good figure into my late teens and early twenties. I was given a wakeup call by the supermodel Cheryl Tiegs, when I was given her autobiography to read by our fashionable friend Phoebe, who was a few years older than Trace.

Phoebe loved that vacuous model/celebrity world and bought into it BIG time with her immaculately dyed and perfectly straight long blonde hair, false nails, a Chanel bag on her raised arm and full, overly-glossed lips, defined harshly with lip liner (all still fashionable I see).

She once said to Trace, "Tracy, there are three levels of good looks – attractive, pretty and beautiful. You're attractive, but I'm beautiful."

At that point I just burst out laughing at her sheer vanity, and if truth be known, my sister was naturally beautiful, while Phoebe had to pay out an awful lot of money for her 'beauty' on a receptionist's modest salary. We just found her amusing and laughed at her insincerity; not in front of her face of course – we were too polite for that. She taught us stuff about clothes and makeup and that you can achieve anything you set your heart on as long as you want it enough. She hadn't excelled in school and her only way out to pay for her lavish and consumerist lifestyle was to marry well. And she did; Trace even introduced them at our local nightclub, Fanny's, and they were married a few years later, after we had all drifted apart.

Phoebe lent us Cheryl Tiegs' autobiography, which had a big influence on my anorexia. Cheryl had been anorexic and bulimic and even used to go through the bins outside her flat and outside hotels to look for food. I read how she had overcome this physically and emotionally by following a healthy diet and addressing the psychological aspects of her 'illness'. This model was inspirational and gorgeous and I remember reading that each piece of jewellery she wore told a story; especially the elephant that she wore round her neck. She advised simple but good pieces of jewellery, and I've followed that rule ever since, though I own very little these days! Her own life-change influenced me profoundly and once I just started being happy with myself, I was no longer so heavily influenced by skinny celebrity role models and the look that was considered so cool. In my late twenties, I would balloon to a size 22, but that would be a different story.

At the Girls' High School, I met a girl by the name of Zoë Heath, who would become a lifelong friend. We always used to joke that we both shared names with key names in the government. Mine was Hattersley; Roy comes from this part of the world and doesn't look dissimilar to my father. Zoë came from a similar background to me and was also horse-mad. Her parents relented before mine, but when we did both get ponies, we spent a lot of time bombing around the country roads, and when we were older, enjoying a glass of my mum's homemade wine and a swim after a long hack. Zoë and I had a playground argument one year, and for a while, we changed 'best' friends with Pippa and Debbie, who'd also had an argument. This is when Debbie and I became close.

Debbie's background was quite different from mine: she lived on an estate in Sheffield, was very bright and got a scholarship. I got my first introduction to boys of my own age at her youth club. I was so nervous, and as I remember, my initiation left me bright red in the face. At the High School, I also met Tamara, and I became very close to her in the fifth year.

Tamara had family connections over in Israel, and in the summer of 1986, we planned to stay on a kibbutz. But Tamara had to be rushed into hospital and she spent the summer recuperating in Sheffield and so our trip had to be cancelled. I often think about how that trip would have altered me and made me much more aware of the world I lived in beyond the 'safety' of these shores.

I managed to get 6 'O' levels and later, after three attempts, got my maths CSE, grade 1. How could I be so crap at maths when my father was a chartered accountant? I believe I have numeric dyslexia, which is called dyscalculia. My other disability is that my hearing is like a radio not quite tuned in. I actually told my French conversation tutor at college about my 'disability', but I think he laughed out loud, probably thinking I was making an excuse for failing my conversation exam. Despite working in live music venues and being a drummer I've always suffered from this condition, believe me.

I always felt 'thick' at the High School and was always in the bottom set, except for French. Poor Miss Barnes, the second set French teacher, had to deal with me. I recall how I'd shamefully make elaborate excuses as to why my homework was not in on time and although she didn't believe me (I even used the 'dog ate my homework' excuse), I think she secretly enjoyed my performance! I loved performing and was once clapped for my rendition of a Shakespeare character in a play that we were reading in class. Most of the other girls were far brighter than me though, and so at an early age I knew my place.

I did learn some things parrot fashion, including several poems and some classic Shakespeare speeches, which are still part of my repertoire. Zoë and I recited a poem one morning in assembly at primary school. It was by WF Holmes, and called *The Old Brown Horse*. It was about a retired working horse whom everyone, including his owner, forgets, and so I made every effort to remember it. Not bad really, as I can still recite it; every line imprinted on my memory from all those years ago. I had a cherished book called *Little Gems of Wisdom*, by Fredric Fewings, which my parents bought for me one year on one of our caravanning holidays. It became my special book and taught me a few important lessons that I have carried with me throughout my life. I gave the book to my stepdaughter: she can also recite it from cover to cover, and I've recently tracked down another copy (it was published in 1975 and is no longer in print), which I will give to my own daughter when she is old enough. Unfortunately, for copyright reasons, I'm unable to share anything with you.

I was rubbish at sport as well as everything else and one year, my report read, "Kay is uncoordinated." How *very dare* she! She could have said that I'm slow at running and not great at hockey but not that word. I thought I was quite good at dancing, inheriting it from my dad, who was a great jiver, but not 'uncoordinated', as Mrs Rankin had reported to my parents. I was not too bad at the high jump, the only sport I'd represent Stanley, my house, in. One year I ran in a hurdles race against faster opponents and instead of being humiliated and finishing last I pretended to fall. All this sort of stuff affects you and moulds you into the adult you'll become. Until fairly recently I believed my 'press' and behaved accordingly. A thick child turns into a thick adult.

It didn't seem to worry Dad that Trace and I weren't very gifted academically. Maybe he thought we'd marry well and wouldn't need a decently paid profession, having a husband who would keep us in the lifestyle to which we had become accustomed. With Mike, it was different. After every term, Dad used to close the study door and then berate him at length for the grades on the latest report he had brought home from school. We'd listen at the door, of course, and afterwards we'd have to cheer Mike up as he was so down. The pressure was certainly on Mike to achieve his grades as Dad had forked out 'big time' for his education, but all he wanted to do was play in a band. Dad later admitted that he worried for our future and providing us with the best education was the one thing he could do.

At the Sheffield High School, we were groomed academically, but rarely touching on the right brain capabilities for us to develop our creative side: we didn't even do home economics or woodwork. But after a recent High School reunion, where I met some of my wonderful old school mates after 27 years apart, and we were let loose around our old classrooms, I realise they have addressed this considerably. The school now has a new performing arts centre, a massively extended arts and music department and even offer guitar lessons. Oh, things could have been so different!

The one thing I would like to put straight though is the level of bitchiness in the school. There didn't seem to be any in our year. People presume that because the school was girls only, bitchiness must have been rife. Wrong. What's the one thing that causes the majority of bitching in other schools? Boys, and the inevitable "Does she fancy him? He fancies her and she's just dumped him!" etc, etc. There was none of this, as there was no opposite sex, and so everyone mainly got along. That said, I don't necessarily agree with single sex schools; they give you a false perception of life, making it harder to understand the opposite sex as you start to form your own relationships. But, let's face it, will we ever understand men, ladies? However, it did enable me to have the freedom to be me without a daily adolescent male presence disturbing my true self-progression. I think otherwise, I'd have got into lots of fights with my pent-up aggression unleashed and frustration about 'just being a girl' would have prevailed.

I managed to get out of the washing up, one of our daily chores, because I questioned, "Why should I do the washing up, just because I'm a girl? Why can't I cut the grass like Mike?" Feminism had hit me early and my parents, not wanting a feminist debate, let my poor sister do it solo. Trace had already broken free of the constraints of the Sheffield High School and went to St Mary's High School, a Catholic school in Chesterfield run by nuns, but with a mixed sixth form. I followed three years later and this is where I would meet my second husband.

My sister Trace was the sister that everyone wanted. She doted on me and took me everywhere with her, including to Fanny's nightclub (underage on my part), a regular haunt that was just a short taxi ride from our house. We were very often joined by my other 'sister' and Trace's best friend, Sienna. We were horrible to Sienna and playfully picked on her. One night, when she stayed at our house after Fanny's, we fed her dog biscuits, telling her that they were sausage rolls. She'd have eaten anything, quite frankly, and on returning home she always raided the fridge, but she was even more gullible than me.

It was Sienna's mother who stopped the bleeding when the drummer from Def Leppard crashed opposite her house on New Year's Eve 1988. Thankfully for Rick Allen, Aunty Billy, who was a nurse and was not fazed by the crash site, even though his arm had been severed, attended to him before the emergency services arrived. He later dedicated an album to her as thanks for looking after him on the night of his accident.

Sienna was still considered the 'hardest' girl in school and my friendship came in quite useful during the one and only attempt to bully me, by a girl in the year above. I forget what the 'bully' said but she was definitely trying to 'assert' her authority over me. Unfazed, I said confidently, "Do you want me to tell Sienna about this?" The 'bully' replied, "Do you know Sienna?" and promptly made a quick getaway!

The first day at St Mary's sixth form was the scariest of my life; I wasn't in an all girls' school now: there were boys too. I went with my friend Claire who'd been at the High School with me and we hung on to each other for the first few months and sat next to each other in English.

Unfortunately for me, I was humiliated in my first English class, after I'd attempted to answer a question posed by the teacher about the text that we were reading. To our right sat Theodore, and Ian Hyland (who would become the entertainment editor of the *News of the World* before its demise, and who is currently with the *Daily Mirror*), and they howled with laughter at my answer. One of them said loudly, "She's about as articulate..." and the other one drew a lorry and held it up so I could see. I never blamed Ian for some reason; nor did I forgive him along the way, but I did blame Theodore. Ian would go on to humiliate famous people for a living instead, adopting the title 'The TV critic with the widescreen mouth', due to his 'outspoken, self-assertive style'. Theodore was one of the cleverest boys in the school: with a high IQ he was considered a genius by Mensa and left school with four 'A' levels, all at grade A. He had shattered my confidence beyond belief and I didn't say one more word in a classroom setting until about four years later.

I was told by my peers that Theodore fancied me. It didn't help much, but I eventually broke my 'silence' when I was in a tutorial group in my second year degree course. I was listening to other people's views thinking, "Hold on a moment, I have more of a valid point to make than these people," and broke my silence. I'll never forget the surprised look on my tutor's face, because I'd spoken. Thankfully, he responded with, "That's a very valid point, Kay," and from that moment on, I started to rebuild my confidence.

Theodore would become my second husband, and before I married him, years later, I asked a mutual friend, Brian P Mitchell, if Theodore was too intelligent for me. He said, "Kay, he wouldn't be marrying you if he thought that." After all those years the spell was well and truly broken.

Despite the blight on my confidence, I struggled on. Academia never came easy to me. I found it very difficult remembering information and didn't have a photographic mind. I could only learn through being shown something and then doing it myself. Pictures helped too and I turned those dreaded numbers into cartoon-like characters. We are all different and have such different skills but it took me some time to realise that. I've come to understand myself and my capabilities now, but back then, I let my peers judge me and put me into that 'thick' pigeonhole again.

I cried when I found out that I'd only got one 'A' level. Well, more descriptively, I threw myself into the nearest corner of the school car park in hysterics, thinking my life was ruined. I was brought back together again by Claire's mum, with lots of love and reassurance and a drop of brandy. I also have to thank a lovely man at Humberside College of Higher Education, who persuaded me not to go back to school and re-sit. In the end, I enrolled on a BTEC HND which included French, which I had failed at 'A' level, as well as English. I left school with only one 'A' level (D in German) and a severe confidence issue.

My education did feed my love of literature though, and I still love the texts that I read. They took me into another world in another time. My love of social history stems from Hardy, Larkin and ultimately George Orwell. I connected with Orwell and his brilliant social observations, which capture his era like a camera, and I read all his books with enthusiasm. He was a middle class boy who put himself into poverty in order to truly understand the plight of the poor. Money has always symbolised power and when money is scarce, fear is abundant. Every waking hour concerned with that primal instinct of survival is beautifully observed in *Down and Out in Paris and London*, when he lived at the bottom rung of society as a *plongeur* (kitchen porter), when he could get work.

My life outside the constraints of my father's rules had started; I left home for a new adventure in September 1988 and I was ready for it.

KAY ROSE-HATTRICK

The College Years – Sex, Drugs & Rock & Roll

To live in a bubble of safeness, is to not experience life to its full.
– Kay Rose-Hattrick

The polytechnics I had applied to wouldn't take me, because I had only got one 'A' level, but I was definitely not going to resit them. I applied to Humberside College of Higher Education to do an HND in European marketing. The college became a polytechnic before I was issued with my HND, and by the time I graduated with a BA (hons) in social science, it had become the University of Humberside.

I lived in Murdoch Halls, an all girls' house. It seemed that I was still being prevented from properly integrating with the opposite sex. The other houses on campus were all mixed and situated on the Cottingham Road site, which was bang right next to the university, meaning that we could share facilities, including the students' union and the library. The day I was dropped off at my halls in Hull was certainly liberating for me, and when my parents had settled me in and had left me on my own, I knew I could be truly me with my new-found independence.

In Murdoch, like in most of the other halls, we were provided with our own room. All were decorated in four different colours (mine was blue), but they all had the same furniture: the same single bed, a desk, wardrobe and drawers, so as to make them uniform. We had to share a communal shower down the corridor, but there was a washbasin in each room. Once I'd made it mine: put up some posters, put my clothes away and arranged my trinkets, I knew I had to leave my new sanctuary and make some new friends. I made the decision to turn right first and knocked nervously at the door next to mine. Little did I know, my neighbour was a French girl, and when I knocked on the door my knock was met with loud shouts in French, which was beyond me, so I panicked. With my severe lack of confidence I ran directly back to my room to centre myself, take some deep breaths and force myself out of my room again.

This time I knocked directly opposite and the flame-haired Jeanette, a mature student and a sweetie, came to my rescue, sitting me down and making me a cup of tea. She took me under her wing for a time, until I'd made other friends of my own age, but remained opposite me for the year in halls, for support. She became buddies with the neighbour to my left, who was a pyromaniac, and who burned the name signs on the doors of the whole floor, except mine and Jeanette's.

For the first year, I knocked around with Justine, Jenny and Alison, and later SJ and Claire who lived on the floor above me in the halls. We would all eat together in the refectory for breakfast, lunch and dinner as we were all full board. Justine, or Ju Ju, as we called her, was responsible for introducing me to my first husband and getting me in to the Smiths, the Cure and fags. We would buy a packet of ten, which would last the weekend between us. I gradually increased my consumption, perhaps to fit in and look cool, but most of our friends smoked too and it was commonplace.

A usual weekend was generally spent getting drunk, like most students do. We would always go over to Hull University's student union for a few then go back over to our union for a late night disco and cheap beer. I liked the university: you could almost touch their intellect, like some prize possession, and I would never let them openly know I was only doing an HND (Have No Degree, as it was cruelly billed on the toilet paper dispensers). One night, when we were out for the usual drinks at the university union, one of my friends from our college was chatting to a pretty young girl at the bar, and for a moment, "she seemed really interested," he told us. It was when he mentioned something about next door that she disappointingly asked, "Oh… are you from the polytechnic?" and without another word, she was off. It was then I realised that there was a 'them and us' attitude, which unfortunately put me off joining the university's drama society to further my love of acting. When I went to enquire, they had made me feel excluded and intimidated.

Sylvain, a French exchange student in the year above me on our course, was my first boyfriend. He studied in Hull for three months and then went back to Lyon to continue his studies. During these months he fell in love with me and even took out a loan to come over to England to visit me after he'd gone back home. Sylvain, who was not only sweet, gorgeous and sexy, was also a gymnast who had competed in French national gymnastic competitions, and he would perform impressive backflips down the corridor for me. I shamefully bombed him out during this visit, when I told him the relationship was over.

The problem was that I felt frustrated and tied down by having a relationship when I'd only just started to mix properly with my male peers. I had just broken free and didn't want to be kept inside that box that a relationship tends to dictate. Sylvain and I remained friends despite our split; he went out with my friend Sam and we both visited him and his family in Lyon the following year. I would never dump anyone else at college as everyone I liked just wanted to be my friend!

After the first year of my HND, Penny, a fellow student on the course, and I decided to go to the south of France to get jobs for the summer to practise our French. That was the plan, and we set off on a National Express coach from London all the way to Nice with only enough money to last us a couple of weeks, and not even a tent. No wonder my dad was once again concerned at my recklessness, but my mum was behind me again all the way. We arrived in Nice with Prince's *Under the Cherry Moon* on my walkman and we soaked up the atmosphere of this stylish city. I'd seen scenes from Nice in Prince's movie, filmed a few years before, and I was a little in awe of the jetset lifestyle it portrayed at the time.

On arrival, we searched for hours for a place to stay but it was the same message everywhere: *"La guesthouse est plein."* We were finally taken pity on by a guesthouse owner who allowed us to stay on his sofa *gratuitement*. The following day, we went to a campsite just outside the city and stayed there under the stars, without canvas, with just our possessions and sleeping bags piled up on a groundsheet. We moved to another campsite in Antibes after a few days, on a recommendation from another camper, and we were able to borrow a very small tent for the duration of our stay and until we secured jobs. On the campsite in Antibes we met some very stylish Italian men who rode mopeds without helmets, and who could speak very little English. I could say the usual "hello", "a beer, please" and "ciao", of course, but also a phrase that I learned on a school skiing trip to Italy when I was fourteen. This phrase has always broken the ice with the Italian men I've met. I don't pronounce it terribly well, I'm told: *"Vuoi ballare con me?"* ("Will you dance with me?"). Learn it ladies: the Italian men will think you're great, believe me!

One night we decided to have an impromptu party at the campsite and I was tasked with getting the booze from town on the back of a moped, driven by an extremely sexy Italian man. Italians are just inherently stylish and cool; they can't help themselves. I was very much English and definitely not cool. Thankfully, neither of us could understand a word each other said, which was good because I must have talked a load of bollocks on the journey there; almost cutting him in half as I held on tightly, chanting the *Lord's Prayer* in my head as we raced along the roads at top speed. On the way back, as I relaxed into the experience and him, I assessed the situation: "I'm in the south of France, speeding along with the wind in my hair, wrapped around an amazingly sexy Italian on the back of his moped. It can't get much better than this!" I thought, with a beaming smile. I felt cool for a change and very much alive.

At the campsite we had seen an ad for the position of nanny and it was decided that as I was better with kids (what?) that I would phone the number to enquire about the position further, the conversation being entirely in French. Penny walked around the harbour asking for jobs on the large yachts moored there. I had more success than her and was asked to go to an interview the following day. I was picked up by Donald Merchant, a Swiss businessman in a black Pontiac, and was taken to a large house in Cannes. There I met his secretary and her baby, whom I would be looking after while she worked. I know what you're thinking: he could have been anyone, but again I had no reason at this stage of my life not to trust people at face value. While the interview was taking place, the door to the sun terrace was opened by a very tall, bronzed naked woman in high heels followed by two men with cameras.

My jaw dropped, thinking, "What the fuck: what situation have I got myself into now?" The naked lady and two men were very friendly and said hello and made conversation as they grabbed some refreshments and went back out the way they came in. Donald quickly explained that his friends were shooting for *Playboy* magazine in the garden. As if that explained everything, as though it was a normal occurrence, but it was so far away from normality in my protected world that it went straight up there with SURREAL! This would not be the only surreal moment of the trip and our association with Donald Merchant. I managed to get back home in one piece, and with a job as a nanny secure, despite Penny worrying at the campsite for a while. She had again been unsuccessful that day in finding work on a yacht.

The only catch for the job was that it was live-in and I couldn't leave Penny on her own. That said, Donald announced that Penny could also have a job in one of his other properties in Super Cannes; once inhabited by Sly Stalone's brother, and where we would both live. The housekeeper was from Tunisia and looked after us like her children, filling us in on our new boss over the time we lived there. While I looked after Donald's secretary's baby, Penny tackled the other villa's garden. Donald obviously liked two young English girls working for him and when we were not 'on duty' he'd take us both out, to the best nightclubs in town; to the places he had met Prince, he claimed. As I'm writing this I realise it was a bit of a dodgy situation, but at the time we didn't feel in any danger from this man and we certainly did not let him anywhere near us sexually. In fact, we used to put him in his place more often than not.

One night we were picked up by one of his friends in a chauffeur-driven Rolls Royce and they took us out to St Tropez for dinner. We arrived at the restaurant, which was rather fun at first and I enjoyed the experience, but the fun turned to disbelief when one of Donald's friends started playing footsie with me under the table.

I went mad in front of the culprit, but his English was limited.

Donald: "Do you realise how much money he has? He drives a Ferrari."

KAY ROSE-HATTRICK

Kay: "I don't care how much money he has, he is not playing footsie with me under the table!"

But they both quickly realised that I could not be bought.

After this incident, Donald rarely took me out and would sometimes cruelly take Penny out and leave me at home like a naughty little girl. One day he announced, "Right, pack your bags, you're going to Geneva." He flew the day before and he picked us up from Geneva airport and took us to what would be our new home for the next couple of weeks. He owned (or at least we think he did) this large, exclusive, modern build on the edge of Lake Geneva, with an indoor sauna and swimming pool and lots of bedrooms. It was my job to clean it and make it ready for sale. Penny got the large overgrown garden again. Every day, Donald would go off to town for the day with a list of things we needed, which always included fags and chocolate, and we were left to do our work. Some nights he'd take us out to the best clubs in town to drink champagne and sometimes he'd just take Penny out, in spite, because I'd had an argument with him that day.

One night, as Penny and I were sleeping, Donald rushed in hurriedly, turning on the main light and shouting, "Get up, get up!" As we were dragged from our slumber, wondering what had happened and wiping the sleep from our eyes, we saw a family of Arabs in full headgear, including wives and children, right in front of us in our bedroom! He explained, "This family are thinking of buying this place. Get up and turn all the lights on." 'Fuck me – another surreal moment,' I remember thinking. Another day, a couple of men who delivered some furniture asked about our boss. They evidently knew him, as he was a well-known European businessman, but it looked as if Donald was not liked and his business dealings not always done with integrity.

Once the cleanup had been completed, we were sent back to France, staying only a few more days before heading back to the UK with a bit of cash in our pockets. I think Dad was cringing when he heard the story of my eventful summer on the way back from Chesterfield coach station – and I had kept some things back from him. My French had certainly improved though and that had been the ultimate purpose of the trip.

Back in Hull, Ju Ju, Jenny, Alison and I all moved into a house on Lambert Street for our second year, together with my schoolfriend Rachel, and this year was the start of the sex, drugs and rock and roll, although not necessarily in that order. I joined the university musicians' exchange and put my name down as a drummer, or rather wanting to learn the drums. David, a good friend at school, and the son of the very funny Bernie Clifton, had given me a practice pad and a pair of drumsticks and I found a drum teacher who had played in the band in the film *Memphis Belle*. He was good, but I'd only had a few lessons before, at Easter 1990, I was approached by a guy called Mick, the lead singer of States of Unrest.

The Easter holidays meant that their Christian drummer was unable to play a gig supporting the band Gaye Bykers on Acid. Despite my protests at having only been on a kit a few times, Mick insisted that we set up and practise. Well, surprisingly, I ended up playing the gig and staying with the group for the next two years, finally infiltrating the 'exclusive' club of the university student.

Mick was my mentor, whether he or I knew it or not at the time, and we spent a lot of time together. He was a mature student and has stayed in education ever since. He got me into realising that this world wasn't the great place I'd come to believe in my safe bubble, and taught me what Thatcher had really done to this country, especially to the miners. States of Unrest were a political band. Mick used to rant on about the atrocities caused by the "good old US of A", and how they were always swept under the carpet and hopefully forgotten by the public. After each set he'd religiously shout, "Don't eat fucking hamburgers, don't drink fucking cola," or at least, something along those lines; the essence of all that is bad (or perceived good) about America. It was a far cry from my conservative roots; Dad was a self-made man, thanks to Thatcher. I rebelled and began to realise that capitalism wasn't all it was cracked up to be, especially for working people.

On reflection, the reality of the world I lived in was exposed to me while I was in Mick's band, and is the basis for everything I am now. States of Unrest were one of the oldest and most respected bands at the university and Mick was determined to expose the truth and make people see the world from a different perspective, imploring the audience not to believe everything that governments and world leaders told us. It would be nice to believe that the powers who run the world are acting in our best interest, but I'm afraid I have learned along the way that this is so far from the truth. It is and always has been about money and power and leading the voter on a merry dance by deception.

In my second year, I started smoking weed and one day had my first 'whitey' with some black hash, which Justine and I had put in some coffee. I was always open to experiment with certain drugs, although I never touched anything but weed during my college days.

It was while Justine was on the phone to a friend that the euphoria come over me and the 'high' had hit big time. At first, it was amazing. I kept picking up a piece of paper and could not understand why it was just dropping back to the floor as I let go, when in my expanded mind it should have flown across the floor. I kept repeating this action time and time again until Justine came off the phone. It started going wrong when we began getting heart palpitations and feelings of anxiety as our minds transcended to a different level, so we crawled into my bed together, hugging each other, thinking we were going to die. I'd put Bryan Ferry on the stereo and wrote a letter to my parents saying, "I'm sorry... I don't normally take drugs..." and ending with "Bryan Ferry, see me out!" Alison came in and just laughed at us when we said that we needed an ambulance. The feelings just wore off and Justine went back to her room.

I told the friend I'd bought it off and he confirmed that I'd had my first 'whitey'; he said that it was completely normal and that if we'd been with him he could have calmed us down in minutes. Generally, when I smoked weed, which was during band practice, Mick and I would stifle laugher in front of Chris and Dave and whoever else was in the lineup at the time, because it wasn't cool to laugh, it seemed.

In my second year, I also was part of a college 'jailbreak' to raise money for Children in Need. The conditions were that you had to get as far away as possible from Hull prison without using any money, and how far you managed to get dictated the amount of sponsorship that you got back for the charity. Several people I knew took part but we had to break into teams of two and so I teamed up with James from Kent. SJ and Penny paired up and made it all the way to Paris. James and I still got the furthest, even though we didn't quite make it to our planned destination, Berlin.

I had visited Berlin in sixth form on a school trip, when it was still a divided city and Checkpoint Charlie was guarded heavily on both sides. People were still being shot trying to cross over to the 'promised land', and only a few months before our school arrived from the West, Lutz Schmidt died too. His memorial cross on a fence by the wall jerked us all into reality. While I was there I bought a postcard of a beautiful painting of a hand on the Berlin Wall, with the white rose of peace breaking through from the other side. It had always moved me, showing such a simple and beautiful possible future outcome for the world, namely love and peace.

It was with this postcard in mind that James and I approached the marketing people at Interflora and pitched them an idea for some great PR for the price of two flights to Munich, while British Rail provided free tickets to London. We would have made it all the way to Berlin, courtesy of the army, "if it had been a weekday," they told us. The army base gave us a hot meal and a few beers to cushion our disappointment and we kipped down for the night by the lockers in Munich airport instead.

Despite not quite making our preferred destination, we got the furthest and raised a lot of money for Children in Need. Our 'jailbreak' adventure also made the front cover of the afternoon edition of the *Hull Daily Mail*; the later edition cut us to page three, I think, with much more worthy news headlining. I also made the Sheffield *Star* and Mum collected the cuttings for her scrapbook.

I graduated in 1990 with my HND in business and marketing, and with some merits. The polytechnic had kicked me off the European marketing course after my first year because I had failed my French conversation exam. Remember me telling you about my hearing disability earlier? My HND allowed me to enter a degree course in the second year and I chose social science, as I have always been interested in people and their behaviour. I loved studying how people think and why they act the way they do. I was particularly fascinated by subgroups who, because they are slightly different, think they are unique when in fact they still continue to 'follow the sheep'. I also moved into a house on Auckland Avenue (owned by the parents of my former Murdoch Hall buddies Nicky and Alison) with Tiffany and Helen. Most of the houses on the street had been bought up by the university as it was so close, and it was nearer to my new campus.

When I was twenty-one, Saddam Hussain invaded Kuwait, which they say 'orchestrated' the first Gulf war. I was affected more than most as my sister, a British Airways stewardess, had flown to Kuwait just days before and was kept hostage for nearly a month. She phoned us as the Iraqis were invading and she told me on the phone that she was watching from her hotel room window as the troops were marching up the beach, confirming that it was gunfire I could hear, although she lied to Mum and blamed the noise on the TV. Soon after this we lost contact with her. At first, British Airways phoned every day, reporting that her group had been moved to the emir's palace. After that, nothing was known and the phone calls from British Airways became less frequent, with nothing new to report.

I even caught Dad crying one day, and I thought, "Oh God, she's doomed!" Dad never usually cried at anything and so it was the break in his resolve that made me worry for her safety as the battle continued to rage on, on the TV. Saddam allowed the women and children to leave Baghdad publicly, and Trace was on this first flight out with Jesse Jackson, the American civil rights activist, on board. She was interviewed by John Simpson on BBC 1 news that night, while she waited at Baghdad airport, looking glowing and glamorous, despite her incarceration. Trust Trace. She told us later that she had been in the emir's palace until two buses shipped them out to Baghdad and freedom. In the middle of the desert the other bus had been stopped, with the BA crew being ordered to step outside and line up, before then being told to get back on the bus. Thankfully, Trace was not party to this experience, which must have been very frightening for those cabin crew, among whom was Trace's close friend.

A few weeks after she returned home, the Foreign Office came to our house and interviewed Trace about her experience for several hours. She had been more observant than most and had taken some pictures of the soldiers guarding the palace through the one-way glass. She had also asked the friendly doctor about the position of the soldiers occupying the palace. They had been provided with one meal a day, which was usually full of rice weevils, and one day they hadn't been fed at all. It had a profound effect on Trace, but she was never counselled after this experience and the affects have caused problems in later life.

During my time in Hull, I turned into an independent woman and a liberal feminist. Feminism for me is total equality between males and females, despite former defined roles, when women permanently wore aprons and their days never ended until they closed their eyes. Times have changed however, and women are now expected to bring home the bacon and then fry it, while the man just has to eat it, as it has already been hunted down for him by a supermarket chain. Don't get me wrong; historically women had their roles as homemakers, looking after children, cooking, cleaning etc, and in the past the men would go out hunting or working, so they had their roles too. However, due to the demand for two incomes to pay the mortgage, utility and council tax bills, car payments, entertainment systems and credit cards etc, there is now no difference, and so I'm sure men must feel somewhat displaced in today's society. I know women feel more pressurised.

A few of my fellow students on my degree course could be described as radical feminists and would not let any man do anything for them; they could probably be better described as misandrists or man-haters. This included one of my female lecturers, who I observed drop her books in protest when an innocent male student dared to keep the door open for her. He'd have given the same courtesy to anyone, male or female; it was just her chip, which prevented her from finding her yin (female side). The radical feminists on our course were mostly gay; not only as a statement but to warn others, like myself, that we could never really be true to ourselves and join the sisterhood if we weren't butch or had a butch girlfriend!

But I was a drummer in an all-male political band and mixed with mainly male musicians, who treated me like a mate and didn't see me as either gender, I suppose. I was a female drummer in demand, as there weren't many of us around. I was quite tight, if a little basic, and I was often asked by other bands to do studio recordings with them. At the time, my brother was running a recording studio in Thorne, about an hour away from Hull, and both States of Unrest and later Soothe recorded there, so thankfully I still have recordings of both bands. I listen to them now and am transported back to those years with fondness, thankful that I experienced them. The live recordings are a little less easy on the ear, though.

States of Unrest regularly played at the Adelphi Club, Hull's infamous music venue, owned by the great Paul Jackson, and I also worked behind the bar there. This was where States of Unrest supported the Manic Street Preachers when they were a relatively unknown band (of course, they went on to become really big) and before their guitarist went missing, presumed dead. They were a lovely set of lads, especially the drummer; a small, sweet, quietly spoken Welshman who told me that it was no problem using their drum kit, except his 'baby', meaning his snare drum, which drummers never generally shared anyway. The Levellers, whom we supported twice, were also very obliging and great guys, unlike PJ Harvey.

The story goes that when you're a drummer you ask the main act what part of their kit you can borrow. Otherwise, you have to erect another kit on an already small stage and soundcheck that individual kit. After your set, you have to break your kit down in record time and generally without much help, so using any part of the main band's kit is always good. I approached her drummer and Polly Harvey appeared from nowhere. Before he could open his mouth, she categorically said no and then flounced off. This story was read

States of Unrest, the Adelphi

out on Radio 6, a number of years later, when I was finally able to express my annoyance at such a disagreeable woman on national radio. Perhaps she heard?

The UK Subs, the 70s punk band who are still going strong, with the wonderful Charlie Harper still the frontman, not only let me borrow their kit but also ended up being perfect house guests. We supported them on stage and afterwards, they were all going to crash in their tour van. It was during the holidays, and all my new flatmates were out of town, so I offered them a place to stay, and they gratefully accepted, as did my own band members.

The following morning, the band went out and bought the makings of a full English breakfast, cooked it for everyone and then washed up afterwards. Being the perfect punk house guests warranted them a mention in *Pop Bitch*, the online celebrity and music newsletter, when, years later, Theodore was sufficiently impressed by my rock and roll past to post it. The UK Subs were welcome guests from then on and they stayed on another occasion too.

On the second occasion, my flatmate Tiffany was somewhat taken aback to find a spiky-haired, black leather-clad man coming out of the bathroom the following morning. I guess all my housemates were not surprised by my friends. They just opened the door, and if they looked 'weird' they called for me. I was the polytechnic representative in the university musicians' exchange, and other drummers used to borrow my kit, so there was a constant flow of musician types in our living room. Despite my exposure to lots of like-minded men, I was never asked out, except by a Sikh guy with gorgeous long silky hair who took me out for a Valentine's meal to Nelly's in Beverley. But although he was lovely, I didn't really fancy him. Generally though, it just didn't happen. I used to wail on occasions, "Why doesn't anyone fancy me, Mick?" He just used to say, "Because they're all scared of you, Kay." I'm not sure if it was true or not, but it's true that I was full of angst and desperation at times! When I did get a snog the relationship lasted no time at all and they just wanted to be my friend. I had three three-month long relationships before I met Ashley, my first husband: Sylvain, Kevin and Sam.

Kevin was an Australian expat about ten years older than me, who lived in Sheffield and who asked me to marry him so he could get a green card. I declined of course; my father would have KILLED me! He was a sound engineer and I got to see a few bands when he was touring. One of his clients, though I never saw them live, was The The. In my opinion, Matt Johnson is one of the greatest lyricists of this age. The The would continue to confirm my realisation that our own government were pulling the wool over our eyes, and were definitely lying to us. Maybe because Kevin wasn't getting his oats, or his green card, the relationship fizzled out, and because of my dating history, I was not surprised.

After Kevin came Sam, who was also older and in his thirties, and to whom I gave my virginity when I was nineteen. We lasted three months and our relationship ended the day I knocked down a teenager. That afternoon, on my way back from college, a schoolkid ran in front of my car without looking at the traffic lights and ended up on the road after hitting my windscreen. I was going very slowly and I had several witnesses to say that he had not bothered to look before he ran out. He was not hurt but suffering from shock, like me. That night was my twentieth birthday party and to get over the ordeal I got very drunk. By the time Sam arrived I was rather incoherent and although I don't remember much detail, another three-month relationship ended that night.

In my third year, I was approached by Paula, who also worked on the bar at the Adelphi, to join their all-girl band. I was the only female drummer in Hull; well, certainly in our circles, and Soothe were keen to recruit me. I continued gigging with States of Unrest for a few months but then I had to make a decision. I chose Soothe.

It was so different working with an all-female cast rather than pure testosterone. Heidi was the band leader and she was very talented; she wrote all the songs and sang and played guitar. Becky played keyboards and Paula played the bass, and we had great fun in practice while swapping instruments. Our band shots were taken on the train track at the back of the Adelphi and we mostly gigged there. This is also where an A&R man (talent scout from a record label) came to see us. His silence suggested he didn't see the potential in us. We recorded a few tracks at my brother's recording studio and we went on a tour, which included the Toby Jug in Doncaster and a pub in York where my whole family turned up, apart from Dad. I don't think he really liked his little girl being in a band and he certainly wouldn't go out of his way to support it.

In my final year, Matt, a friend doing psychology at the university, practised a technique on me. It was my first real guided meditation, and it had a profound effect on me. The technique he used is the basis for all hypnosis and regression and I still use it when I want to go into deep meditation quickly. After talking me through each part of my body and sending it to a relaxed state, so that it was just a heavy weight and not part of my body any longer, he took me on a mind journey. The places I visited with Matt that night took me deep within myself and then blasted me back out again into a different reality. I still use the same place I visited that night, which I conjured up in my mind all those years ago, as my safe haven. When he had finished, he was as amazed as I was, and we went round to the shops together in the snow, discussing the experience we had just shared, both of us totally high, without the use of other substances.

I became a little obsessed with tarot card readers during those years. I went to see so many different ones and none of them could tell me anything, really. One guy even gave me another half an hour on the clock because he said I was blocking stuff. "Not me, mate, I'm open-minded. Perhaps it's because you're a fraud?" It must be said that two independent readers predicted that I would conceive three children and one would be either aborted or miscarried. They both seemed clear on this.

My four years in Hull were certainly eventful: I'd been a drummer in a political band, I'd taken drugs and had my first 'whitey', I'd finally lost my virginity and still graduated with a respectable 2:2, the drinking man's degree. I was quite pleased that I'd actually managed to pass at all, let alone not come bottom. I learned more than social science and what I had observed of the society I lived in during my years in Hull. I also went through a big transition; destination independence and autonomy from Dad.

KAY ROSE-HATTRICK

Sacked – Preparations

for an Adventure

3

 Watch out for those people who quickly lull you into a false sense of security;
they can pounce on you when you least expect it!
– **Kay Rose-Hattrick**

After college, Tara, a close mate, and I remained in Hull and moved into a house together as our other friends went home, to London or to a new city to start their post-degree lives. While she got a job for the council I found a job at Humberside International Airport, not that it had that many international flights. I must have impressed the marketing manager, because I got my first proper job on the information desk. As part of my remit I had to plot out flight plans for any flight leaving Humberside. This was quite scary really, as we had to inform all the airspaces that planes would be crossing through. I also had to make sure that the weather charts were collected every morning and photocopied for the pilots.

I worked with a woman called Bella, who was an angel to your face, but who obviously took a great dislike to me, as she was the one who got me the sack in the end. In my disciplinary hearing, my lateness was cited. I hold up my hands to that one as I'd slept through my alarm on a couple of occasions and had been awoken by Tara saying that work was on the phone. I had to be at work by 6am on the early morning shifts and you already know that I don't do mornings very well. It was a long drive too: on the other side of the Humber and I had to cross the bridge at nearly a fiver every day.

It was the other two reasons cited on my final warning which made me realise that Bella wanted to get rid of me. The immigration officer, who would have lunch with me when we were on shift together, told me later that every time I made a wrong move, Bella would be to-ing and fro-ing to the marketing manager's office, reporting on what I had done.

So the reasons for my dismissal were:

1: *"My lateness"*
I hold my hands up to this one and can't deny this reason.

2: *"My comment to other airport staff regarding hangovers"*
I had said to one of the baggage handlers, when he had enquired about my weekend, "A bit too good!" Come on!

3: *"My inability to service late night shifts"*
I remember going through the rota with Bella, as I was still in Soothe at the time, to see whether I could play in the gigs we'd booked. She was as nice as pie and said not to worry as I could always swap shifts with her or the other girl who worked there. What a cow!

The lateness was enough to sack me but these two other reasons made me realise that people aren't always what they seem and to always watch your back! I've always wanted to go back and do a *Pretty Woman* on her: "Remember me?" I'd say, "You got me sacked," and see how she responds. I don't know what it would achieve, except put a ghost to rest and pull her up on her devious nature.

About the same time as I got the sack from the airport I also got the sack from Soothe. Heidi started getting funny with me and got a bloke in to drum for them instead. So I moved back home, as there was now nothing keeping me in Hull.

My old housemates, Alison and Nicky, had decided to go travelling round the world and they asked me to join them. I needed to widen my horizons and turn into a woman. There weren't even any fellas to keep me tied to this country. I was single and desperate for an adventure. I got a job at HMV in Meadowhall in Sheffield, known locally as Meadowhell, because it's always so busy. My sister's old schoolfriend, Vicky, was assistant manager there and looking for holiday cover. HMV was one of my favourite jobs ever, and I spent my days shrinkwrapping CDs and ordering calendars from Viz whilst smoking copious amounts of cigarettes in the back, when you could still smoke in the workplace.

At HMV I met Paul, whom I was to meet again in a rave club years later, when we would become good friends. I always thought back then that he viewed me as a little rich girl with little depth, and although he was always sweet to me, I'm sure he always laughed with the others about my naivety. He has told me since that this was not the case at all. I was certainly very gullible and nothing's changed.

I started saving frantically and I got a job working at my local pub, The George and Dragon, then owned by Dot and Tony Andrews (RIP), and I worked there most evenings as well. My mum would bring sandwiches to the pub for my dinner as I went straight there from HMV.

Nicky, Alison and I travelled down to London one Saturday to book the round the world tickets at an independent backpackers' travel agent. I was so excited once the itinerary had been planned and the flights for each leg booked. We were to fly to Bangkok on 24th March 1993 and then:

Bangkok – Hong Kong
Hong Kong – Perth, Australia
Perth – Sydney (internal)
Cairns – Christchurch, New Zealand
Auckland – Los Angeles
New York – London

We had given ourselves only ten days to go overland from LA to New York, and then back home exactly one year after our leaving date.

(M)ETAMORPHOSIS –

AROUND THE WORLD IN 355 DAYS

I shed my adolescent skin and flew free to the edge of world and paradise,
captured in my memories forever to remind me of who I really am.
— Kay Rose-Hattrick

I was nervous as hell before leaving home, not knowing where I was going to lay my head for the next year. Packing for a year was also tricky, but not so much as packing a three bedroom house into a van, as I would do years later. But a dilemma nonetheless. I knew it would be hot on the first leg of the journey in Bangkok and Hong Kong, but it would be autumn in Australia and warmer clothes would be necessary. I had to be realistic; there would be no room for Jeremy Peapod, my trusty teddy bear, bought on the day I was born, who still comforts me. I was so stressed, but when Mike called me over and cracked an egg over my head I no longer had my travelling worries in mind; just a release, first by way of tears and then anger, berating my brother for his actions. Of course, his intention was to distract me.

Dad drove me down to Heathrow Airport and I met up with Alison and Nicky, with their parents in tow, who were understandably anxious about their little girls travelling round the world and what that would bring. In my family, my mum was behind me 100%, but my father was reticent and tried to dissuade me at every opportunity. Years later, he admitted he didn't want me to go because he was unable to control me over such a long distance. My argument was that I needed to find myself, and it wasn't likely to happen by getting the first job that I applied for and getting tied into a mortgage. I wanted to experience life first.

We celebrated my 23rd birthday on the plane with a bottle of complimentary champagne, kindly given by the airline. We arrived in Bangkok and delighted in the adventure of a new city, so different from where I'd previously ventured to in Europe. We got a taxi to Khao San Road, which every backpacker knows is the place to be, and which is highly recommended by the traveller's bible: *Lonely Planet*.

The Khao San Road was full of hostels and agents and restaurants and bars showing all the latest movies, and travellers all with stories to tell about the best place to book your trip, where to go and where to stay. This information is invaluable when travelling, as it is real time as opposed to being a year out of date, even if you're using the latest edition of the 'bible'. New places are discovered all the time and other places listed lost favour among the hardened backpackers. If you haven't done so already, read *The Beach* by Alex Garland to get the picture.

I wrote a diary during the time I was away, but unfortunately, I lost the first diary, which covered this period of my travels, so it's all from pure memory. I suppose therefore only the important parts of the metamorphosis will remain for posterity: the memories I have locked deep inside, and which had a profound impact on my development.

After several days of adjusting to this different world and settling into our new way of life on the road, we left Bangkok and headed north to Chiang Mai, which promised treks with breathtaking mountain views and visits to remote Thai tribes. We arrived in Chiang Mai and booked into a delightful hostel with a garden courtyard, where proper English tea was served by the very pleasant proprietor. We met up with our party, a mixed group of nationalities, and took a minibus up to the mountains until we could go no further, except on foot.

We started to climb higher through forests, with our slim guides, who were used to the trek, almost running through the trees with all the cooking equipment and supplies on their backs. We all found it tough, but I had been building up my stamina by doing my Cher step aerobics video in preparation, and so I was able to keep up. Nicky, however, couldn't, and kept stopping, her heavy breathing preventing her from going very fast.

We broke the long trek on foot and rode a short distance on the back of some elephants. Alison and I rode on Mai, whose owner spent the whole journey spitting and stabbing poor Mai's head with a blunt knife. We shouted at him to stop but he just laughed in our faces, so we responded by laughing at him, while cursing him for his actions in a language he didn't understand. Thankfully he dismounted and left Alison and I alone on board, which Mai took advantage of, making a beeline for the river. Well, we all know what elephants do in water, and we got completely soaked, laughing at the beautiful experience. At least Mai was 'free', if only for a short while.

After the elephant ride the trek carried on up another mountain and we were exhausted. The news from the guides that the village we would stay in overnight sold ice-cold Singhas (Thai beer) brought us enough energy from our depleted banks to run the rest of the way. It was true: they did sell beer at the local shop/kiosk and Alison and I had nearly downed one by the time Nicky had made it up the last stretch that we had just sprinted. She was overweight, and those extra few pounds and her asthma brought her to the decision that she should return to Chiang Mai the following day and await our return. I would truly empathise with her when I too was overweight, climbing another mountain in south-east Asia years later.

After our long trek, we washed where all the villagers bathed, at the pump in the village square, and the locals seemed happy that we were there as they laughed and joked with us, despite us not being able to speak each other's language. That night, we all slept in a wooden structure, side by side, which was also where the opium doctor would visit us later, to sell her wares to the new party in town. Our guides were actually incredible cooks and produced a banquet of rice, vegetables and meat every night.

The 'doctor' was, however, our evening's entertainment, and I did partake of a couple of pipes that night, as did many of our party. Well, you're not going to miss out on such an experience surely? I suppose the best description of opium for me was that it made me feel really mellow and very chilled, and it helped with the biting bugs in the mattress that night too!

The following day, Nicky was taken on the back of a motorcycle to the bus stop, to catch a bus back to Chiang Mai, and the rest of us walked further into the mountains. The countryside was breathtaking; we walked through forests and fields filled with poppies waiting to be harvested for their opium. We arrived at a village by a large river, inhabited by the Sharon people and whose hospitality was second to none.

That night, we ate wild boar and drank local moonshine, which had the desired effect of loosening our tongues and our singing voices for that night's entertainment. A kind of Eurovision in which we had to sing a song from our own country, but the only song Alison and I could think of was 'Auld Lang Syne' (which is of course by Robert Burns, who was Scottish!), and rehearsed it on the toilet, pissing ourselves at our poor performance. We found out that every nationality present that night sung this at New Year. What would you choose as being typically English, anyway?

The following day, we took a boat down the river to our pickup point; it was incredible and very relaxing after two days of hard trek. When we got back to the hostel the friendly proprietor told us Nicky had checked into another hotel and gave us the address. After a shower and change and a painful Thai massage, which made us feel great afterwards, we took a tuk tuk to the five star establishment.

We made our way up to Nicky's new room, which was quite luxurious, paid for on her dad's credit card. We asked her if she wanted to come back to the hostel and go out for dinner with the trekking group at a local restaurant, but she declined and we left her to her decadence for the night.

A few days later, we travelled south to Sarathani and across, by an unseaworthy-looking ferry, to Koh Samui and paradise. At the island port we were bombarded by people insisting that their accommodation was the best, but we chose to stay between the two main places, Lamai and Chewang, and where Ashley, my first husband and I, would later honeymoon. It was so cheap, but beautifully clean, with huts right on the beach, shaded by coconut palms. Geckos, who would sit on your knee for hours, roamed in abundance and the ocean was teeming with brightly coloured fish that are only seen in warmer seas, and which I'd never seen before with my own eyes, except in books and nature programmes.

We enjoyed glorious sunshine until the night of the famous Thai water festival in mid-April, when the rains came and didn't stop for days. This festival is pretty crazy as everyone continually throws water on each other for 24 hours, including the local police, who really don't seem to mind getting wet. We had been to a bar in Lamai that night with some guys we had met at our lodgings and we didn't know it was the start of the water festival until a local started to throw water over the tourists. Once 'war' broke out, we spent most of the evening running to the ladies' toilets, collecting water for our next victim. Laugh? I was in tears with laughter that night, it hurt so much. I think I filled up my laughter banks for a lifetime. I also had my first snog of the trip, with a guy called Louis.

We grudgingly left Koh Samui, as we had to catch a flight to Hong Kong after three weeks in Thailand. I wish we could have stayed longer, as returning from a simple existence to a large cosmopolitan city was quite a culture shock. On the first night, we booked into a hostel in Kowloon, run by a friendly chap, but as he showed us the room, a cockroach was seen scurrying across the camp bed. We drew straws for who was going to sleep on that bed and of course, mine was the shortest! Cockroaches would be in my Room 101, with their greasy hard bodies, the noise they made when scurrying away and being one of the only creatures that would survive a nuclear blast without a problem.

The guesthouse, or rather his spare room rented out to tourists to earn some extra cash, was situated in the Chungking Mansions, a potential deathtrap of a tower block. Hundreds of backpackers crammed into guest houses in the 17 storey building, with varying degrees of cleanliness and price, but undoubtedly the cheapest accommodation in town. The next night, we moved to a cleaner hostel for a little bit extra. It had an en-suite bath that was so small it was more like an oversized sink.

Hong Kong was impressive, but very expensive and we could only afford to drink during happy hour, which is when we met Rob, whose father was the director for Federal Express Asia and who had a penthouse suite on the island. His father was away for a few weeks and he said we could go and crash out there during our stay in Hong Kong. Well, from a sink to a swimming pool overnight! You never do know who you're going to meet and Rob was our knight in shining armour.

We followed the usual tourist trail and went to Stanley Market, visited the casinos in Macau, a Portuguese colony on the Chinese mainland, and Rob showed us round the city. Although I have good memories of Hong Kong, I just wanted to be back in Thailand, living away from the hustle and bustle of city life. Hong Kong was so pricey that we had to live on McDonald's, against my better judgement, and we only went out for one Chinese meal, as a thank you to Rob for putting us up.

From Hong Kong we flew to Perth, Australia. My sister visited within the first few days of our arrival. Trace still worked for British Airways and could request trips as part of her roster. I saw her about four times in total during my time in Australia.

I loved Perth – the weather was fabulous and the people friendly; not that we were mixing with many locals. We hung out with many different nationalities at our backpackers' hostel. They were mostly on a gap year before they had to join the 'real world'. Alison and I booked onto a trip up the coast to Monkey Mia, where we fed dolphins in the sea and were taken to 'the edge of the world', to remote stretches of beach where we rode the sand dunes in our 4x4 minibus. On this trip, we met a wonderful bunch of people, including the 'comedians': Bruce, a Kiwi, and Mike, a Canadian, and we had a ball.

Nicky had declined to join us again but Alison and I were pleased because she didn't get stuck in like us and comments like, "Next time I travel, I want to see the world from five star hotels" left us knowing that she hadn't come on this trip for an adventure or self-exploration, as we had. Alison and I had just secured jobs in an Italian restaurant but Nicky had decided to return to the UK, so we used our internal flights to Sydney to see the sights with her before she flew home.

Sydney is an incredibly impressive city for sure, with the Harbour Bridge and the Opera House dominating the landscape amid the skyscrapers. The 'bible' had suggested that a good place to find cheap backpackers' accommodation was the Kings Cross area of the city, which was also the red light district and where the strip clubs were situated. Prostitution is legal in Australia and Kings Cross is where it happens, attracting hundreds of people a week to its bustling midst, mainly Japanese businessmen, sometimes with their wives in tow. Kings Cross is also where Alison and I lived and worked for the next few months. Nicky went back to the UK soon after arriving in Sydney, but not before treating us (I think on her dad's credit card) to a show at the Sydney Opera House.

As I'd previously worked for HMV, I took my CV and reference to the Sydney branch first of all. No luck. Then to other shops and restaurants, but still no luck. A fellow backpacker had said that they were always looking for waitresses in the strip clubs, so I went to the Pink Pussy Cat and Alison went to Porky's to ask for work, and we were both successful. Alison's establishment, Porky's, was a little bit more upmarket than the Pink Pussy Cat, which became clear in my first week.

Alison came into my club to have a chat and as we chatted we heard a tinkling sound next to us. We both looked, unable to believe what we saw, which was a man urinating on the floor. We looked at each other again, before looking back to the place he was openly peeing. Understandably disgusted by what we saw, we immediately alerted the barman and security guard. If there is one thing I regret it would be that we said anything. The drunk didn't deserve what happened next. He was beaten almost senseless in front of our very eyes and then thrown onto the street. Alison and I stood there helpless, unable to stop this mindless violence, but knowing it was because of us. It made me feel quite sick.

The club was seedy, and so I left once a job in the Love Machine, a much more upmarket establishment that was directly across the road from Alison's club, had been secured.

Butch was the good-looking but arrogant barman at the Love Machine and, because he couldn't charm me, he could be quite nasty to me. My fellow waitresses, from New Zealand and Holland, were lovely but the other one, I forget from where she originated, was a bit of a cow. As our first job of the evening, we were expected to clean the mirrors on stage with newspapers, which gives them a great shine, and then to pounce on people as they entered the club, to sell them drinks. The waitress would make 50 cents on each drink sold and keep all the tips, so it was a competition with the other waitresses to secure punters and keep them happy so that they would only buy drinks from you and you alone. Nicky, a Kiwi, and I took it in turns to approach each person entering, where as the other girls were more ruthless and would push past you to get their commission.

There was a definite hierarchy within the clubs, starting with the bottom rung, which was us, the waitresses. We had to wear black and white, with no low-cut tops, as we were only there to sell drinks, and if a prostitute came over, we had to make ourselves scarce. We were also there to fetch and carry for the prostitutes before work, buying them dinner or whatever else they required. The prostitutes were mainly lovely, except one called Lola, who demanded I get her a sandwich. On a number of occasions, the brothel manager had picked her up on her manner, for not saying please, and the situation had pissed us both off. It culminated with her starting a fight with me on my last night working at the club.

The first time I was attacked by a prostitute, however, was by Marlina. One night, when I was not working, I went over to Alison's club with her boyfriend, Fergus, whom she had met when we had first arrived in Sydney. I was just chatting to him, while Alison worked. The next thing I knew, I was pulled round and punched in the eye, which sent me flying into the mirrored walls, which cracked on impact with my head. I hadn't even seen who had attacked me, but I was whisked into the office upstairs straight away, to sit with the big boss. Marlina eventually came into the office and I fearlessly shouted, "Is that the fucking whore?" What a stupid and naive girl I was, as from that moment on, I was escorted round Kings Cross by security guards for a whole week, and they all told me,

"When she says she's going to kill you, you should take her at her word!" I still had little fear, and was still angry with her.

Thankfully, her boyfriend was the barman at Porky's, and we got on well so he persuaded her that I was OK, and that I wasn't trying to nick her 'clients', by explaining that the guy I had been talking to was just Alison's boyfriend. She even apologised for giving me a black eye and I was let off 'house arrest'. The second time I was punched by a prostitute was only weeks later, by the rude Lola. I must have said something to piss her off but she was such a cow, and as she threw the first punch I put my knee up, so that she couldn't get too close and hit my face. Everything seemed to turn into slow motion as she threw more punches. I thought, "Oh no, not again!" but I felt strangely calm and she didn't hurt me at all. When we were pulled apart I ran down to a bar where I was meeting friends and realised that I'd actually pooed my pants in my fight or flight response.

After the incident with Marlina, I understandably avoided Alison's club on my night off. One night, I was invited to join some people sitting on the pavement near our backpackers. Other people joined us over the few hours we were there, including a lovely girl called Erren, a young street prostitute. She had been kicked out of home by her mum, and then later by her auntie, and had ended up on the streets, finding prostitution her only way of making a living. She said to me, "Kay, I live on these streets and I'm going to die on these streets." I was intensely moved. I had wanted to continue my studies and become a social worker when I got back home, but after meeting Erren and hearing a story from another pavement buddy, Tom, an ex-junkie and prostitute, I didn't think I would have been emotionally able to deal with this type of career. He told me that his life had been changed when a good friend of his had jumped to his death from a tower block. It was the death of his co-worker that ultimately saved him and moved his life forward, with a sudden jolt.

I became numb after a time working in the clubs, being exposed to so much sex and porn, and to a world which could be quite violent at times. I was required to live a nocturnal life, sleeping for most of the day, as we didn't climb into bed until at least 3 o'clock on most mornings. We did make quite a bit of money, but people had started to treat me differently when they knew where I worked; in an almost superior way, judging me for what I had chosen to experience.

Most people asked me why such a 'nice girl' was working in a place like this. There were some great people working in the clubs; the strippers were mainly friendly and were amazing dancers (most of them professionally trained), with stunning costumes. Most of the prostitutes were also kind and a good laugh, with the exception of a few bitches. It was probably the safest place for us, to be living and working in 'the Cross', because we knew all the club security guards and they looked after our backs, even when we weren't aware of it.

One night, I served two softly spoken Arab men, who tipped me well and who also commented on why I worked there. Later, I saw them in the cafe that we frequented for breakfast after work, and one of them read my palm. They were very charming and attentive and asked if I would like to come back for drinks at their apartment in Darling Harbour, a particularly exclusive side of town. Despite warnings from my colleagues about the dangers of leaving with them, I left with them anyway, thinking belligerently, "How *dare* you tell me what to do; these people are much more respectable than you." They were only looking after me, and it was only later that I realised my fellow co-workers' true essence. Again, I was being truly naive.

The Arabs and I caught a taxi to their apartment, which overlooked Darling Harbour. I was offered some wine, which I accepted, but I wondered why the older guy had opened two bottles of wine; one for himself and one for me. This was the first alcoholic beverage of the night for me so I was not impaired. I was then offered some hash, which we smoked while we chatted politely. I was shown into one of the bedrooms, where the older guy produced a gold bar and said that it was a present for a friend. As this was happening, the younger guy was having a conversation with someone on the phone. It sounded like an argument, but may have only been the usual tone of people conversing in Arabic. Then he disappeared into the other bedroom.

As we chatted he poured wine from two separate bottles. I thought this was a little odd, so I asked him if he would like to try some of mine. He declined so quickly and fiercely that I had a 'flash' and 'something' told me to *get out, right now*. As I rushed to the door, picking up my shoes, but in too much of a hurry to put them on, the other guy emerged from the other room completely stark naked. I pushed the older one away, as he stood in the way of the door, and ran up the street as fast as I could, in fear of my life. As I ran past a large house, a security light came on, and not knowing what else to do, instinct told me to go back, and so I banged on the door, in fear of the Arabs following me. I was so scared.

The door was opened by a doctor and his wife, perhaps in their sixties, and very respectable (Darling Harbour is a very exclusive part of the city), so you can imagine their surprise when they opened the door to a very upset English girl, claiming that she'd been drugged in the middle of the night! Despite this, they welcomed me in, heard my story and gave me a cup of tea while we waited for the police. The policeman who subsequently picked me up and took me to the hospital, insisting I needed to take a drugs test, wasn't so nice to me, especially when I told him that I worked in a club down in Kings Cross. He had instantly judged me, unlike the beautiful couple in whose house I had thankfully found sanctuary.

The drugs test came back negative and the unforgiving policeman dropped me off at our hostel. Sheepishly, I returned to our room, where Alison berated me for being so bloody stupid, and she was right. Although I had not been harmed, or drugged, it freaked me out big time, and I started to realise that the so called dregs of society with whom I mixed were truly good people. They were only there to protect me, as they did all their 'family'. The two Arabs in question came to the club the next day, bringing the denim jacket I had been too distracted to pick up. I didn't speak to them as I was still very wary, but it seemed odd to me that they would turn up like that. Perhaps it was to show silly me that I was indeed just paranoid and that they had presented no danger to me.

I still don't know to this day if I *had* been in any danger with these men, but the worst case scenarios of me being either raped or murdered has crossed my mind. I believe that overwhelming feeling to leave that apartment when I did that night was a sign from above. 'Something' spoke to me that night, for sure; something beyond just my inner voice. Who would have believed me, a brothel worker, over two respectable Arab gentlemen with gold bars stashed in their bedroom? It actually doesn't bear thinking about and taught me some lessons:

1. Don't judge people by the size of their bank balance.
2. Money **should not** command respect.

And that old adage:

3. Don't judge a book by its cover.

Although first impressions do count, that couple didn't judge me; they instead listened with empathy and open hearts. They were truly angels sent to protect me that night, while the policeman was judge and jury and saw me only as a transient brothel worker, and it suited him not to see the truth.

Shortly after this, we left Sydney and the clubs behind and travelled north to Brisbane to visit Sian, our friend from college, who was living and working there. The plan was to continue north but I had no money, the last of it having gone on a 'sure bet' that Fergus had given us.

Australia is dangerous for gambling as many betting shops are located in the pubs, so the more drunk you get, the more likely you are to do a stupid thing and put up most of your money on a 'sure bet'. They just don't exist. Needless to say, I went back to Sydney nearly penniless to find work, while Alison headed north to Ayres Rock and to continue her travels, before heading home to a friend's wedding. When I got back to the hostel in Kings Cross, I saw an ad for an au pair's position, and I was asked by the mother, Gabby, to go over to Beecroft, a suburb of Sydney, to meet the family.

What I saw looked great and I soon moved all my stuff into my annex room in their house and started working. My charges were Kate, 10; Ben, 8; and Sarah, 6; today they will be in their late twenties and Kate will have turned thirty! Gabby worked for Australian

Airlines and Ross was an officer in the Australian navy, but they never had much money so I had to be very resourceful with a chicken, making it last for several meals. I baked every other day; biscuits and cakes for their packups for school and for after-school snacks. I certainly learned how to cook there and even cooked for Ross's captain and some of his officers when they came to dinner one night. I made my first pumpkin soup for the captain's table, following Gabby's recipe.

To earn extra money I also took a job at the Black Stump, a restaurant about two miles from the house. I wasn't a very good waitress, as reading back in my diary, I'd forget to put drinks or puddings on the bill, and on occasions I was made to pay out of my own pocket. I was able to live off my tips while every bit of money was put into the bank to pay for my 'escape' and to continue my planned travels.

Saturdays were supposed to be my day off, but Gabby would always wake me and ask me to go shopping with her, so I didn't really stop, or have any personal space, and this did get to me. I think I was suffering from post-natal depression of sorts, when you have sole responsibility for the welfare of young, impressionable children and the pressure builds up, without any valve for release; especially when they're not your own and unconditional love doesn't kick in automatically. The kids played me up a lot, except the darling Sarah, who would sit and brush my hair for hours for a mere 50 cents. I had very little time away from them, except my evening job, and I became quite isolated.

At the time I also received a call from my mum to say that Nan, Dad's mum, had died (Amy Proctor RIP). I would not be able to attend her funeral and felt very alone with my grief so far away from my own family. Most of my travelling friends had left Sydney and I didn't get out much, except with Amanda, my old college mate's sister, who lived in Sydney. When I'd been away for six months, Trace requested another trip to Oz, which coincided with the kids going on holiday to their grandparents', and so I was free to party.

It was 23rd September 1993, the day they announced that Sydney had won the Olympic bid, and the streets were full of celebrations. I spent a very alcohol-fuelled night with Trace at various favourite haunts in the city until the early hours. The following evening, she and the rest of the crew were picked up by the airport bus outside the hotel and I was left standing on my own again. I started crying as she got on the bus and I didn't stop until I got all the way back to Beecroft, to an empty house, as the family were not due back until the following day. I felt so lost that night.

Needless to say, I was feeling quite sad at the time. Enter Philip stage right. He gave me a huge confidence boost and showed me some much-needed affection. Philip was Gabby's little brother, an aid worker in Afghanistan, over visiting family before flying back to the 'war zone'. He stayed with us for a couple of days and I fell for him! He was about ten years older than me, with a certain kind of sex appeal and a cheeky charm you couldn't help but have fallen for.

We spent his last night, when everyone had gone to bed, cuddling and kissing and talking about the meaning of life while he brushed my hair and I purred like a kitten. When we finally went to bed I heard him come out onto the patio and try the door to my annex room but I pretended to be asleep. You see, I knew that if I had opened up the inevitable would have happened, and I would have given him my heart as well as my body. He left the next day and, after Gabby and the kids dropped him off at the airport, he called me and we said our goodbyes knowing that we would have taken it further if the situation had been different. He actually gave me such strength and restored my respect in the opposite sex.

During my time as a nanny I was just making money and biding my time until my travels could be resumed, and I did get quite depressed, as my diary suggests. Reading over my diary immediately flings me back without any paddles to my emotional angst of the time. Oh, and I've only just come up for breath. I ask my 23-year old self to do the talking now.

Diary extract – 5ᵗʰ October 1993

As I sit here in my room, prisoner within my own soul, I long for summer days and new hope. I long to be ecstatically happy again, again, or for once? Days pass me by unnoticed; misspent time that I could have spent doing: what? Living, maybe; loving, maybe, but not just damn existing and pushing past the days in order for it all to be over. Why am I here, then? Definitely not to feel like this. Duty and security keep me trapped. I hope my depression is short-lived.

I think back to that night in the reggae pub on Koh Samui, soaked through to the skin in the pouring rain on Lewis's knee; happy, laughing, nicely numbed through Mekon and Singha and tingly from the sun with someone who didn't love me, but who did like me, and that was all I wanted. Days and warm evenings out on the terrace with the guys drinking a beer, having fun, exchanging jokes, taking the piss out of Mike and laughing at Bruce, laughing at his little stories which were definitely 'lost in translation'! Alison and I on the balcony with the trek after a wonderful day spent; washing our hair in the river, riding elephants – shouting at Major Gozzer, Mai's 'owner'. Singing songs by candlelight, drinking moonshine, smoking opium – feeling free and wild and good. Literally pissing ourselves over our attempt at an 'English' song. I haven't laughed like that in months. Will I ever again?

On the edge of Eagle's Bluff, 'the edge of the world', which seemed so immense, but so far away from problems and stress. Feeling I could jump and that I wouldn't fall, but fly forever. On the beach with sand as fine as icing sugar, jumping down the dunes, splashing about in the sea, away from civilisation, and only the four wheels of the minibus to remind us we would soon be taken back to the hustle and bustle of the world. We were at total peace with ourselves, with friends and memories that would never die and which would carry us through times like this. Alone and so far away from my true loved ones. Feeling the way I did when Mum phoned me to say Nan had died. I felt so lost and so far away from her, not being able to do anything, just feeling alone and lost and completely sad.

KAY ROSE-HATTRICK

Being in Philip's arms and feeling so contented and happy and never wanting to move, but knowing I would never be there again; just many more women in my place, probably feeling exactly the same as I did. I didn't want more from him, just that moment out of his life to give me warmth and security and to keep me going for a little longer. Sienna's letter, asking what it was all for, yes, exactly what? For these wonderful moments and memories that are the only things left. Memories and images which don't portray feelings that were experienced. Just lots of faces in the same rat race called life.

Being beaten up by a prostitute. What did that teach me? Never to mess with a pro? Yes, but what else? For a while, I was part of their lives, living as they do, working with them to earn a buck, mixing with the same crowd. Maybe not as desperate as them; there was always a way out and it was never going to be a permanent thing. To be able to see that they weren't the dregs of society, but people with feelings and hopes and dreams. Not people to look down on and pass on the other side of the street because they weren't good enough to mix with. They just had their own problems and they dealt with them differently, like by punching me out! But Greg's a good person, so Marlina can't be all that bad. Just a vicious cow!

You have to laugh or else you'd spend the whole time crying. For people like Erren you should have a place in your heart for them. A place of hope; a knowledge that someone, somewhere cares, even if it doesn't really help them at the time. Sitting in the playground the other day, watching the kids, I felt so disheartened. They will grow up in a certain way, full of prejudices and full of materialistic greed. They have no possible chance for it to be any different because of this society. I want my kids to grow up good, to love everyone and everything and never to be jealous or greedy.

I didn't realise how low I had become. I felt alone and unloved and not secure enough in myself to support my progression. As I've got older I've learned not to take life's knocks to heart as much and I've come to realise that what I think I need, for the greater good of me, is not necessarily what I do need! All those moments I experienced moulded me into the person I have now become, and although I was so desperate for answers back then, over time, those questions have been answered. Not fully, I might add, but the things I had felt so desperate about in the past resolved themselves as I endeavoured to learn the lessons from each period of my life, in order for them never to be repeated. It took me a few attempts though, and some lessons have been repeated; mainly with men.

Another entry from my diary:

I wish I could believe and accept that my life is perfect.
I wish I could look at life through rose-tinted spectacles.
I wish I knew what my soul is yearning for.
I wish my love for someone was not unrequited.
I wish I could find peace in my heart, body and soul.
I wish I had more faith in myself and God.

To me, life at the moment feels like one long road to oblivion, full of downs and not many ups. I seem to have so many knockbacks; things go right for a while and then things seem so desperate, a complete lost cause. Of course, there is hope; if there wasn't, then life would be so meaningless and the only sure thing would be an end to this little life in this big world.

I guess I owed a lot to Lenny Kravitz at the time, as his songs, which I was listening to constantly, gave me hope and the self-knowledge that there were others out there like me, questioning things which just didn't add up.

It continues:

Yes, I want to be loved and I know what it's like to love, but not be in love. I am a completely free spirit but am I ready to love? I've got so much love to give to the right person. The problem is, when is he going to appear in my life? Tomorrow, a week, a month, a year, a decade or more from now, and how am I possibly going to make it through this period of longing? I know I'll know him when he comes along and there will be only one man for me. I remember sitting on the bus, the 286 from Sheffield to Holmesfield, daydreaming about what my future husband was doing precisely at that moment: eating, sleeping, working, making love... maybe thinking the same thing as me?

Looking back now, I am grateful for the time I spent with Gabby, Ross and the kids, but I was so isolated and desperate to go on another adventure, and I was on my own this time. Trace had requested a trip to Australia for Christmas and brought Mum and Dad over with her so we could spend some of the festive period together. Gabby and Ross were great that day: they took me to meet them from their flight, having packed a picnic with beer and fizz to eat by the harbour on the way back from the airport. They arrived the day before Christmas Eve and left the following day, flying out to Hong Kong to spend Christmas Day. I'd booked lunch on one of the boats in the harbour and Mum, Dad and I caught up on my year so far, while Trace slept off her shift in the hotel. It was so good to see them, and I was in very high spirits as I had finally saved up enough money to continue my travels and leave my childcare responsibilities behind. I had three months left to have some fun.

On Christmas Eve I said goodbye to my family at the airport and went straight to Amanda's house to spend Christmas. That night, we went out with her friends to a restaurant, which is where I met Robert, an expat from Norfolk who was in his early forties. I didn't much like him on first meeting as he took the piss out of me a little too much, but I suppose that was his way of showing interest. As the alcohol took effect, I was now free of responsibilities: I just wanted some fun. Robert was the first guy I had any sort of sexual relationship with and it was new to me.

On Christmas morning, Amanda gave me a stocking full of useful travel presents and we spent a fabulous day on the beach. It's quite weird for a Brit experiencing a hot

Morning picnic in Sydney, Christmas 1993

Christmas, but I'd celebrate on a beach again, for sure. Robert joined us on the beach and from then on, we were inseparable. Perhaps it was that few men had shown me affection before, but after we had spent a sex-driven few weeks together, he asked me to marry him. He bought me an amethyst ring and I even went into the emigration office to pick up the forms to be nationalised. I was caught on a wave, but it didn't take me long to open my eyes to the fact that I would never be his wife. I had far too much living to do.

I had just under a month of my trip to go before my flight departed for Los Angeles, and I was keen to do some travelling. Robert, of course, didn't want me to go and said that if I waited an extra week in Sydney he would take me to see Lenny Kravitz. But when I refused his invitation, as I was keen to get back on the road again, he told me that Lenny was playing Brisbane while I was there. I didn't have enough money for luxuries like tickets, even to see my idol, although I would have loved to. I had a tight budget and lots to see. However, if you'd asked me at the time who I would choose to share a sauna with out of anyone, I'd have picked Lenny Kravitz, for sure.

I'd been to see him play in the UK with my college mate SJ, and he was at the height of sexiness. I think he was going out with Vanessa Paradis at the time, who, let's face it, is drop-dead gorgeous and has had relationships with all the coolest men on the planet. So what I'm saying is that, not in a month of Sundays would I have had the faintest chance of wooing him away from the likes of Vanessa; not in my tatty swimsuit anyway!

I left Robert in Sydney and travelled up to Brisbane to stay with my college mate Sian, who was living with a woman called Sherry. I'd met Sherry on our last trip to Brisbane and we'd instantly hit it off. On arrival, she whisked me away to her gym at the Hilton for a sauna. I told her she was dead posh for having a Hilton gym membership, but apparently the rates were very competitive.

As we walked into the sauna, my heart sank, as there were two Americans chatting in the corner: "Blast!", I thought we were going to have a real heart to heart. I was dying to talk to Sherry about my failing relationship with Robert and how, in my mind, it was over. She had even promised me a chat earlier that day, as it was quiet. I quickly resigned myself to the unexpected situation and continued to chat, knowing others were listening too. One of the guys in the corner asked if it would be OK to put some eucalyptus oil on the coals and we nodded and smiled. Their energy was good and they were sociable enough to not have that underlying strain. It's difficult if you are in a room with strangers and no exchange has been made, not even a nod or a smile, and when you can cut the atmosphere with a knife. It didn't feel strained in this situation and I was intrigued as to who these guys were.

I could just about make them out in the dark, steamy sauna. I asked myself, "What are two, young, hip Americans with a nice energy to them doing in the Brisbane Hilton sauna?" With occasional fleeting glances across the room, sometimes catching their eye and smiling and sometimes getting away without being detected, I started scanning them, as I couldn't work it out. I'd noticed one of them had long dreadlocks and loads of tattoos, but it still hadn't clicked. It was only when the Spanish-looking one got up, and the other one stayed and wanted to chat, that I could give him my full attention and get to the bottom of this mystery.

It didn't take long for Sherry to jump straight in and ask what I'd been dying to ask all along: "What are you doing here?" I think the rest went like this:

Hip American: "I'm here on tour."

Sherry: "Oh, are you in a band?"

Pan over to Kay who is managing to go white despite the temperature in there. The penny had finally dropped.

Hip American: "No, I'm a solo artist."

Kay (managing to stay calm, despite her heart beating at a rate of knots!): "Oh, I do recognise you, actually."

It should really have been, "I carried a watermelon." It just felt like that *Dirty Dancing* scene, with a pointless comment.

Sherry (still oblivious): "So what's your name then?"

Kay and Hip American (in unison): "It's Lenny Kravitz."

After that, I lost the power of speech, through shock, but wouldn't have got a word in edgeways with Sherry anyway. He too was a chatterbox and the conversation went on to where we were all from. I just about managed to gain enough control to say, "Sheffield." He replied, "Oh, I've played in Sheffield a few times. I liked Sheffield." I thought, "Oh, how sweet, you're actually a really nice, down-to-earth guy, despite your position in my mind as demigod. His songs had taken me through some of my darker moments and I knew this man had to have a big, vulnerable heart, like the rest of us, in order to write them. Talented too, and incredibly sexy!

I'm so glad he was such a lovely guy, because I loved his songs and they became real after meeting him. At some point, Sherry invited him round for Sunday dinner at her sister's in New Zealand. He told her that he really would love to but had a tight touring schedule. He was the type that really would have, if he could. He said that it had been really nice to chat with us and, although he had to go to do the soundcheck, would we like to come to the gig later that evening? Now, does a bear shit in the woods or what? He went to get changed and asked us to write down our names so he could put us on the guest list.

I ran into the changing room and borrowed a pen off some poor woman, who probably only heard these words, and in no particular order: "Lenny Kravitz, pen, guest list, OUTSIDE!" I managed to stop myself from shaking enough to be able to write down our names and then regained my composure before handing them over to Lenny. He thanked me and said goodbye, clutching the piece of paper. By this time, Sherry was in the plunge pool. "All OK?" she asked. "Yes," I replied excitedly. For that moment I was in seventh heaven. I'd not only met the guy I would have chosen to share a sauna with out of anyone in the world; he'd also been fabulous and we were on his guest list. Sherry then asked the obvious: "Where's he playing, and how do we get our tickets?" Oh shit! Amid the excitement I'd forgotten to ask those simple questions, and now my moment of bliss was instantly clouded by a dumb mistake.

It took me back to my driving test in the days where the examiner would just ask you a couple of questions about the highway code, before he or she passed or failed you. I'd driven really well and I knew I'd passed until it came to the theory, when, in my panic, I had forgotten everything that I had learned and just blurted out the first thing that came into my head, knowing it was wrong. But as I stood there, frozen, I thought, "Great, you were so nearly there as well!" Thankfully, my examiner was great and gave me big clues to all the road signs and passed me first time.

And thankfully, Sherry was using her left-hand (logical) brain and we found out from the gym staff where he was playing. We went down to the lobby and got the number for the venue and, as we were putting the coins in the payphone, who should walk down to reception but the man himself. He was accompanied by his manager and I walked up to him as cool as a cucumber saying, "I'm really sorry, but where do we get the tickets from?" By this time a group of young girls were surrounding us, demanding his autograph, so he asked his manager to take down our names again and phone them through, finishing with, "I really want these girls to come."

His friendly manager told us that he'd phoned our names through to the venue about five minutes ago but that he would have to do as he was told. He also informed us that all we needed to do was give our names to the ticket office at the venue. As we were leaving, Lenny looked over from signing another autograph for the ever-increasing circle of fans, smiled and said, "Enjoy the gig, girls."

When Robert phoned me later that afternoon, I started the conversation with: 'You'll never guess who I've just shared a sauna with!"

"Who?" he reluctantly asked.

"Lenny Kravitz," I announced.

The phone went quiet until I said, "Robert? Robert? Are you there?"

He finally responded, saying, "How can I compete with that?"

It was at that moment that I knew our relationship was definitely over. Come on, compete? Why would he think there was any competition between him and Lenny? Remember Vanessa, his girlfriend? I wanted him to be happy for me in meeting someone I admired. It smacked of jealousy and insecurity. I wanted someone to love me, not stifle me.

Sherry and I took the train to the gig that night. We walked straight up to the ticket office and said that we were on the guest list. "Whose?" the assistant replied. "Lenny Kravitz's", I announced. I'd been on other guest lists before and it was usually with Kevin, the sound engineer, or Toxin, the UK Subs' tour manager, but this was rather different. We did make an obsessed fan cry before the show had started though, when we told her that we had shared a sauna with him earlier that day!

I've dined out on that story a few times now and some people always joke if they've heard it before, saying, "Oh no, not the Lenny Kravitz story again!" But whenever we play the 'claim to fame game', this story is obviously going to be told.

From Brisbane, I took a bus up the east coast of Australia to Hervey Bay, where I'd arranged to stay with Robert's friend Mick, another expat, who looked after me while on the mainland. At the local backpackers' hostel I booked on a trip to Fraser Island, which was just off the coast, and we were put into small groups to tour the island in a four-wheel drive. In our party there were four Swedish guys, two Danish girls and Toni, another

English girl, and we took it in turns to drive the vehicle as we explored the island. We had bought food but most of our budget was spent on alcohol.

Fraser Island was amazing, and our first stop along the way was Lake McKenzie, a freshwater lake. The water was crystal clear and the beaches as fine as caster sugar. We were warned not to swim in the ocean, as it was shark infested, including by the great white, so we kept to the inland lakes to bathe. There were no roads on the island, and when we did run out of beer, we used the beach as a motorway to the nearest bottle shop. We travelled at breakneck speed before the tide came in, which would have trapped us miles from our camping spot.

From Fraser Island, I travelled up the coast to Airlie Beach and the Great Barrier Reef. Unfortunately I only had a few days before I had to catch a plane to New Zealand, but I still managed a day's sailing and snorkelling around the Whitsunday Islands.

I flew over to Christchurch, New Zealand on 15th February 1994 for the final leg of my journey, and only a month to go before I returned home. Christchurch is a beautiful city and I spent a few days there before starting my travels. At my backpackers' hostel, I shared a room with two Swedish girls, Marlin and Katrina, and we quickly became friends. To spend the time before our bus departed, we watched the famous Christchurch Wizard in the square and watched a wonderful open air production of Shakespeare's *A Midsummer Night's Dream* at the university. We had booked on the Kiwi Experience bus together, which left from Greymouth and which was the most convenient way for us backpackers to do a tour of the South Island.

On the bus, we met our other travelling companions, whom we would spend the duration of the trip with. The other passengers had been on the bus for a while and it was quite cliquey, so those of boarding at Greymouth became good friends. We were: Renate from Brazil, Kim from Derbyshire, Paul, Chris and Blake from Canada and not forgetting Katrina and Marlin from Sweden, and of course myself.

The bus took us through the most remote and breathtaking scenery I had ever seen. We stopped off at the glacier at Franz Josef, before continuing to our wilderness stopover, taking in the best views and shouting at our bus driver, John, to stop for photos along the way. We eventually arrived in Queenstown, a ski resort during the winter but an all-season action town offering such delights as bungee jumping, white water rafting, river surfing, hang-gliding and horse riding etc. The original group shared an alpine lodge with lots of other Canadian men we had met on the bus and it was party all the way. Looking back at my diary, there was always lots of drink involved.

I love Canadians; they have a similar sense of humour to us Brits, unlike the Americans we met, ie, they took the piss out of each other. Canadians also get very offended if you think they are from the US, but you can tell in a moment if you ask them to say OUT, as they have much flatter vowel sounds than Americans. I wasn't ready to do a bungee jump in Queenstown, but went river surfing for my adrenalin rush instead. We were given body boards and had a quick lesson before descending the river, reaching a couple of grade 3½ rapids by the end of the ride. Six is the highest, so quite a challenge with just body boards and no experience, and on the first rapid, I fell off my board and nearly drowned. Luckily, I was saved by our instructor in the nick of time. The next rapid was a breeze and I felt totally exhilarated by the experience by the time the bus picked us up. It was all filmed for posterity, the cameraman originally hailing from Nottinghamshire.

Kim, Renate and I went horse riding through amazing countryside past Sam Neil's ranch, and we went on a day trip to Milford Sound. If you know your fjords from your sounds, it's actually a fjord, and we spent the afternoon being followed by about thirty dolphins swimming alongside the boat out in the Tasman Sea.

We were all loth to break up our original group, but by the time we reached Christchurch again, most of our party had left the bus. I had planned to meet up with Robert in Auckland and so booked on another Kiwi Experience bus to travel up the north island with Katrina and Marlin. At Lake Taupo, I eventually plucked up enough courage to do a bungee jump. I'm glad I did it. Leaving New Zealand, where AJ Hackett first invented the experience, without doing one would not have been right. I looked over the edge at the boat on the lake where I was to jump, which was just a dot, and thought, "What are you doing, you crazy girl?" I was scared, even though I knew it was safe, as Katrina and Marlin had jumped before me and had survived. In the end, I just flung myself off that high platform with my eyes tightly closed, as I'd been previously told of retinas detaching during jumps. I had to just let go to get the T-shirt!

I had been invited to visit Sherry, who was over on holiday at her family home near Hastings, on the east coast of New Zealand, and I caught a local bus from Taupo. They lived in Hawkes Bay, a wine-growing area, and they took me to a vineyard during my stay. I spent a fortune 'tasting' the wine that day. The family were so welcoming and we stayed at Sherry's sister Dawn's house, visiting her father for dinner one night. He made the best cream desserts ever! This is where my diary ended. For some reason, I didn't write anything else from this moment on.

After leaving her lovely family, I travelled up to Auckland, arriving at a city centre backpackers' hostel just before Robert, who had arranged to visit me, arrived from Sydney. We started arguing soon after we met up again and I remember phoning Mum up from a payphone in my hostel as Robert slept upstairs. She was concerned for me after my announcement that I was to marry him. My sister had had a blazing argument with him as she clearly didn't want to lose me to Oz. I told my mum that I thought I was here for a reason and by that time I was certain it wasn't to stay down under and marry him.

For what would be our last trip together, Robert and I went to the Whitsunday Islands, north of Auckland. But he refused to join the rest of the group, isolating us, only wanting me for himself alone. I wanted to have some fun and meet new people before I left for home the following week, and knowing the relationship was over, I didn't want to be with him any more. Our relationship broke into even smaller bits as a result and by the time I took him to the airport to catch his plane I had told him it was **over**. He didn't take it well, but I felt very unwell and a tannoy request went out for a doctor among the passengers in the terminal building. The doctor, who responded to the request, urged me to go and see a registered doctor, before flying myself. Thankfully, we were distracted from our 'break up' and Robert left, on a plane back to Australia. I would never see him again.

I caught a taxi to a locum doctor near the airport, who diagnosed an infected cyst in my salivary gland. We were both worried that I had no health insurance to cover me for the USA, whose airspace I would be entering, as it would have cost a fortune for healthcare. He showed me how to drain my cyst, which I did throughout the journey, feeling very poorly throughout the long flight to LA. I did pick up though, when we made a fuel stop in Tahiti, which was certainly the highlight of the journey. As we left the plane to sit in the small rustic airport while they filled up on fuel, we were greeted by local women in grass skirts who hung garlands of flowers round our necks; something I had only ever seen before in films. I'd love to go back to that island one day, and stay for longer than just a few hours next time.

When we finally arrived in LA, we were told there had been a terrorist threat in London and that all flights there had been cancelled. This meant that my flight to Manchester was now full. The passengers on staff discounts were all obliged to stay overnight in a hotel in LA as a result. Trace had bought me a ticket using her staff discount (as her sister, I only paid 20% of any flight during all the time she worked for BA) from LA to Manchester for Christmas, to ensure my swift return to Blighty. This was instead of going overland to New York, as my 'round the world ticket' had dictated.

I had literally no money left and my credit card was declined by the hotel we stayed at. Thankfully, my room tariff was paid for by a kind fellow passenger and BA employee, who was paid back by Dad when we arrived in the UK the following day. My time in LA was brief but I did get to see the Hollywood sign from the plane window, which was enough for me.

I got back to England, ten days short of a year; the year I got my wings and gained a day (having crossed the International Date Line). Mike had made me a welcome home sign and Mum and Trace had the champagne on ice. This stage of my metamorphosis was complete and I had changed from a girl into a woman, losing much of my naivety along the way. Things would never be the same again; I would have itchy feet for the rest of my life.

Husband no. 1 – Ashley

5

Love is perfect. It's us that's not.
– Kay Rose-Hattrick

Almost immediately after coming back from travelling I met Ashley Bright (RIP), my first husband. I had gone down to see Ju Ju, my college mate, at her London flat for the weekend and she was having a party at which Ashley was also a guest. The first time we spoke, in the kitchen in her bijou, one bed Highgate dwelling, I knew I had met someone very special. His smile, which lit up his face so brightly, rocked me to my foundations and back up again. He was spiritual too; he just didn't fully understand it. Ashley was truly interested in me and I in him and we immediately clicked and chatted all night. We didn't want to part so soon, so I went back to his 'swinging flat in East London', as we playfully referred to it, and which he shared with his flatmate, Brendan. That weekend, and into the week that followed, we spent as much time as we could with each other, and from then on we met up most weekends.

For the next year we took it in turns to travel to London or Millthorpe to see each other. I was on the dole for just over a month. I enrolled on a back to work programme, a bit like in *The League of Gentlemen*, but our 'restart officer' was nothing like Pauline and really nice. Most of the class had enquired about the course, but some were forced to attend as they hadn't had a job for some time. On the first day, about ten minutes in, when the tutor was introducing us to the programme, a guy walked straight into the classroom without looking at the tutor or saying anything; not even a "Sorry I'm late." As he walked past her desk he threw down a piece of paper (presumably his curt letter to attend, or else) and sat down at an empty desk. We were all amazed that he'd been so rude.

Some of the others in the class were dressed in suits and had been made redundant, desperate to get back into the workplace. I felt quite sorry for them and it was a bit like a scene from *The Full Monty*, with age not on their side, unfortunately. I myself was chuffed to have help with my CV, which so needed it, and to have stamps for job applications paid too: wow, a bonus. I suppose I thought I had the job market at my fingertips; I'd just not yet decided quite what that job was going to be.

I'll always remember the reaction of the tutor and how brilliantly she reacted to his entrance; I think we may have even applauded her. There was only a brief pause as the guy sat down in front of her, but it seemed endless, and no one drew breath for those few seconds, all of us taken aback by the attitude of this unbelievably disrespectful and immensely rude man. "In my office, now, please," she commanded, assertively. We all watched as he grudgingly sulked into her glass-panelled office and the door was shut behind them. We could see, but couldn't hear; all of us making assumptions about what was being said. It lasted a minute, and he went towards the exit and she took her place at her desk, beautifully calm, and said firmly, "I am not having him disrupt my class and ruin it for everyone else." She told us he had received an 'if you don't attend Job Start then you will have your benefits stopped' letter and was angry. (I think it was only about a three week course anyway.) His attitude made the tutor angrier though, and he knew it.

I couldn't believe the attitude of this man, taking it out on someone who was trying to help him, and who certainly hadn't sent the letter. He just couldn't be arsed, and unfortunately people like this give being on the dole a bad name. I know there's not much opportunity out there, but you have to open yourself up to all eventualities as you never know what's lurking round the corner, and it could be quite pleasurable. She then carried on, without a trace of being flustered. She was a good role model in how not to take shit, and that's probably why I remember it so vividly.

Shortly after this course, a position opened at Dad's accountancy firm, where he was the feared senior partner, to cover maternity for the receptionist. I travelled in with him, and had to endure Terry Wogan every morning, but I didn't see much of Dad during the day as I was tied to the switchboard. I met some great people there, especially Kim, one of the partners' secretaries, and Julie, who worked downstairs in finance and whom we sometimes dropped off back home in Dronfield. Pat, who shared the office with me part time, also shared her treats of shortcake with me every Thursday and Friday, which was the highlight of my week.

One day, I wrote a poem about my experience of being a receptionist on the long, drawn out afternoons when there was nothing to do except wait for the sound of the switchboard to call: no escape; just to wait, and wait, and wait. Thankfully I knew this would not be forever.

One day its shrill voice will call to someone else.

Another captive enslaved by its environs.

Let me tell you, it could be *sooo* boring but Kim or Julie would cover for me for toilet breaks and we had a little light relief. One afternoon, however, we got a phone call from Julie downstairs who said the tannoy was on and she could hear Kim and I having a giggle in the background. Thankfully, it was muffled so you couldn't hear what we were talking about, which was in fact contraceptives. I told her that my mum and dad had three planned children and never used contraceptives. Can you imagine if everyone in the building, including those in client meetings, had heard us? It's not really something the senior partner wants advertising to all his employees by his daughter. Phew, we quickly turned off the tannoy and howled with laughter at the hilarity of the situation. Despite my workplace boredom, the money enabled me to commute to London every fortnight.

Ashley proposed on the day of the 1994 Wimbledon women's finals, only a few months after we met. Dad had got tickets from a draw at work, and after Martina Navratilova won again that year, we met up with him for dinner in London. That night, Ashley pulled me aside to pop the question, urging secrecy between us until he had done things properly and in keeping with tradition. I think he said something like, "If I was to ask you to marry me in a few months' time, what would you say?" I responded positively but it wasn't made official until:

1. He had bought the ring; sapphire and diamonds from Hatton Gardens.
2. Asked for Dad's permission for my hand in marriage, formally, and behind closed doors.
3. Got down on one knee to officially propose to me and slip on the ring, symbolising our commitment to each other.

Our engagement was finally made official on Christmas Day 1994. The marriage proposal was only kept secret from Dad up until then as I *had* to tell the closest to me at that time, Mum and Trace. They were as thrilled as I, finally getting the son and brother-in-law they had always wanted. I knew I had not been 'in love' with Robert; our engagement had just been a sham. With Ashley, it was different. He was gorgeous and everything you would want in a future husband: handsome, thoughtful, intelligent, talented, witty, kind-natured, playful, lovable and with no baggage, just unconditional love.

"Where does it all go wrong?"

Even after our engagement, Dad made us sleep in different rooms when Ashley came up to visit me. But I moved down to London the following year and lived with Ashley and

KAY ROSE-HATTRICK

Brendan for a few weeks, before we all moved into our brand new residence down the road in Forest Gate. Brendan only stayed for a couple of days, after I'd found a fag down my brand new toilet. It was only a one bed flat, and quite small, and we wanted to start our life together without Brendan getting in the way! He'd had loads of time to look for a new pad himself, but Brendan being Brendan, he'd left it until the last minute. You couldn't be mad with him for long though, the adorable Scot with a soft, lilting voice.

Gladys Dimson House was a listed building. It had been an orphanage, then a maternity hospital and then it was turned into flats, mainly for hospital employees, of whom Ashley was one. At the time, Ashley was a manager at the local hospital, and only in his late twenties. The building was in its own grounds and had two ponds, which were home to swans and toads, among other aquatic life. One night, we took a midnight stroll around the gardens with a friend who was visiting us for the evening. Under the moonlight, we came across literally hundreds of toads, some babies, some huge adults, but all incredibly friendly. I spent most of the night sitting with several of them on my knee and the toads and I refused to move for hours; lapping up this surreal but beautiful experience. From then on I became bonded with these warty dudes.

Soon after moving down there, I got a job working for an IT recruitment agency. My job was to 'coordinate the candidate recruitment and selection process for senior information technology-related posts', or so it says on my CV. I was quite successful and the only one who could keep my boss, Paul, in order, or so I was told.

Paul and I had a love/hate relationship. When I was in favour, as a treat he'd take me to the West End in his red Porsche 911 to meet his clients. On these days I was made to take off my thumb ring as he said it brought down the tone of the company. I grudgingly obliged, grumbling about how it suppressed my creativity and individuality. We had some great banter between us though, and I could give as much as he gave me without worrying about the repercussions of putting him in his place, despite him out-ranking me. One day, he took me out to lunch and he decided we would continue drinking all afternoon as the big boss was not due back from the head office in Leeds that day.

When we went back to the office at the end of the day, to pick up our stuff, Paul was ushered into the office, red-faced, as his boss had returned prematurely. He quickly made up the story that I was threatening to leave and so he had kept me in the pub to persuade me to stay. After Paul, I was called into his office. The big boss told me that he was sorry that I felt that way, and would a £2k pay rise persuade me to stay? What a result! I stayed at Lorien for about a year and mainly enjoyed it, although the work wasn't very challenging. I did learn a very useful skill at Lorien though, when they paid for me to go on a touch typing course.

For weeks, after work, I sat in one of the many places on Tottenham Court Road that offered touch typing courses, sitting in front of a large screen with the computerised voice of a woman on loop saying, "A tap B tap C tap D tap" etc. I remember thinking, "I'll never get my head round this." But the repetition worked, and I finished the course having acquired a highly sought after skill, in my opinion. It's extremely useful for anyone to learn, despite their profession, and especially now I'm writing a book! Now I can't look at the keyboard as I type, as I mess up; I just *feel* the letters instead.

Lorien was a great company to work for, with a very strong 'work hard, play hard' ethic running through its workforce, all the way from the top. Every month, they funded a lavish night out with all expenses paid; usually to a restaurant, but one night we were taken to the *Alien Resurrection* show at the Trocadero in Piccadilly Circus.

The show started when we were greeted by a guy dressed in army gear, who 'worked' on the spaceship we were supposed to be 'visiting'. He asked us to wait in a chamber for what seemed like an eternity, and in the distance we could hear gunfire and 'alien' screams. We waited some more and our office group reacted in different ways. It was like watching a psychology experiment. The boys were mainly acting cool and manned up to the situation, which had become quite 'real' as we got even more into 'character'. I wound myself up so much; deep down knowing that it was just a 'show' but at the same time getting caught up in the energy of the situation, so the adrenalin kicked in and I started to have trouble breathing. It was the waiting which was the killer and brought on the heart palpitations.

Finally, the army guy came back and announced that 'aliens' had in fact escaped on the ship and that we needed to evacuate immediately! Fuck me – it was so real to me by this time, and as we were led down the dark corridors of the spaceship with only the red emergency light guiding the way, and the girls holding onto each other out of pure fear, an alien appeared from nowhere, screeching and writhing on the spot. It was made even more visually dramatic by the infrared paint on the 'actor's alien' costume and the strobes lighting up the fearful creature. After we escaped through the exit, I was so high on adrenalin, let me tell you! This 'experiment' shows beautifully that anyone, including myself, can be relatively easily manipulated to think and believe something that is not really the truth.

A different type of scary was experienced on another weekend, when we crewed a boat over the English Channel to France. It was billed as a team-building weekend and we certainly worked as a team in a storm on the first night, crossing the channel. One of the guys who worked at Lorien was a keen skipper and he successfully captained the boat there and back without mishap, despite our boozy lunch in France. What an experience it was to be in the middle of the channel on a moonlit night: telling ghost stories to each other with the nearest vessel, a ferry, only a few sparkling lights in the distance. With the rain and waves lashing across the boat, and only being kept safe by the harnesses that we were strapped into as we were thrown all over by the motion of the angry sea. We were at the mercy of the English Channel and all the elements that night, far away from any help, and I felt very free. And the adrenalin high was present again.

Although the perks were good, the work at Lorien just didn't stimulate me and it wasn't long before I left without even securing another job. A friend had told me there was a vacant post working for her employer, BTEC, the awarding body who had issued me with my HND. I was successful in interview, which I think was thanks to the half of Valium that Ashley's dad had given me to calm me down, so that I wouldn't go into a panic like I usually did in interview situations. I started working with Rowena in the London regional office soon afterwards.

First wedding day with Mum, Dad and Trace, my chief bridesmaid

With a job secured, Ashley and I set a date to be married on 24th August 1996, at St Swithin's parish church in Holmesfield. As I'd only just started working at BTEC, I had only accrued a few days' holiday, so I had to organise the wedding at long distance, often returning to my parents' to finalise plans. As a child, I had visions of my ideal wedding day, where I wore flowers in my hair and walked barefoot through the long grass. Remember that image for later. I certainly didn't want a big meringue or the usual wedding dress from a bridal shop, so I only bought one wedding magazine and saw a version of my perfect dress straight away. A friend put me in contact with Lucy Bennett, a dress designer who designed and made my dress, and we became very good friends through chatting over a bottle of wine after the many fittings.

Lucy also made the dresses for the four bridesmaids: Trace, Sienna, Ashley's sister Carol and Charlotte, my cousin Adele's little girl. The girls looked stunning in their long, fitted blue numbers with Charlotte in cream and a blue sash. Lucy made the dress exactly how I wanted it and I had flowers in my hair, but I wore dainty cream ballet pumps for the ceremony, afterwards changing them for cream Doc Marten shoes that Lucy had covered with the lace from the dress. Lucy and her boyfriend even came to the wedding in the end, as we had developed such a good friendship.

During the ceremony at St Swithin's church, I cried with an overwhelming love for a man as I committed myself to him in the eyes of 'God' and the 'law' and all our close family and friends. I loved Ashley deeply and I believed it would last forever. After the ceremony, we left in an old cream Rolls Royce, which took us to Baldwin's Omega and our reception. The Omega is said to be the best mass caterer in Sheffield and it was no exception that day, as David Baldwin carved the sumptuous joints of meat for the wedding breakfast in view of us all. Dad hadn't spared any expense and guests enjoyed a free bar all day. After all the family and Mum and Dad's friends had been invited, I think I was allowed one table for my own friends, which of course included my old schoolfriends Zoë, accompanied by her fiancé (now husband) Matt, and Claire. SJ, my old college friend, was also there, with her new partner and now husband, the very funny Adrian from Manchester.

I had made the decision to keep my maiden name once married and as a feminist to the end, I wanted to retain my own identity. Before I did my speech, I was introduced by the master of ceremonies as Kay Hattersley. I didn't like the traditional proceedings of a wedding where the bride has no voice. This decision would later cause problems with the family, but I joked that I sounded too much like a furniture polish: "You can hear the ad," I said, "Stay bright with K-bright."

After a fabulous wedding, we honeymooned in Thailand, flying into Bangkok and then on to Koh Samui, the island paradise I had visited a few years before. This time, we stayed right on the beach and Ashley got his first taste of travelling, which he loved. Ashley lost his wedding ring in the sea one night while we were night swimming. The sea algae lit up the dark ocean like fluorescent tubes when they were disturbed, lighting our way while we searched frantically for the 'needle in a haystack'. He took it really badly when he had to accept his ring had been claimed forever by the vast waters. Looking back, could it have been a sign that our relationship would not last forever?

We returned to married life in London and my new job. At BTEC I was the 'first line contact for further education customers in the London area and responsible for the organisation and administration of seminars and workshops in the London and Anglia regions' (again taken from my CV). I stayed in this post for a year, during which time Rowena and I were joined by the serious Tim, who took Anglia off me, but I knew how to crack his face and we became good friends. I met some other great friends here too, and most Fridays a group of us from different departments, but mainly student services and always including Pete from Lincoln, would meet for a few drinks after work. A few drinks was generally a few too many, but we always had such a laugh together.

The company was going through a restructuring, as we had just merged with the academic awarding body London Examinations, and a job came up in the marketing department, which I leapt at, despite it being a sidestep and with no pay rise. This was far more appealing to me as I'd enjoyed marketing at college. I was responsible for coordinating all the exhibitions we attended all over the UK, including Northern Ireland. I also attended most of the larger ones to set up, which included a trip to Belfast with the office manager, Kath, who was based in Birmingham. What a trip that was!

Julie Walters was in town filming the 1998 *Titanic Town*. She wasn't staying in our hotel of course, but many of the film production crew were, and even the wardrobe department were occupying the corridors. Kath and I got chatting with the 'dolly grip' and another grip and had a drink with them one night, quizzing them about the role of all the grips involved in the process of making a film: fascinating. We also toured a few of the other pubs in Belfast after we'd finished at the exhibition for the day. We could feel the presence of tension still lining the streets, but were safe at all times. This was confirmed by the taxi driver, who took me to an off licence to get a bottle of Irish whiskey and then on to the airport, and we chatted at length. Belfast is a beautiful city and I was glad of the opportunity to visit and have so much fun with Kath, while work was paying.

I generally didn't have any help lugging exhibition stands around the country, but the boss's secretary, Jane, became my partner in crime and a lifelong friend. We were very often found bombing around London in the back of a black cab with a rather large exhibition stand and boxes of materials in tow. I didn't like her much at first meeting; I found her a little aloof, but we bonded one day when talking about her passion for camping, and I saw her as a nature lover who needed to be out in the countryside and away from the city, like me. She became my bezzy mate and we had such a laugh together; it was painful when we were pulled apart due to another restructure, when the marketing team were moved to corporate affairs and I was given a new boss.

The BTEC marketing team moved down to Russell Square, right next door to Senate House, which was used in the adaptation of George Orwell's *1984* starring John Hurt. It felt like Big Brother was watching you every time you went out to the courtyard for a fag, as its imposing facade looked on. I love George Orwell and had digested all his books by this time in my life, so the significance and meaning of *1984* was all the more apparent in my mind as I looked up towards the ironically named Ministry of Love every fag break.

My new manager, Aletha, a Canadian, was perfect in every way: in appearance, character and intelligence. Her gazelle-like demeanour made me feel fat, clumsy and incompetent but she was a lovely girl and she taught me a lot, especially about structure and organisation, making lists and producing forms for everything. She also invited companies to bid to be able to deliver our exhibition stands and materials all round the country. The company who also printed our books won it, and Barry became my contact and a star. He made life so much easier for me, and the company was based in Worksop, only up the road from my parents. I combined a business meeting and trip home whenever I could. In my new role, I also helped organise the Edexcel Student of the Year Awards, where the best of the students in both academic and vocational subjects went through a rigorous process, so that we could find the ultimate student of the year. This is when I was putting on the pounds like there was no tomorrow, at one stage reaching a size 22.

Our patron was the Duke of Kent, and every year part of his duty was to hand out the student certificates at the awards ceremony. Aletha had given me the job of handing the framed certificates to the Duke on stage. I was briefly pulled aside by his aides for my etiquette lesson in dealing with a Duke, which didn't really go in, and I remember just smiling and saying, "Hi," like I would with anyone, as I took my position next to him on stage. That year Nick Ross, of BBC's *Crimewatch* fame, was the master of ceremonies, and instead of calling out the students in order he ignored his script and welcomed *everyone* up saying, "Come and get your awards." As a result, everyone piled on stage, but not in the order I had stacked the heavy, framed certificates that I was handing to the Queen's cousin. He didn't notice until I gave him a certificate with a boy's name on for a girl and snapped at me about it.

We were alone on stage and his aides were not party to what I said. I whispered to him, explaining what had happened, but he didn't seem to understand and still looked annoyed, and so I exclaimed, "There's nothing I can do about it!" while giving him an annoyed look back! He thought better than to challenge me further; it's unlikely he is spoken back to very often by a member of the *proletariat*, but I was certainly not going to be spoken to by anyone in that tone, even royalty.

I was given a video of the day and I was huge, but I comfort ate as I was quite depressed at the time. I hated London and commuting to work every day. London is an unforgiving city and despite all those people it can be the loneliest place on this planet. I wasn't used to this, being brought up in the north where people still spoke to each other and helped out when they could. In London, people could be struggling with buggies, or old people could be struggling with their bags, but you could bet your bottom dollar that commuters became blinkered.

Mum came to visit me after I cried down the phone to her one day about how low I'd become. I met her from the train station and as we got on the tube not one person got up to give up their seat for an old lady. When she finally got a seat Mum almost immediately stood up again for a pregnant lady. Young men and women bowed their heads to avoid my glares after I asked loudly, "How's your arthritis, mother?"

Tube and train travel was pretty dire and was always plagued with incidents. I understand that the number of tube passengers has increased by a third since I lived there, too. One evening, I got on the Metropolitan line, as it was always quiet and guaranteed a seat, and someone was 'chasing the dragon' in full view. I only found this out from a fellow passenger a few seats away, who quietly talked me through the process of preparing the heroin before smoking it.

One day, I chastised some kids on rollerskates who were terrorising a German couple on the Docklands light railway from Greenwich to Stratford. They were being so rude and I told them off for disrespecting our guests in this country. The boy was mouthing off at me so I stuck out my foot, smiling as the doors opened and he went flying. He'd certainly had his comeuppance and he knew it!

"It was him!" he shouted, placing the blame on someone else.

"I know it was you, I saw you!" I responded.

He suddenly went quiet and skated off with his head down, hopefully thinking twice about voicing his xenophobic remarks in the future. I didn't care; I was not going to be bullied or abused by anyone and certainly wasn't going to pretend things hadn't happened, like other commuters would.

Another day, I boarded my usual train into Liverpool Street station and incredibly, got a seat in the main part of the train. Most days, you and a fellow traveller had to prise open the doors of a driver's cab where two trains had been pushed together, in order to squeeze onto the already heaving train. You weren't supposed to be there, of course, but they seemed to turn a blind eye to it. There was much more space there and when you arrived at your stop you could walk through the main car to get off. Just for that short journey I would often strike up a conversation with someone who had helped me with the door; unheard of in the main body of the train. Opening the door, which was a two man job, developed camaraderie between passengers and barriers were let down for a while. On this occasion, the driver's cab was occupied by schoolkids, who rushed into the car full of people and sprayed us with a fire extinguisher, soaking everyone around with foul-smelling water, before taking cover back in their sanctuary.

I looked around and the guy next to me was even wetter than I was, but continued to bury his head in his newspaper as though nothing had happened. When we stopped at Stratford station a short time later, the kids got off. As they piled through the train carriage I confronted them, voicing my disgust at their behaviour. As the other boy had before, they denied their part in it, thinking I must have been stupid, but nonetheless a typical teenager response. Not one person in the cab said a word, apart from one northerner who reassured me that the smell would go away, as it was only stale water. I couldn't believe my fellow commuters but soon realised that I could never rely on them for help in an emergency.

London and I never got along, although I realise I did experience a lot in the five years I lived there. As the years progressed, my behaviour and ways altered. I used to rush everywhere at top speed, and when I went home to my parents' one weekend, Mum and I went to Marks & Spencer in Chesterfield. Whilst I tried on some clothes in the changing room, she chatted to the assistant. I asked her later, "Did you know her, mum?" and I was amazed that they had never met in their lives. People talked to each other up north and I was shocked at what I had become.

Ashley was a home bird, a typical Cancerian, and we didn't stray too far from the flat very often. At weekends, I refused to travel into central London as my weekly commute was quite enough for me. Every weekend we would visit his parents and sit in his mum and dad's kitchen; me being shy and quietly sipping a gin and tonic while they mainly talked about hospitals. They had all worked or did work for the NHS, except his sister Carol. I hated going round there as I always felt stupid and unable to join in the conversation. I had a very bad self-image at the time: I was size 22 and felt fat, frumpy, stupid and trapped in a city I despised. His mum was a proper mum though, and was always so lovely to me. I still have very fond memories of her. His sister Susan was nice to me too, but his other sister, Carol, and his father could be a bit difficult.

On one occasion, I had a package in the name of Hattersley delivered to their house and, as a result, Ashley's dad didn't speak to me for about a week, until I had apologised for not using my married name. It was totally different for his own daughter, though. He actually berated Carol for not keeping her maiden name when she went up the ranks to be a sergeant in the Met. One rule for him, it seemed.

In 1998, my father went into hospital to have his piles removed and found that he had bowel cancer as well. It was a massive blow to the whole family, especially Dad. I'd not seen him so scared and vulnerable since Trace had been taken hostage in Kuwait, but this time he feared for his own life. It was hard for me living in London with my dad so far away, but I was there for him during this period, as were his whole family. After the operation we all visited him as he lay in his bed, seemingly attached to every machine in the hospital. Our strong, dependable father was a shadow of his former self, understandably so considering that the surgeons had removed most of his bowel and redirected it to a hole in his side.

He did recover and was given the all-clear, but he still has to endure his colostomy bag, especially when it splits in public. It split in Sainsbury's recently and the stench was overpowering; as if he'd just squatted in the aisle. It doesn't bother me; I'm just concerned for him as I know he gets really embarrassed. Though no one would really know who'd dealt it unless they looked into his face and saw his supreme discomfort, but no one looks at each other anyway. The shopping trip is cut short and Dad rushes home to sort out his bag. I admire anyone who lives with this condition every day; it takes such a strong person to move forward from this. Though unfortunately, you aren't left with many options, are you?

I found it difficult being so far away from my parents but for Christmas we would alternate between Millthorpe and London and I always looked forward to the ones up north. I felt I could never be myself with Ashley's family after one year when we sat down at the table for Christmas dinner and I picked up a cracker to pull.

At that moment, Carol announced, "We don't pull the crackers until the end of the meal."

"Oh!" I said.

"But isn't the whole point about wearing your hats during the meal and looking slightly stupid? We do it at home," I added.

She sharply replied, "You're not at home now!"

I just wanted the ground to swallow me up, but I couldn't get emotional about it at the time. That Christmas, I pretended to be asleep on the chair that was renamed the 'sleepy chair' after that. It was the place where I used to find solace and escape. In fact, that's where I did spend a lot of time, asleep. I'd often say, "I'm going to escape to my dreams," as my life was not going the way I had pictured it going and I needed to get away.

The Lenny Kravitz song 'Fly Away' was a track I was listening to constantly and it is what I ultimately desired to do, as I had come to hate the city even more. Ashley and I spoke at length about travelling and then leaving London to start a new life in the country and it all seemed set. In September 1999, our dreams were realised and we set off for three months on a trip that would take us to Singapore, Malaysia, Laos and Vietnam. I gave up my job at Edexcel and was given a fantastic sendoff; I felt overwhelmed by how much my work colleagues, who were now good friends, told me they were going to miss me. Ashley's job was kept open for three months and we also kept on the flat. I really did think I was finally going to escape London, but not before rebuilding my confidence on the road again.

When Ashley and I talked to his family about moving out of London, Carol announced, "I'd like to move outside London, but I've got to consider my parents," meaning that Ashley and I also had a duty to stay close by because of their age. But what about my parents; did they not count? Especially considering Dad had only just had a serious health scare? Before we went travelling I asked Ashley if we could start a family and perhaps try while we were away. He fiercely cut me down and dismissed the idea immediately, saying that I shouldn't be so stupid. OK, sorry, it's just what married couples generally do after nearly four years of marriage, surely? But at least I was free again and away from that city for a while!

The Quiet American

Travel expanded my mind; seeing something pure, beyond economic success, which made me humble. I realised that our lives in the west have become far too complicated. These beautiful people reminded me of the simplicity and power of love itself.

– Kay Rose-Hattrick

Ashley had always had a vision about being in New York in the 1960s and hailing a yellow cab. "In a previous life," he had wondered. He also felt a strong connection to the Vietnam war; a war called the American war by the Vietnamese. It was a very humbling time for us both, seeing people in complete poverty but with such zest for life and with smiles beyond material satisfaction. They even welcomed their ex-enemies with open arms, despite the casualties of that futile war being evident on every street corner. Agent Orange victims crawled among the tourists, offering their wares with love still in their hearts.

Agent Orange is a blend of tactical herbicides the US military used as part of its chemical warfare programme, Operation Ranch Hand, during the Vietnam war. Between 1962 and 1971, American forces sprayed over 19 million gallons of the chemical in Vietnam, Laos and parts of Cambodia, in order to remove trees and dense foliage that provided enemy cover. Concerns about the health effects for both the war veterans and the indigenous population still continue. Interestingly, Agent Orange was manufactured primarily by the multinational giant Monsanto Corporation, who were the first to genetically modify crops.

We had three months to rediscover ourselves and it was my opportunity to regain my energy and rebuild my confidence. It felt good travelling again; that freedom of just having a rucksack on your back and not knowing where you will lay your head from one day to the next. Travel didn't fill me with anxiety. I was now very happy to embrace this freedom after my previous travel experiences. It was Ashley's first adventure, as he had only ever having been on package holidays in Europe before, and he was a little anxious; but then, he was about most things. He would always worry that he'd be found out as someone less capable than he had shown in interview and, therefore, unable to cope with the level of responsibility he held at the hospital. I often had to reassure him that he was perfectly capable. But he was just a 'whittle', as my mum would say.

My Burmese friend and car mechanic, Gerry, had visited Singapore with his wife a few years before and they told us that the city was just too sterile. But looking at the dirty London streets deep in litter I thought: how could they be too sterile? They were right: in Singapore it's even illegal to have chewing gum and the streets almost gleam with cleanliness. Ashley wrote a diary throughout this period, which has helped me remember a lot of detail about the trip and which has brought back so many good memories. After Singapore, we headed north on the train into Malaysia, first to the Cameron Highlands and the tea plantations then to the east coast and paradise.

To get over to the Perhentian Islands you have to get a boat from Kuala Besut. A speedboat picks you up from the boat and takes you the short distance to shore. The sea is crystal clear, with sand as fine as sherbert, and the coastline is filled with bars (mainly alcohol-free, due to it being a Muslim country) serving that day's haul, fresh from the barbeque. We dined on marlin, swordfish or shark washed down by the best milkshakes ever, also a speciality on the island. We had a little hut with an en-suite bathroom, which we shared with tree frogs every night. Although they were cute, I insisted Ashley take them outside one by one before we went to bed. If truth be known, I didn't want them snuggling up with me in the night, if their toad cousins were anything to go by! It was on this island that I swam with a shark and giant turtle.

I've always been petrified of sharks; since *Jaws*, really. I watched it as a five year old when it first came out at the cinema, accompanied by my siblings and my Auntie Sue. I remember screaming when the head rolled out of the bottom of the boat. When I followed a very sleek reef shark that day, fascinated by its grace and power, it was only when I stuck my head above the water, took my snorkel off and saw that my party were like little bobbins miles away, that I panicked! After a surreal few minutes of quietly swimming with the shark, I realised that these waters were full of them and strangely, now, they had all turned into great whites, ready to eat me. I had a long way to swim with my head above water, not able to see what demons lay below, but thankfully the adrenalin considerably increased my swimming speed on the way back. I can safely say I have never swum that fast, either before or since. Despite this, and getting completely burnt to a crisp that day, I would have stayed on those islands forever, had I had my way. But we were eager to continue our travels and get to the country we were both most looking forward to: Vietnam.

After a few nights' stop in Penang, where some mosquito bit me on the eye during the night, so that I woke up looking like I'd gone at least five rounds with Mike Tyson, we went back to Singapore to catch our flight. We had pre-booked a hotel in Hanoi for a couple of nights and chose to stay longer in a room you could tell had been previously reserved for the top Soviet government men visiting the country. The decor was dated and in some parts shabby, but opulent and very eastern European.

The streets of Hanoi, meaning 'river within', were full of cycles, motorbikes and cyclos (bike taxis) and you took your life into your hands when crossing them. A beautiful city, and our first taste of the Vietnamese people and the country's food and culture. We didn't get to see the great man Ho Chi Minh though, as he was over in Russia getting a makeover; his dead body was undergoing further preservation by the same people who had dealt with Lenin. From Hanoi, we headed north to the coast and went on a long trek through the forest. I still carried a lot of weight, which made it very tiring climbing the mountain, although the pounds were coming off quickly thanks to the vegetables and rice diet. To reach the mountains, we had to go on the back of motorbikes, which took us through villages and along dusty country roads at top speed. I once again held on very tight to my skinny driver and made myself forget my Western programming about the dangers of high speed motorbike travel without a helmet. After that hair-raising journey, whenever I got on the back of a bike, which was often in Vietnam, I just enjoyed the ride. I had finally let go.

On the way back south we stopped overnight in Vinh, a very eastern bloc-like city in the Nghe An province, Ho Chi Minh's birthplace. The city is full of concrete housing towers littering the landscape and there's really nothing to see there, so there are few tourists, which is the only reason we could afford the best, and it seemed, only, place to stay. The hotel manager gave us his personal attention and we chatted at length. I don't think I saw any other guest while we were there. The train to Hue was very pricey, so the hotel manager flagged us down the bus. We'd never have managed it on our own as local bus travel was something not normally done by westerners, or indeed encouraged by the government. I don't know what he said but the angry-sounding bus driver ended up taking our money and we were allowed on.

I must say, the bus driver got angry about everyone stepping onto his bus; it was more of a performance, and the audience loved it. Normally a seat would be occupied by three people, but they made an exception for us as we also had rucksacks and were fat compared to the locals. We were immediately welcomed by someone handing us a fag and a drink of water, which went on for the entire journey. You also 'crashed the ash' (offered them cigarettes in return) and everyone was very happy with the arrangement.

I wrote the following piece years later, to try and win a trip to Vietnam, although I never sent it. I guess it summed it all up in 100 words:

We left Vinh Ho hurriedly, on a local bus flagged down by our hotel manager. An hour outside the Soviet-style town, the bus gave up the ghost and so we were left stranded miles from anywhere: a fully loaded bus, a Vietnamese phrasebook and we were the only westerners for miles around for a total of eight hours.

Damn, what's the word for toilet...? "Phong ve sinh", which is only understandable if the intonation is correct. My success in the language granted me a pee next to a couple of disgruntled sows.

Word soon got around that there were two 'fat' and very 'white' tourists, not normally seen in these parts. We were overwhelmed by the hospitality of these people. A couple of hours into the breakdown, we had been accepted, and were invited as guests by a fellow passenger to a meal of rice, vegetables and duck eggs eaten in one of the locals' small living quarters.

The meal was bought by Jung, a young fellow passenger whose English was marginally better than our Vietnamese, and who looked after us throughout. Ashley thanked him with a Manchester United shirt he had. Football is the universal language when all's said and done, especially Manchester United, and he was thrilled with it. After the meal, the kids arrived from nowhere, pulling my hair and earrings and telling us that we were really fat. And their parents came along, too. Communication went beyond words that day, and we all understood each other with laughs and jokes and poking, being told we should start a family. When we finally arrived in Hue it was early morning, and as we got off the bus, everyone waved frantically as they pulled off to their next destination. It was an experience not encouraged by the Vietnamese government, who recommended keeping to the tourist buses at all times. I'm glad we didn't.

Hue was beautiful: set astride the Perfume River and with the Forbidden City its focal point, where only emperors and their concubines had previously had the pleasure of its beauty. Now it stands a shadow of its former self, but still impressive, and picturing the opulence is easy. Because of its tactical position, Hue saw some of the bloodiest scenes in combat during the Battle of Hue, which was part of the Tet Offensive. The city was virtually destroyed and more than 5,000 communists were killed.

We met Quan, a cyclo driver, on our first day and we agreed that throughout our time in Hue we would only use only him and his cyclo to see the sights the city had to offer. He told us in whispers about what life had been like for him and his family following the war and during the communist regime, looking around as if still being spied on. Two days later, he invited us to his home to share a meal with his family as his honoured guests. It was already raining when we met him on bikes we'd hired from our hotel, and we followed him to the other side of town, where shacks with corrugated iron roofs became the landscape. His home was no exception. All his family lived in the one room and all washing and calls of nature took place outside, by the lake.

He had bought beer and several members of his family came to drink and chat with us. They offered us hors d'oeuvres that we couldn't quite fathom out, but being polite guests, we tried everything put in front of us and it was all delicious. We were treated like kings in their very humble abode, and we were later invited to Quan's father's house, a brick-built dwelling not far away. There we dined on other interesting dishes, including frog's legs, while the entire family, including uncles, aunts and lots of children, looked on. It was really weird being the centre of attention for so many people, because we were fat, white westerners. We were encouraged to sing some songs but it seemed they'd never heard of 'Ticket to Ride' before, although our rendition was not the best. Ashley gave the kids some playing cards and a wonderful and memorable night was had by all. This had not been in the traveller's bible: it went so far beyond that. We were honoured by the experience.

Overwhelmed by their hospitality, we left in the rain on our bikes and cycled back to our hotel. The next day, the rain was still coming down and the ground floor of the hotel had started to fill with water so the staff moved everyone up to the first floor rooms. The rain continued to fall, and by evening, the roads had turned to rivers. From our window on the second floor we could see people being rescued by large amphibious vehicles. People were being pulled out of trees and from the tops of roofs. Thankfully for us, our hotel still managed to feed all their guests with vegetables and rice, as they had a boat and were able to row to the hills to get food for the duration of the floods. We heard that other tourists in other hotels had not been so lucky. Spirits were kept high by singing on the stairs up to the second floor every night after eating dinner – the playlist coming from all over the world.

We listened religiously to the BBC World Service, thinking that such a major incident would be reported and that perhaps we would get more information about the extent of the damage, but nothing. Ashley rigged up a drink can and caught water out of the window to wash and clean our teeth in, as the water supply had been affected. I suppose this is where I learned to bathe in such a small amount of precious water. After about the third day, the rain stopped and the floods slowly started to subside, revealing that the river outside the front of the hotel was in fact a forgotten road. We ventured out, but not too far on the first occasion, and managed to speak to our parents and let them know we were OK. Ashley's dad had heard about it from some obscure news report, but it had not been mentioned in the mainstream press. Funny, if a flood had caused this much devastation back home it would have been headline news internationally.

The aftermath of the flood was indeed devastation. We saw a bloated cow floating down the Perfume River and lots of rats lying dead by the side of the road. All the tourists in Hue were desperate to escape. The airport was stretched to capacity, but our plans were to cross the border into Laos, and we had to wait until the road was passable again. Hue became like a ghost town as all the transients left the sinking ship for safety. We tried to find out whether Quan and his family were safe, and cycled down to his side of town, but understandably, we were met with hostile stares and jeers of "Hey West, fuck you!" and suchlike, and so we thought we should abort the mission. The news was bad and reports were that there were almost 400 dead in the Hue area alone.

It didn't take long for businesses to re-open and the big cleanup to begin. By the time the next lot of tourists were shipped in, by various means, the streets were back to normal. One woman who owned an internet cafe spent three days perched on the top of computer tables protecting her expensive equipment from the looting that had taken place during the floods. She had no insurance and it would have left her with nothing if the looters had made off with her computers. The locals just bounced back with smiles on their faces, despite what had happened.

One good bit of news to arrive via email was that my sister was pregnant and due in July the following year. We were over the moon with the news and I cried through joy, amid the carnage around us.

A week after the floods, with the city almost ghost-like from the exodus of the tourist population, we heard that the road was passable again and so we were able to continue our planned route across the border at Lao Bao. After a very long journey, we were turned back at the border for not having the right exit visas in our passport, and so we had to return to the local town, Dong Ha, with our 20-stone fellow passengers. Their weight had been increased by the dozens of cigarette cartons stuffed down their clothes, as they were smuggling contraband across the border!

Back at Dong Ha, we met a guy called Tommy who said he could take us to the government office to get our visas, and who generally looked after us until the following day, when we could continue our journey. It turned out that Tommy had been an interpreter for the US army during the war and had spent 18 months in a re-education camp afterwards.

Re-education camp (Vietnamese: *trại hịc tắp cại tạo*) is the official title given to the prison camps operated by the government of Vietnam following the end of the Vietnam war. In such 're-education camps', the government imprisoned several hundred thousand former military officers and government workers from the former regime of South Vietnam. Re-education as it was implemented in Vietnam was seen as both a means of revenge and a sophisticated technique of repression and indoctrination, which developed for several years in the North and was extended to the South following the 1975 Fall of Saigon. An estimated 1 – 2.5 million people were imprisoned with no formal charges or trials. According to published academic studies in the United States and Europe, 165,000 people died in the Socialist Republic of Vietnam's re-education camps. Thousands were tortured or abused. Prisoners were incarcerated for as long as 17 years, with most terms ranging from three to 10 years.

– Wikipedia

Once the passports had been stamped by a very disagreeable immigration officer, we were able to get on the road again. The journey back to the Laos border took us along the Ho Chi Minh trail and by the Khe Sanh base. We'd stopped off at the base the first time we'd passed, and had walked around the museum filled with war memorabilia. Outside, Vietnamese vendors sold the dog tags, still with chains attached, that had once belonged to American servicemen, or so they told us. We crossed the border on foot, and as we walked through the Vietnamese side there, was no one to be seen. We called out, but not getting a response from anyone lurking in the office, we crossed to the Laos side. This was manned, and the smiling staff stamped our passports.

There was nothing around and so we started to walk in the only direction; we presumed towards town. We were picked up by two guys on motorbikes who, for about 50p, took us to the cafe and bus stop, where we heard that we'd missed the bus for the day. Thankfully, a guy with a floppy straw hat offered to take us to Savannakhet, about 300 km away, in his truck for $5 each, and we gratefully accepted. After he'd finished his lunch, and us our first Lao beer, we got on our way.

The so-called road was just a series of dangerously deep potholes, which needed much negotiation and so the journey was slow. Along the way, we saw dozens of vehicles overturned due to these potholes, so we were lucky. Thankfully, we had a very careful driver. We passed through *"incredible countryside, through villages full of chickens and dogs and waving children, through bright green rice paddies and clouds of fragrant wood smoke from cooking fires..."* (extract from Ashley's diary). We stopped off on the way for our first taste of Laos food, bought by our driver, and which we believed to be chicken accompanied by sticky rice – the staple in this country.

The final 26 km was on a flat, newly tarmacked road and so we sped along, reaching our destination late in the evening. We checked into a very cheap hotel then went out for a few beers at a friendly nightclub. From Savannakhet, we travelled north to the capital, Vientiane, which was influenced strongly by the French, and where we found a great French restaurant selling wine and *assiette de charcuterie et fromage* (dish of cold meats and cheese). I'm afraid I didn't think much of the Lao food. It was the sticky rice, which accompanied everything and which seemed equally as dry as the meat dishes widely offered. Everywhere in Vietnam, we ate well and really enjoyed the food, so it's not me being fussy, but Lao food: no thanks. So the French restaurant was no copout. We were just in need of good bread, cheese and ham and wine to feel our bellies properly full. At this little restaurant in the square, we met an interesting travelling couple. Royston Ellis was an independent travel writer and Lady Beryl was 85, and told us she had been an actress in Berlin and had seen the Nazis come to power. There is always someone interesting to meet on the road! Years later, I found out that Royston had been John Lennon's inspiration for writing 'Paperback Writer'.

After Vientiane, we travelled north, cycling on hired bikes through beautiful mountainous terrain to secluded Buddhist temples with crystal clear lagoons, down long dusty country roads in the back of a pickup to an exquisite waterfall where poinsettias grew wild. We saw a duck being caught, killed, cooked and eaten by some locals while we watched from our balcony. We watched alms (giving materially to another, usually food, as an act of religious virtue) being quietly given by locals to a procession of Buddhist monks in the early morning light and we paid a visit to the opium doctor and smoked weed, which gave us both cartoon dreams.

Our journey back to Vietnam was not as comfortable, as we had opted to go back to the border by bus. Before the tourists had even boarded the vehicle it had been occupied by many of the locals with their vast produce, which filled every part of the bus, including our footwells, so you were unable to move around. We were sat in a fixed position for the duration of the journey: about nine hours in total. This is when my knees were damaged for life. I couldn't straighten them for the greater part of the horrendous bus journey, until I opted to lie down on the bags of onions piled high in the aisles, and got some sleep. During the journey the pissed up driver (we'd seen him drinking) stopped for a toilet break in the middle of nowhere, and before everyone could get back on the bus he started to drive off. We had to literally throw ourselves back on top of the Red Bull and onions, despite our pleas to "stop the fucking bus!"

By the time we got off the bus at the border we were all covered in a thick layer of red dust, which seemed the least of our worries. As we passed back through the Vietnamese side of the border, the guard scrutinised our passports and quizzed us as to why our passports had not been not stamped on the way through. The guard took us into an office and a lovely female interpreter explained to the guard that we hadn't got an exit stamp because there had been no one there to stamp it. They couldn't believe that it was their system that had broken down, so we got a lecture about 'proper conduct' and, as they couldn't send us back to the Laos side, they backdated our exit stamps and sent us on our way, after lots of form-filling.

Ashley decided to go and spend some more time at Khe Sanh combat base, so he negotiated a return motorbike journey while I got on the local bus with the other westerners and the fat, cigarette carton-ladened locals and headed on towards Hue. I eventually arrived back at the hotel we'd stayed in during the floods, with several people in tow, and they greeted me with open arms and upgraded us to a room with a balcony and a bath for the same price. Ashley arrived in Hue shortly after, and was also welcomed like a long-lost son. The following day, we hired cycles and went to see if we could track down Quan, our cyclo driver. Our reception in that part of town was much better this time, so we managed to leave a message with his neighbour. Later, when we were just about to leave with friends to a nearby restaurant, a slim figure walked into the hotel bar, taking off his hat and smoothing down his hair. It was Quan, and we both rushed up to him and gave him lots of hugs, thankful for his safety.

We told the others we'd catch up with them later and he took us to a run-down bar where we shared food and beers. He told us that all his family were safe and that they had escaped to the high school on higher ground for four days during the floods. His father had been ill, but was much better now. Before we left, he insisted that we both drink a last beverage with him, which looked like cold tea, but tasted like a mixture of sherry and whisky. It was actually rice wine, fermented for 100 days with cobra venom and five snakes placed in the bottle to continue the fermentation. He said it was good for strength. I didn't know about that; it just got you pissed! We met Quan at 7am the next day, to say our final farewells prior to the departure of our bus to Hoi An. We went for coffee and he gave us cakes for the journey and a model of a cyclo as a present. What a gorgeous man, whom I shall never forget.

Throughout the journey, we were entertained by wild and almost unbelievable stories from Nicolai: *"A loud and confident Kiwi, with a British passport, who is related to James Joyce, has met the likes of Henry Kissinger and Bill Gates and who now writes for* Forbes*"* (extract from Ashley's diary). Nicolai was travelling with Christian, who was a quietly spoken Frenchman, and we spent a lot of time with them both during our stay in this beautiful, sleepy riverside town. Hoi An was full of bicycles and French and Chinese architecture; an interesting combination.

This was the town in which to do lots of inexpensive retail therapy. On every street corner, you were harassed by tailors wanting you to go to their shop to get clothes made. We followed one tout back to his stall in the busy marketplace, where dozens of other tailors offered a similar service. We were treated like VIPs, seated with drinks and catalogues from every high street clothes shop and designer you could imagine. All you did was pick one of the latest designs, they would measure you, and you went back for a fitting the following day. Your garments, at a fraction of the retail price, would be ready for collection shortly after. The quality was excellent too, and I still wear the wraparound trousers I had made there.

On our last night in Hoi An, Ashley and I went out for a drink with Nicolai and Christian and we spoke about our spiritual beliefs. I was searching for something in my quest with life and needed a bit of guidance to take me on to the next level. They both suggested that I read *Siddhartha* by Hermann Hesse, which I did when I got back home, and which introduced me to Buddhism. We had been observing the Buddhist way of life on our travels and we saw how happy people were. My interpretation of Buddhism, is that it teaches you to find happiness within, and is more of a way of life than an organised religion as such. God does not stand in 'judgement' of us from outside, as we are all essentially one entity. To be true to yourself is also to be true to God or the Divine.

We left Hoi An and the guys and travelled south via Nha Trang to Ho Chi Minh City, still referred to as Saigon by all the locals. Apparently, and thanks to Ashley's diary, I know there were 2.5 million scooters, 1.5 million bikes and 1 million cars, so an extremely busy city; very vibrant and very friendly. Whilst we were there, we visited the War Remnants Museum, a sobering account of the American war, as told by the Vietnamese. I remember the photos of the smiling US special forces holding Viet Cong heads, and a GI carrying the remnants of a man. The hardest to deal with were the deformed babies in bottles, which were caused by Agent Orange and the dioxin contamination that followed, and which affected the whole population. As we came out, a man without an arm sold us a map of the city.

The destruction of this war was still well and truly evident on most street corners, with amputees crawling around flogging photocopied bestsellers pertaining to the war or war memorabilia to tourists. They were always smiling, despite their pain. Some of the tourists were ex-US servicemen who had returned to make amends to these beautiful people. Humble and generally with war scars themselves, mainly psychological, one Aussie we met had developed bowel cancer through the local water he had drunk during his tour of duty. Incredible really that the Vietnamese seemed to be all-forgiving, considering that it had happened only a few decades before.

The one thing that was different about this city was that there was not one branch of a certain famous hamburger chain. The local fast food was pho, a delicious soup with noodles, vegetables, beef and fragrant leaves, and which replaced the usual burger joints. From Saigon we went further south, down to the Mekong Delta on a longboat, passing gangs of children on the riverbank, who were all waving and shouting "Hello… hello… hello…" until they were probably as hoarse as us. Even the parents waved and shouted and some even performed comedy dives, as much for our entertainment as the kids'. By the time we got to our landside destination, our arms had gone dead. We were unable to wave without holding them up.

We didn't want to leave Vietnam and the people we had grown to love and respect, and Ashley's diary says it all:

> It's hard to believe that after all the good times, we've left Vietnam and are now back in Singapore. The contrast on arrival with what we are used to is quite unbelievable – this place is orderly to an unhealthy extent; palm trees trimmed and planted with mathematical accuracy, no markets, no people, no ducks, no cyclos, just sterile, modern and dull. We both miss Vietnam so much.

We flew back to London a short time later. At the end of the diary, which Ashley wrote on the plane home, he concludes:

> …And that's the end of the adventure, the end of the best thing I've ever done in my life. This is Ashley Bright at 7.15 GMT and 33,000 feet, fed up and missing wonderful Vietnam, signing off… 11.12.99.

Ashley and I had such a wonderful time travelling together; it changed us both, but I was reborn more confident, worldly wise and slimmer, and a change to our current situation was inevitable. On reflection, I think I had undergone another metamorphosis, but this time I think I had morphed into a butterfly/dragonfly hybrid, and shed some more skin, like a python after a growth spurge.

(♦)UT OF THE SMOKE – SEPARATION

I picked up on the energy of London and I didn't like who I'd become.
Seeing little empathy from my fellow commuters every day,
I began to question our humanity and came to realise that I didn't belong there.
– Kay Rose-Hattrick

Our travels had a profound effect on both of us. We had become much closer as a result and I believed that we could start our new lives together away from London. This had been the plan when we'd given up our jobs, but as time went on, and Ashley went straight back to a job in the NHS, it became clear that he was reticent about moving out of London and leaving his family. I got several temporary jobs, including binding reports on Fleet Street, sending out holiday brochures to Sunday magazine readers and being the receptionist at Marie Curie HQ for a few days.

We still had the energy of our travels driving us and Ashley did scan the broadsheet ads for suitable positions around the country. Nothing seemed to suit, and as the months progressed we became static again, morphing back into our previous lives as though nothing had changed. Ashley's job had been left open so it was only my life that had changed post-trip. I finally got a longer contract in the conference and training department at Mind, the mental health charity's HQ in Stratford, very close to where we lived. Stratford was very different back then, before the Olympics and when the shopping centre was still full of closed or cheap shops. I saw what it looks like now on a BBC *Apprentice* episode, and it's changed greatly. It was close enough to walk to work, and I did on some occasions, but I mainly drove, as they had their own locked car park at the back of the building, next to Stratford station. Either way, I no longer had a stressful journey to contend with every morning so my day would start quite chilled.

I loved working at Mind and the girls, Helen and Katy, were a real laugh, and became good friends as well as colleagues. In fact, all the people who worked in our building, just round the corner from HQ, were a blast. The conference team's job was to organise training for mental health professionals on all aspects of mental health and we would generally split the different courses between the three of us. Helen was our boss, and I loved her immediately. Usually I am inept in interviews but she brought out the best in me and I felt at ease, especially when I saw an Eddie Stobart spotter's badge and admitted to spotting myself. Well, it passes the hours when motorway driving!

To make sure a course ran smoothly, we were required to attend the training sessions at various venues across the city. The job was easy, but interesting, especially when you met the mental health professionals on the course you had administrated. A pair I recall with fondness were the world's leading experts on hearing voices, Marius Romme and Sandra Escher from the Netherlands. I learned a lot about this condition from those two beautiful and passionate people, although I never told them about the voice I had shouting at me, to "get out", when I was in Australia.

> Marius Romme is best known for his work on hearing voices (auditory hallucinations) and is regarded as the founder and principal theorist for the Hearing Voices Movement.
>
> Romme has stated that schizophrenia 'is a harmful concept' and that delusions, hearing voices and hallucinations, so-called 'symptoms' of schizophrenia, are not related to an illness but may be reactions to traumatic and troubling events in life.
>
> – Wikipedia

Sandra bought me a hippopotamus, which we affectionately named Marius, before they took me out for beers to thank me for running the course.

It was during another one of these courses, while the participants were in session, that I had an epiphany that changed my perception, and indeed the course of my life.

A few weeks earlier I had met a girl called Nadia from Dronfield Woodhouse, where I was born, at a bar while out with my old Edexcel workmates one night. Of course, I was fated to meet her and our first exchange came after I tried to engage with a guy at the bar about the rudeness of the staff in the toilet: he ignored me, but she didn't. We continued to talk, realising we had lived in the same place, and now, with so many miles distancing us both from where we had grown up, we still shared the same space. We both complained that life down in the Big Smoke was a far cry from where we had been raised, and where people still talked to each other. The conversation then went straight into spiritualism and it was clear to a rookie, like me, that Nadia was far more knowledgeable about the divine stuff and energy exchange than I was. She was a tarot card reader, so I asked her for a reading and we exchanged numbers and arranged to meet at her house the following week.

I had always felt alone on my quest as those close to me were not interested in alternative thinking. One exception was my group of Edexcel drinking buddies, who hailed from all over the country, whom I continued to meet up with for a few pints most Fridays. When it was getting late and we'd all had quite enough to drink, we would discuss stuff beyond this realm. They agreed with me one night when I announced my theory.

I said that I believed life to be just an experiment and that the gods or powers who were holding our strings laughed at our antics, while we lived ignorantly below, thinking we were free and actually had control of our own lives. In the 1980s, I had once watched a scary programme about a doll's house. The family were normal people, living normal lives while their daughter played with her doll's house. It was only at the end of the show that you realised the noises they started to hear were from the family that lived outside their house. Imagine a doll's house within a doll's house within a doll's house, repeated infinitely. The concept that our reality is not necessarily the true reality, and that there is a much bigger picture outside our reality, flashed through my mind even as a child watching that show.

A line from *Lord of the Flies* by William Golding (originally from Shakespeare's *King Lear*, of course) became embedded in my memory after we had read the text at school: "As flies to wanton boys, are we to the gods. They kill us for their sport." All these things were real to me and made sense, but there was certainly more out there than I could fully comprehend. I was eager to find my way down my spiritual path and fulfil my destiny, as I had always believed I was here for a reason. These things were imprinted on my memory to remind me of the truth and to wake me up out of my slumber.

A few days later, I travelled across London to Nadia's house, who read my tarot cards. We spoke about many esoteric things that day, but not about my failing marriage and the increasing number of arguments about leaving London. It was the cards that said that I would split with Ashley and move back up north. Following the reading, we went out for coffee, to talk more about our spiritual journey. As we left the coffee shop I asked her if she had read *The Celestine Prophecy* by James Redfield and she had. I think many spiritual journeys are started with this book, especially now they have made it into a film, although the acting is fairly wooden. Nick, a close friend of Ashley's, had suggested I read this book and so I purchased it in a bookshop in Glastonbury town centre during a long weekend that we spent with him and his pregnant wife, Sarah.

It changed my way of seeing things, and Joe and I, my alternative friend from work, would practise seeing the energy of the flowers in Russell Park during lunch hours. (Yes, I agree this might sound bonkers to the average Joe.) Joe would later introduce me to reiki, so I was able to understand how energy flowed, but it was this book that had introduced me to the universal energy. As the film unfolds, it shows the viewer that we are all one-energy, with the ability to flow among other energy sources, living or otherwise. In the film, the main character goes on a quest to South America to discover the prophecies and learn about energy for himself. In a mountainside retreat, he is shown by one of his teachers how the flow of energy works and they meet a woman in the forest, who the main character quite fancies. He starts to flirt with her, but his unwanted attention makes her feel very uncomfortable. In the film, you can see the energy flowing between them, especially his unwanted attention/ energy, as it tries to dominate hers. In the end, the young woman balances the flow and she is able to regain her position, while he is left wondering why his advances were thwarted.

We all know people who drain our energy and whose company leaves us feeling exhausted and a bit vulnerable. Unless you put up a protection before you see such people, I suggest you keep clear of them altogether. Unless the energy exchange is balanced and flowing freely, they are never going to be good for you to be around. I realised this a long time ago and I have to be quite discerning when choosing whom I share my space with.

Nadia suggested that I read *Conversations with God – Book One* by Neale Donald Walsch to continue my quest. After parting, I went straight to the bookshop and bought the book. As the title suggests, Neale Donald Walsch has a conversation with God, asking all the questions I would have asked if speaking to God. In turn, God answers all his questions with stuff that made sense to me. I was reading this that day outside the training course, when I had my epiphany (a moment of sudden and great revelation or realisation). In the book, God says that there are certain people in this life whose mission it is to help others to seek the truth. As I read, "You know who you are," I burst into tears, thankful I was alone, as I was unable to stop crying for some time. It had been like a bolt of lightning and shook me to my core, so I knew it to be real, and at that moment I was at last sure of my mission in this life: to be true to myself and others while seeking the truth.

I suppose it was a bit like in the film *They Live* by John Carpenter, when the main character finds some sunglasses in a disused church and puts them on to find that aliens have taken over the world. It's worth a watch to understand the concept (and probably more real than we'd like to think), and the fight scene must be the longest in film history. It wasn't that I started to see aliens, but like him, I just started to see things more clearly, and the stuff that had happened to me in my life up to that point made more sense. I floated back from central London that day, seeing life from a completely different perspective to the average commuter, who was probably worrying about getting a seat on the tube at rush hour. I felt as though I'd been let into a secret, which would fully reveal itself in time. I never told anyone about this, including Ashley, and only disclosed this in later life when I was surrounded by likeminded people. Normal people would have thought that I was mad.

I'd always known that my life had a purpose. I was unsure of where my life would take me, but I knew it was not with Ashley. This new determination gave me the strength to leave London. I was sure that this life was no longer for me, especially as it was clear that Ashley, who wasn't in a hurry to look for alternative work outside London, had got back into the steady routine of the hospital again. The contract for Mind was coming to an end and a permanent post was now on offer. I had been encouraged to apply for it by Helen and Katy. I went home to Sheffield for a week to do some serious thinking, and during this time I spent my days reading Alain de Botton's *The Consolations of Philosophy*, doing my Penny Smith's Ashtanga yoga video, and generally relaxing in an environment much more laid back than I was used to down south.

Before my retreat north, I told Ashley that I was happy to compromise again and continue to live in London, if only to keep our marriage together. I enjoyed my job at Mind and I would have got the permanent job. He snapped that there was no point. By the time I got back, we'd both done a lot of thinking and both admitted that we'd taken off our wedding rings that week. We made the decision that we wanted different things and I believed that he was happy for me to go. He continued to reinforce his refusal to leave his home town, saying that he didn't want to leave his family and friends, so a job in another city would never have been on the cards. I couldn't continue to live in this capital of ours without that light of escaping being a possibility, so I planned to leave solo. So on 3rd July 2000, I left my first husband and cried all the way back to Derbyshire.

My brother Mike and my sister's husband at the time, Craig, hired a van and came down to Forest Gate to collect all my things, which had been divided achingly equally between us by Ashley. I was so upset, but had already given Ashley the option of me staying and he hadn't taken it. In floods of tears, we said our farewells and he gave me a letter and the rambling man, a bronze charm that he had bought in Vietnam, and which he gave me for my future protection. Later he had admitted that if I had said, "I don't want to go," he wouldn't have let me, but neither of us said a word.

I literally cried all the way from Forest Gate to Millthorpe. When I got home, I opened the letter from him and cried some more. The letter reinforced his feelings and made it crystal clear to me that this is what he truly wanted. I was left in no doubt that our relationship was at an end. I really believed that he didn't want me any more and that was heartbreaking, but liberating at the same time.

The letter read:

As we know, life is full of surprises and it would be great if we could stay in touch as friends. At the moment, we're one of those couples that just can't live together. We need to be apart, to be happy as individuals. What's the point of staying together if we're both unhappy?

...so I'll say my goodbyes now, love. You are a fine woman and you will find someone with whom you can be happy. I know that. Take good care of yourself, never doubt who or what you are and believe in yourself. I shall never forget you.

It seemed so impersonal, and could have been from someone I had just been dating for a few months, not someone I was married to. I really did think he wanted me gone. I remember sitting on the front step at Berry Hill, having a fag with Mum, knowing that I had done the right thing, but that my heart was broken. My father even stepped over us to get to his regular appointment at the pub. I remember thinking, "Can't you forget your pint and change your routine, just this once, to stay with your daughter?" on a day that was one of the toughest of my life up to that point. A Capricorn through and through: you could set your clock by Dad, he's so achingly routine, but then again emotional Kay was always left to Mum, who made everything seem better. What I also needed was Dad to say that everything was going to be all right, nothing more. Even a hug would have been good.

My niece Amy was born two days after I returned to my parents', sharing Ashley's birthday. He did say that she waited for her Auntie Kay to get home.

Life went on and I was pleased to be free of the metropolis of London town, although I was so sorry that my relationship had failed. Even though I still loved Ashley dearly, I knew I had a mission and it seemed that it was not with my first husband of only four years. But there was a new baby around and many distractions. I was more chilled and didn't speed everywhere, as I had down there. I went back down to London not long afterwards to attend the wedding of his best friend and ex-flatmate Brendan, to Bunty. That weekend, Ashley tried to woo me back, but I was still under the impression that he just wanted to be friends, so it didn't quite compute with me. He'd bought my favourite wine, cooked my favourite food and for the whole weekend was incredibly attentive.

Ashley wrote another letter after I returned to Sheffield, filled with how much he loved me and the great times we had shared and saying that he ached for us to be back in each other's arms again. And then...

I honestly thought that if we separated, you'd be happy again for a while then you'd come back and we could plan a real future. How unbelievably wrong I was. In no other relationship have I misread a situation so badly. Never have I doubted a decision to get out until now.

His plan for me to return had backfired, because I had genuinely thought that he didn't love me any more and that I had to move on. I didn't know how to respond to this letter as I was in shock, as well as being pissed off that he orchestrated our breakup to prove a point. As I didn't respond, he sent me a final letter, listing eight reasons why I was a bitch, and that he realised the relationship was over. The final reason reinforced his previous point:

> *Yes, I encouraged you to leave but always because I believed that, while some time at home would make you 'happy', you would love and miss me enough to return. You will never understand how painful it was or has been for me to do this but I had to know. Was it where we were or was it 'us'? You have answered my question. You are happier now without me than you ever were. Nothing I say or do will change that. And despite the fact that I engineered this test, you alone failed it and confirmed what I knew all along. You were never in love with me, you just loved the attention and the thought of being in love.*

My dad said, "If he really loves you he'd be camping out on this doorstep to get you back." He never ventured near. He pulled me apart in this letter and even now, when I read it again to write this, I feel almost compelled to hate myself. He used to say to me when we were together, especially when I brought up moving out of London, "You'll never be happy, wherever you go." I almost started to believe this, but I was happy back in Sheffield, which would once again become my home. Remember the old adage: "If you love something, set it free." He did all right, but it made me think that it was him who wanted the freedom. Before he could catch me again I had flown: ready to start a new life.

CREATIVITY, SPIRITUALITY & THE NHS – RICHARD, REIKI I AND PARK HILL

8

Just as a candle cannot burn without fire,
men cannot live without a spiritual life.
– Buddha

I met Richard in the George and Dragon, the pub I used to work in before I went travelling, but which had since been taken over by Norma, as Dot and Tony had retired to Dronfield. Richard was a friend of the family and we just got chatting at the bar one night. He was a landscape gardener, and offered me work helping him out during the summer, doing a number of different gardening jobs; something that gave me the confidence to express myself creatively. I didn't think I had it in me, but with his encouragement, I started glass painting, pot painting and planting, including helping him with some big jobs, which I was very proud of. Richard was a very talented man, with piercing blue eyes and curly black hair. He was fun to be around, and for a time we were inseparable. I started to feel like myself again for the first time in years.

I started losing weight. I also bought Carol Vorderman's video and followed her month-long detox programme. By giving up dairy, meat, alcohol, wheat, caffeine and fags I lost about two dress sizes and felt fantastic. Not that giving up fags aided my weight loss, but I was once again free of them – for a while.

Before meeting Ashley I had been very interested in essential oils and their properties. I would put oils in my bath or create massage oils blended with uplifting fragrances. Ashley said he didn't like those "yucky" oils in his bath and even refused massages from me, so I stopped using them. I now regained my interest and started practising again on returning north. It was during this time that I also became Reiki I attuned. Whilst I was still in London, Joe, my alternative friend from Edexcel, had given me distant reiki healing as part of his Reiki II training attunement. That evening, I lay down on my bed across the city from him, aware that I was being filled with healing energy, and feeling quite high after the treatment. So when I saw an advert for reiki in our local parish magazine, I took it as a sign to enrol on the weekend Reiki I course. After all, there is no such thing as a coincidence, which I would come to truly understand. Reiki literally means universal life-giving energy, and is not easily understood by many people because energy is invisible to most.

One way I describe energy and how everyone knows its presence is by using the example of a football match. Once the match is over and the crowds disperse back to where they came from, their energy still remains, like ghosts. You only have to visit Bramall Lane, the Sheffield United football ground after match day to experience this and know that energy is tangible; the air still charged with the football fans' life force for some time after the match. Have you ever walked into a room directly after someone has had an argument, but those around are behaving normally again? There is something not quite right, although on first sight, nothing seems apparent. The negative energy has been unleashed and you can 'cut the air with a knife', finding out that a disagreement has indeed just taken place.

Positive energy has been used for healing since time began, and the laying on of hands is taught as part of our Bible stories. To be reiki attuned opens up your chakras so that the practitioner can be used as a vessel through which the energy flows, and which they then direct through another person in order to heal them. Chakras are your energy source, a bit like the Duracell bunny, and we all know we need energy to perform. Each chakra has its own colour and, like a vortex of energy, controls different parts of the body. When you're ill, you may find it difficult doing any small task, complaining of lack of energy. The aim is for all seven chakras to be aligned and spinning the right way, which, interestingly, is different for males and females. Anyone can be reiki attuned and no one should be considered special as a result. An attunement only means that your blockages have been cleared, enabling the energy to flow freely. Reiki is similar to when you get a good cuddle from someone, which is a positive energy exchange embracing LOVE. We all know we feel better after one of these too!

At the very end of my month-long detox, and the weekend course, I was taken into my reiki master's healing room, eyes closed, so I had no idea what she was doing until years later when I too would be master level attuned. What I did experience that day was something incredible; a force that flowed through me and brought bright colours swirling around my chakras, opening me up to the force of the universal energy. It was quite far out and left me high for weeks afterwards. Back then, I practised the techniques shown to me as part of my course at every opportunity and it set me further along my spiritual path.

At the very end of summer 2000, Richard and I went to visit a job in Huddersfield. The top end of the garden had already been flattened and laid with concrete flagstones, but it was the bottom end that they had invited Richard to quote for. This part of the garden was just a jungle of brambles backing onto a bridleway, which was clearer than the actual garden. When I looked at his impressive, hand-drawn plans I thought he was mad if he was going to create such a vision, and I told him so on the journey back to Sheffield. He was confident that he could achieve what he had promised and we started work.

I've never grafted so hard in my life doing such manual labour, which firstly involved removing all the brambles and then levelling the ground. We found masses of boulders and rocks, a concrete washing line post, a bee's nest and bits of oddments that had been buried for years before we could even start moving earth. We then made raised beds out of railway sleepers and steps with the same material that led down to the next level. After filling the beds with tonnes of topsoil, which had been delivered on the front drive, completely covering it, we were able to go and choose the plants.

The garden centre had the most amazing display of buddleias, known as the 'butterfly bush' to most gardeners, due to their attractiveness to butterflies. They certainly liked them that day, as that area of the garden centre was teeming with red admirals, peacocks and the painted lady, which I remembered from when I was a kid, when butterflies were very much a part of our summer scene.

We took about ten plants home with us, hoping that the butterflies would follow too. We also planted many different perennial shrubs and pansies and geraniums that would give instant colour. I planted nearly a tonne of daffodil bulbs to ensure an impressive spring show. We lined the paths so that weeds and grass would not grow through and gravelled the top and bottom areas. This finished, we were finally ready for the unveiling, with a bottle of bubbly shared with the clients, who could scarcely believe the transformation. Neither could I. That day, we walked away from that couple knowing we had done a great job; we knew they were pleased and we were proud of what we had both achieved. I learned from Richard that you could achieve *anything*, even seemingly unachievable things, if you had *vision* and the *right positive attitude*. And not listen to others! Thanks for that, Richard.

As summer turned to autumn and the weather became more inclement I decided to move indoors and start making things to sell for Christmas. Norma, the landlady at our local pub, had agreed that we could organise a Christmas craft sale in November. I pretty much sold out, and took commissions that kept me occupied right up until Christmas itself. I spent every day in Mum and Dad's conservatory painting wine glasses, vases, tealight holders and ornate wooden candle holders, with help and encouragement from

Richard. Things had started going wrong between us, and I wasn't very nice to him and our relationship fizzled out soon after. Little did I know that he was seeing someone else behind my back anyway, whom he would marry not long after.

I finally got round to updating my CV and making appointments to visit temping agencies to find a proper job. I only visited one agency, since my typing wasn't bad and I had a lot of experience in administration, so they sent me to my first interview at Park Health Centre, to cover a temporary post. Pat, the secretary who interviewed me, liked me and I could do the job, so in January 2001 I started work in the NHS as a temporary administrator for South East Sheffield primary care group (PCG). By April, it had become a primary care trust (PCT).

I had experience of marketing and putting on events so I was paired with Dr Jillian Creasy, a GP, who is now my Green councillor. Jillian and I were a great team and we boasted the best PLI (protected learning initiative) in Sheffield. We arranged for protected time so that GP surgeries could close one afternoon a week and we organised learning and continuing professional development for all members of the practice. Did you ever wonder what GP surgeries in Sheffield do on Thursday afternoons?

Every couple of months, we would put on a large event for all South East PCT practices at Bramall Lane, the Sheffield United football club ground, and which was sponsored by approved pharmaceutical companies. GPs could collect their professional development credits after each event; otherwise they wouldn't have attended. For all other staff it was a good afternoon away from the surgery. We put on a nice lunch and lots of varied workshops for all in the afternoon. The evaluation always focused on the temperature of the room or lunch so if that's all the constructive criticism we got, the rest must have been up to scratch. At Jillian's request, I organised a facilitators' training course and those involved with PLI, including Jillian and myself, became trained facilitators, meaning that we could run discussion workshops at the event.

I have always been good at putting on events. I think because I had done so many in a professional capacity in London, Sheffield was like a walk in the park for me. I think that I am just a natural hostess, and my nurturing side comes out. I want everyone to have an equally good time. I want to look after people, as I believe everyone is special; just because one participant was a receptionist and the other a GP made no difference. I remember my first session as a trained facilitator, when I had a group of lovely receptionists and two GPs, one of whom was particularly difficult, but thankfully, he left early. I was nervous as hell, which was intensified by his refusal to enter into debate on a pre-agreed subject and him being generally difficult. An important observation that fuelled my fire and made me realise that arseholes were not exclusive to any profession, but were abundant in some! He didn't put me off either, and I continued to facilitate sessions, but still remained nervous beforehand.

In 2001, the USA came under attack by 'terrorists', and we were all shocked beyond belief when we saw, on the news, footage of two planes flying into the Twin Towers and of a plane getting dangerously close to the Pentagon. It was more poignant for our family as my sister had been flying into Washington that day. I immediately thought, "Oh no, not again!" as my sister was caught in the crossfire!

Whilst I was temping, we later employed another temp from my agency. She was called Jenna, and we later found out that she was the step-daughter of the owner of the recruitment agency. Jenna had been brought up in South Africa and was quite abrupt in manner. A pretty girl, with long blonde hair and very easy to wind up; she was even more gullible than me. I was in charge one day, as Pat was on holiday, and I asked Jenna to go down to the post office for some stamps. She refused. I asked her again and she refused again. This time, I was quite annoyed as I couldn't believe she was refusing to do part of her job. It turned out that she didn't like going down to the post office because her posh accent always made her feel uncomfortable in there, where there were pub ashtrays on the counters for customers.

You see, we worked next to Park Hill flats: revolutionary in all sorts of ways when they started building them in 1957, but now I personally think that they look outdated in the Sheffield landscape, although they are nonetheless a listed building. By choice, I wouldn't even walk through the flats during the day, as there was a feeling of potential danger lurking, but peering up at the balconies (some looked derelict) some tenants still produced the most amazing summer flower displays. The place was run down and had that eerie feel of days past, past its prime. Understandable that Jenna, whose background was so far removed from that of the residents of Park Hill flats, felt nervous. She stood out with her long blonde hair and posh British/South African-twanged accent. So I went along with her to provide moral support to buy the stamps!

Jenna had a friend called Fozia who was also living with her parents and desperate to have her independence, so it was decided that we would start looking for a place together. On first meeting Fozia, I loved her: gorgeous, funny, a little crazy and she turned out to be the best flatmate I've ever had. Fozia insisted that we start our search just off the 'fashionable Ecclesall Road', (or Eccy Road as it's known locally), which is mainly occupied by students, due to its close proximity to town and the universities. It's fashionable with the rich too, as there are trendy wine bars and restaurants and exclusive boutiques lining the street. We met one Saturday morning to view a property on Denham Road, just off Eccy Road, and fell in love with it. Unfortunately, another couple had just viewed it and they were likely to take it.

That afternoon, Jenna and I continued our search further out of town and away from the trendy area and found a few properties to view. When we told Fozia later, she said, "Location, location, location, girls!" and we knew she was right. Thankfully, the Denham

Road property ended up ours, and despite the agency we dealt with being based in Leeds, the property was actually owned by the Druids.

The Ancient Druids were once judges, kingmakers, scientists, magicians and priests and their modern counterparts may be viewed likewise. The word itself (Druid) comes through both Brythonic tongues (Cornish and Welsh), meaning either knowledge of the Oak or Wizard, or Wise man in Gaelic (Irish and Scots).

Druidry itself is both a philosophical viewpoint and a religious worldview, although it would be fair to say that many Druids also view themselves as Pagan priests.

The Council of British Druid Orders

www.cobdo.org.uk

As tenants, we were offered all sorts of health benefits, for example financial support for eye tests, and we received their quarterly newsletter, but we never met any of the Druids themselves. We did feel looked after, over and above what you would expect from your average landlord. Surely the Druids wouldn't let anything bad happen to us?

We moved in together in the autumn of 2001 and I finally regained my independence from my parents. I was 31. It was a great little terrace house, with a small garden and a cellar. My room was downstairs at the front, Fozia's above mine, and Jenna, because she had seen the advert, bagged the large attic room at the top of the house. I had no close friends in Sheffield except people from work. Although we would occasionally have nights out, as it got closer to Christmas, I knew I was in for a fairly lonely ride so I purchased some Bach's heather remedy, which is good for loneliness, and it did help a bit. Fozia was a trainee solicitor, and with her friendly and open demeanour had lots of friends. Although I was invited out on many occasions, I preferred my solitude over pretending I had a large, but borrowed, social network.

I was happy enough to lie in bed watching a film with a bottle of wine as my only company. I would love to have the house to myself so I could crank up the music and dance wildly around the room, often talking to myself in the mirror about where my life was going. Richard was on the scene again, albeit once a week. But he was a married man, already having troubles with his wife.

Soon after moving in, Fozia met Luke through work and it wasn't long before he was round most nights. Fozia, Luke and I always had one day of the week when we would have a smoking night. Sometimes we called it the 'Monday night club', sometimes the 'Tuesday night club', but by the end, we had hosted that night on every day of the week.

Luke would roll the joints, as Fozia and I were useless, and she used to joke that we were his *punkawallahs*, fanning him while he built another spliff. Jenna would sometimes join us, but would rarely buy any. It was mainly the three of us. I never felt like a gooseberry, just one of the club, and we three became close.

I loved Luke with his titian hair (as Fozia would insist it wasn't ginger!). He also became my divorce lawyer on both occasions, and he saved me a lot of money. I especially loved the beautiful Fozia, an amazing girl who was always dressed to perfection, even on a tight budget, with a voice that was soft, soothing and sexy. She used her charm to win around any situation and taught me how to use my feminine ways to do it for myself.

Boot and I, 2001

A month after I moved in to my new bachelor flat, Berry Hill, my parents' house, had a new occupant and so we had a new member of the family. This was in the form of a beautiful, black and white border collie, whom the owner/breeders officially named Wath-on Christmas Boot (he was born in Wath-on-Dearne), but we just called him Boot or Booty. I had wanted a bitch and to call her Jess but we were all drawn to the little boy, who was far more affectionate than the others, and fell in love with him immediately. The breeders mainly sold working dogs, but they said if any of the litter would make a domestic pet, it was Boot, and they were happy for us to adopt him.

I don't think Boot ever had any border collie instincts, unlike Kelty, who as a Shetland sheepdog had had them in abundance, although that was her downfall. I observed this when we were walking through the sheep-filled fields back to Berry Hill from the George and Dragon one evening. I had alerted Mike to the fact the field was full of sheep, that Boot was a border collie and, surely just as a precaution, a lead might be sensible. Mike did this walk often and he reassured me that the dog wasn't remotely interested in sheep and he was right: Boot didn't even notice that they were everywhere. He was far more interested in the stick that we were throwing (fetching sticks was his love), than pursuing his purpose as a border collie.

Boot settled well into our family and we all loved him dearly, especially my niece who was only five months old when he came to live with us. One day, when Amy was still a toddler, my mum, sister and I noticed she had left the room, and so we went to find her. A photo was taken of the priceless, unscripted moment when we found her sitting next to the pup in his basket, just keeping each other company. They became close and he was very protective of her, but he didn't like other children much and so was barred from the George and Dragon after snapping at a local's toddler. He loved going to the pub for a pint with Dad and so he had to change locals where there were fewer toddlers!

Whilst editing this part of my book I also heard the news from my sister that Boot (RIP) had died. He'd had his last fit (an abnormality in his brain) and his heart couldn't cope. He was twelve years old. I wanted to dedicate a part of my book to him and his memory and this is the point where he comes into my story. This world is certainly a sorrier place for Boot not being here. He was buried on 'Booty Hill' by Dad and Roger, Trace's current husband, with a black cross bearing the inscription 'Boot', painted in white by Amy to say farewell to her long-time companion and friend.

At work, the primary care group had turned into a trust, and I applied for a job in the newly formed organisation. I did all the publicity for our various training courses and I know my ability to produce an eye-catching poster granted me a permanent post. It was certainly not my interview technique that got me the job, as I was constructively and kindly told by Helen, one of the panel members, in my feedback later. I am rubbish at interviews and have failed lots of them due to my acute nervousness and lack of self-confidence to really be able to sell myself. They still gave me the job because they knew I could do it, and not because I convinced them I could in the interview.

At this time, Sheffield NHS was split into four areas: North, with an HQ at Firth Park; West, based at the Hillsborough Barracks; South West, based at at Fulwood House, and South East Sheffield primary care trust, based first at Park Hill and then later at Orgreave, near Handsworth. If you know Sheffield, you'll get a feel for the area, but if you don't, let's say they covered the breadth of Sheffield.

Let Wikipedia tell you what a PCT did.

An **NHS primary care trust** (PCT) was a type of NHS trust, part of the National Health Service in England. PCTs were largely administrative bodies, responsible for commissioning primary, community and secondary health services from providers. Until 31 May 2011 they also provided community health services directly.

– Wikipedia

To the patient, the structure of PCTs meant nothing and was just another change by the government that didn't really affect their frontline care. They still visited their GP, who may refer them to hospital, and from the surgery they could access community nursing teams. These included district nurses for the elderly and health visitors for the newborns, plus physiotherapy, mental health services, dentistry and sexual health services etc. And if they needed to call 999 for an emergency, they still could. Patients did begin to get an understanding of the PCT towards the end of its life, just as community services were working well and they were getting used to things. What it meant to patients was better health care at the point of access and a lot of money was thrown into the community to improve health care services. But I do believe there was also a lot of wasted money. Money in the NHS seemed quite abundant back then, but then Sheffield spent heavily too. Each PCT in Sheffield led on different areas, with South East being responsible for children and young people, sexual health and dentistry among other things, and I was responsible for the communications in these areas.

My job title was communications and events coordinator, and this is where my official communications training started; a particularly steep learning curve. On becoming a PCT, a new chief executive had been appointed, one who refused to sit in the same office as the admin staff and who changed the dynamics of what had gone before overnight. We grew and grew and moved to our new base in Handsworth, on the site of the 'Battle of Orgreave' a site which still carries the energy of injustice and the brave fight by all those miners persecuted and beaten to a pulp that day by Thatcher's Britain.

On 18th June 1984, a picket was planned by the NUM to stop lorries leaving the coking plant at Orgreave. Orgreave is next to Handsworth, just on the border with Rotherham, and accessed just off the Parkway, Sheffield's slip road to the motorway. That day, South Yorkshire Police, who were joined by other forces including Nottinghamshire and the Met, escorted the convoy of NUM members and supporters from across the country into Orgreave. They were then led on foot into a corn field facing a thick blue line of police, probably ten deep, as one man later described it for the BBC's documentary *Battle of Orgreave*. The miners were well and truly in the Police's trap: there were police dogs on one side, mounted police on the other and a steep banking so that the only way out was into Orgreave village. The documentary exposes the violence that occurred that day as the miners were forced up that route.

Some of the miners caught on film told their story about the real turn of events that day. One photographer, a woman, tells how she was saved from being hit on the head with a truncheon by a police rioter. It's convincing enough for me to see in those miners' faces that rioting was not on their mind; they claimed that it was the police who were rioting that day. They wanted to sit down peacefully in the road, to stop the trucks coming into Orgreave. Of course, a more biased news report was broadcast to the nation that night, reporting that the miners were throwing 'missiles' and 'rioting', leading to the arrest of 95 miners (but who were all eventually acquitted).

In 1991 South Yorkshire Police had to pay out over half a million pounds to 39 miners who were arrested at Orgreave. With their bad press in 2012 with the Hillsborough investigation, people understandably demanded answers about Orgreave too. This tragic day captures Thatcher's Britain, using bully boy tactics to control the mob. Her legacy, for many, is that she is responsible for creating a police state.

Over the five years I worked at the Orgreave site, I watched the slagheaps being landscaped, eroding the visible memories of what had gone before. Remember I talked about energy remaining? The site's energy gave me enormous strength to fight my oppressors all the way.

Geranium Fellows OBE was our new chief executive. I thought she hated me, but on reflection, I believe was incredibly intimidated by me. She used to make a beeline for me at parties as she didn't know anyone else. I must say I was rather worried when, at a health conference, she once asked me, "Who's that guy over there, Kay?" I replied, shocked, "That's your cancer lead (GP in charge of cancer), Geranium!" She also used to look me up and down as though she had a bad smell in her nose, a classic controlling trick. She had a team who jumped to her tune 'or else', and their sycophantic behaviour suited her down to the ground. Control is the suppression of all creativity, to make a person feel stupid and inferior and not let them believe that they have any valid input. I would come to realise that this bullying behaviour was rife in the NHS.

You could always tell when Celeste, my line manager, had been bullied. She'd come back from the senior management team meeting and try it on with us, a red tinge lighting her face. I know we wound her up by saying that some of the new directives were nonsense and that they would be a waste of our time and money. But she always pulled the 'management card', and so we dutifully complied on every occasion. Geranium wasn't someone who could be challenged, which is why she probably had very little to do with me. But being left alone suited me. I spoke my mind and was no sycophant.

When we first moved into Orgreave I shared an office with Gill from accounts, and we had such a giggle. I would spend my lunch hours scanning the internet for any spiritual sites, especially sites dealing with 2012 and the end of the Mayan calendar: the ultimate shift to a higher vibration, and not the end of the world, as some sites suggested. I came across this beautiful story, which made complete sense to me, and I just have to share it, with kind permission from Michael Lightweaver.

A Galactic Fairy Tale, by Michael Lightweaver

A long, long time ago in a galaxy far, far away there were all of these little light beings just hanging out enjoying life in that joyful and timeless dimension. And then one day a very large, magnificent angel came to them. He had a very serious look on his face. He was looking for volunteers for a very important cosmic mission.

"We have this small – but very special – planet out at the edge of the Alcyon galaxy called Gaia. It is quite unique like a beautiful garden and it is teeming with hundreds of thousands of different life forms. It has been something of an experimental station in the galaxy and it has a most interesting humanoid life form that incorporates the very highest and lowest frequencies known in the cosmos. It is in fact the very epitome of dualism. On the one hand it is an incredibly beautiful life form and is capable of carrying the highest frequencies of love, light and joy known throughout the whole Universe. On the other hand it is capable of carrying the densest and darkest frequencies the cosmos has ever experienced – frequencies which the rest of creation evolved beyond aeons ago.

Here is the current situation. Within the domain of time, this planet goes through periodic cosmic cycles. It is now coming to the end of two major cycles – a 2,000 year long age of Pisces and the 25,000 year long cosmic year in its journey around Alcyon, the central sun of the milky way galaxy.

With the completion of this cycle, many things are coming to an end and many things are about to begin. But most importantly, the planet is experiencing an infusion of light that is dramatically increasing its frequency. As during any major time of transition, there will be a certain amount of turbulence. Some of this will be geological, for Gaia herself is a living planet and is also evolving. But much of it also involves the hominoid species that dominates the planet.

This will not be a particularly easy time for the species – especially for those who are sleeping and those who are vibrating at the lowest frequencies. As the frequency changes it will create insecurity which in turn will create fear.

The first era of evolution on this planet was the physical era and the key word was survival. The second era, which is now ending, was the mental era and the key word was logic. The third era, which is now beginning, is the era of the heart and the key word is love. This is the highest frequency.

Those who currently hold the reign of power on the planet are of the old order of the physical and mental. To the extent that they can make a graceful transition to a heart centred and divinely guided life, it will be an easy transition. To the extent that they are unable to do this, they will experience much turmoil.

So this is the current situation of Gaia. The reason I am here is to seek volunteers who would be willing to incarnate in humanoid form on the planet at this time to help make this an easy and smooth transition. We have sent prophets and teachers in the past. Very often they were brutally persecuted or killed. In other instances they were set up as 'gods' to be worshipped and these humanoids built elaborate religions and rituals around them and used these religions to control each other. They did everything except follow the simple teachings that were offered.

So this time we are trying a different approach. No more prophets, saviours and avatars that they can use to create religions. This time we are sending in thousands – actually hundreds of thousands – of ordinary light beings with only two assignments:

1) Stay in your heart. Regardless of what happens, stay in your heart.

2) Remember who you are, why you are here and what this is all about.

Now that seems easy enough, right? Unfortunately, no! As I have said, duality has reached its peak on this planet. This species has perfected the illusion of good and evil. The greatest challenge you will experience is to remember Who You Really Are, Why You Are Here and What This Is Really All About. When you remember, you will be able to stay in your heart, regardless of external events.

So how will you know when you are forgetting? It is easy. Watch your judgements. The moment you notice that you are in a place of judgement you will know that you have forgotten Who You Really Are, Why You Are Here and What This Is Really All About. That will be your signal.

Now here is the challenge. Life on this planet will require a great deal of discernment – wise evaluation of what is true, what is appropriate and what is for the highest good, both for yourself and for the planet. In many ways discernment is similar to judgement. However, you will know when you are in judgement and when you have moved out of your heart when you are in a place of blame.

We know how challenging this planet can be. We know how very real the illusions on this planet appear to be. We understand the incredible density of this dimension and the pressure you will face. But if you survive this mission – and it is a voluntary one – you will evolve at hyper speed.

We also should say that we know that some of you who will go to this planet as starseeds, will never germinate – never awakened to the remembrance of who you really are. Some of you will awaken and begin to shine, only to be choked down by the opinions and prevailing thought forms around you. Others will awaken and remain awake and your light will become a source of inspiration and remembrance for many.

You will incarnate all over the planet; in every culture, every race, every country, every religion. But you will be different. You will never quite fit in. As you awaken you will realise that your true family isn't those of your own race, culture, religion, country or even your biological family. It is your cosmic family – those who have come as you have come – on assignment to assist in ways large and small in the current transition.

True brotherhood and globalisation in its highest form will come only in remembering Who You Really Are, Why You Are Here and What This Is Really All About. It will come as you return to the true temple of Divine Presence, your heart, where this remembrance takes place and from which you are called to serve the world.

So, are your ready? Good!

Oh, and by the way, there are a couple of other minor things I should mention...

Because of the density, you can't operate in that dimension without a space suit. This is a biological suit that actually changes over time. There are many things we could tell you about this but our orientation time is short so I think you can just jump in and experience it. You should be forewarned, however. There will be a danger that if you forget Who You Really Are, you may think you ARE your space suit instead of the fact that it is simply your vehicle in that dimension. Once there, you will notice that there is an infinite variety of space suits and a great deal of attention given to these. However, in spite of the infinite variety, because this a planet of duality, they all fall into two basic categories called 'genders'. Again, we really don't have time to go into this now. But you will find your relationship with your own space suit to be most instructive and interesting.

The other little thing is this. In order to operate in that dimension, you will also receive a microchip called a 'personality'. This is like an identity imprint that, along with your space suit, will essentially make you different from everyone else. This will allow you to participate in the hologram there – something they call 'consensus reality'. Once again, there will be a real danger that you will become so engrossed in the holographic personality dramas that you will forget Who You Really Are and actually think that you ARE your personality. I know it sounds rather unbelievable right now, but once you get there...

Again, there is so much more we could tell you by way of orientation, but we think you can learn the rest experientially 'on site'. The only thing that is important is to remember Who You Really Are, Why You Are Here and What This Is Really All About. If you can do that, everything else will work out fine. But take note: So few really DO remember this they stand out as 'different" and others called them 'Enlightened' or Awakened' and similar terms. Strange isn't it?

Well, good luck & bon voyage!

Michael Lightweaver
www.mtnlightsanctuary.com

Things were making more sense to me spiritually and I started seeing the number 33 everywhere I looked. I took it to mean something, as De La Soul had told me often enough that three was the magic number, and it was my favourite number as a child. But when I looked at a clock it read 33 minutes past, every time. I didn't Google this phenomenon until much later and I now realise I'm not on my own; there are many of us! It still happens. Oh gosh – it's just happened again as I write this bit and glance over to the clock. I rest my case.

So my life was quite all right, but lacking one important element: love. Enter stage left, Theodore, my old friend from school. Things would never be the same again following his email.

The 'Love Square' –
One Crazy Week in May

9

Love confuses and bemuses; it's our heart that shows us our true path.
– Kay Rose-Hattrick

heodore Googled me out of the blue one day while I was at work, apparently because he was bored, finding me through a corporate document I had written and posted on the internet. His email popped up into my inbox saying, "If you are the same Kay Hattersley who went to St Mary's, then how the devil are you? If not, apologies!" After receiving the message I told Gill about the 'as articulate as a lorry' story, but needless to say I responded pretty sharpish.

Theodore was living in Brighton and working in the public sector. It was also quite a surprise that he had contacted me the week before I was due to visit my old Edexcel workmate, Jane, at her home in Brighton, where she had moved to from London some time earlier. Through my study of reiki, I have learned that there is no such thing as a coincidence and everything happens for a reason. In our daily email correspondence, during the week, I told him that I was going to go down to London before travelling on to Brighton, as Ashley and I were going to talk about our divorce. Our friend Nicolai, whom Ashley and I had met in Vietnam, would also be there visiting.

We arranged to meet while I was in Brighton and he bought a new mobile so we could contact each other while I was down. This was the start of the 'love square' week; a week that would bring complete upheaval to my life as I knew it. It started with Richard. He had married since we split up, but as things were not going well with his new wife, we had rekindled our friendship. I didn't see him as a married man at that time: he was my Richard and I had come first.

The day I left for London was the day I said goodbye to Richard, as my lover, for the last time, although we didn't know it then. He wanted me to keep in touch during that week as he was worried that he would lose me to Ashley. I told him that I just wanted him to be happy, either with his wife or with me, but that he needed to make that decision for himself once and for all. It certainly wasn't fair on anyone this way.

I drove down to London and was greeted by Ashley and Nicolai as I pulled into the car park behind the flat we had shared. I had lost a lot of weight since I had last seen them, thanks to Carol Vorderman, and I was looking better than I had done for years: thinner, happy and confident. You could see it in both their eyes at first embrace.

That night, Ashley was supposed to be going home to his girlfriend's, but we'd all had quite a lot to drink. We looked at photos taken in Vietnam and caught up on one other's lives. That night, as we had a cuddle, I didn't realise that it would be the last time I would ever set eyes on him. When Nicolai left the following day we had a heart to heart that culminated in him saying, "What's the point of divorcing, Kay; we'll only have to get remarried." And that's how we left it. I cried as he waved me out of the gates, until he couldn't see me any more, and then I continued on to Brighton, believing that my husband and I would finally be reunited. He promised to stay in touch throughout my stay and that we'd seriously talk about our future plans on my return to Sheffield.

It was great to see Jane and the two boys she'd had since leaving Edexcel, as well as her boyfriend and now husband, Nick. It's always the same with Jane; one of those good friends where you pick up where you have left off, despite the meetings being years apart. She's so funny and always true to herself and therefore others. She's a Libran – my polar opposite. Like any opposites, you can have a love/hate relationship, and where you clash you can also complement each other. Jane and I certainly complement each other. I told her about what had happened in London with Ashley and the saga about Richard. The following day, I arranged to meet up with Theodore.

It wasn't a 'date': we just went to a local pub and caught up, after many years. It was great to see him again and he creased me up all night. The next time we met I went round to his flat and then on to a club. When I first arrived, I pulled out a pre-rolled spliff and I recall the smile on his face that said, "Thank goodness Kay Hattersley isn't a stiffy." It was going to be a late one as we were due to watch our schoolfriend Brian P Mitchell, who would be performing at the comedy club later. I had therefore arranged to stay the night at Theodore's, purely as friends.

Theodore had always made me laugh. Even at school, when I kept a wide berth for fear of the jokes being at my expense, he could take me and his fellow classmates close to tears. After that spliff, I don't think I've belly laughed so much in my life. He was so charming that night, and even when it came to sleeping next to me he continued to behave like a gentleman. My estimations of that man grew accordingly and I spent a lot of time with him over the week, culminating on the Thursday, when I asked if I could kiss him!

During the week, concurrently with my growing affection for Theodore, I was communicating with Ashley and Richard. I told you it was a 'love square'. Ashley had been texting throughout the week, reflecting about the times we had spent in Brighton together and with Jane and Nick. As the week went on, the texts became less reminiscent and by Friday teatime, he sent me the text that would completely change my options for the future once again. Although I'd already changed them with 'the kiss' the previous night. It said that he realised his life was with his girlfriend, that we wouldn't work together and that I should find happiness with Richard. As I read it I cried, looking over to where Theodore was telling yet another joke, and I thought, "I love that man." I could see our future together, and I knew I was also not on the rebound.

Richard's texts throughout the week had been from a jealous man. "Why aren't you responding to my texts? What were you doing, and with whom?" I kept my replies lighthearted as I knew I couldn't dump him by text. I had been prepared to dump him for Ashley at the start of the week and Theodore by the end!

Theodore and I made love that night for the first time and I knew it was right. The day after I got back, I told Richard that I was in love with Theodore and that our relationship was definitely over. He didn't take it well but he had essentially made his position known throughout the affair. He always went back to his wife.

From then on, Theodore and I took it in turns to travel to either Sheffield or Brighton, except when he was visiting his son Conrad, who lived with his mum in Gloucester. The weekends we spent together were always booze-fuelled and like a scene from *Sid and Nancy*, but I knew he was the man for me.

KAY ROSE-HATTRICK

Husband no. 2 – Theodore

The Mathematics of Kay, by Theodore

10% her mum, 14% her dad
63% happy, 37% mad
12% Mike and 5% Trace
4% clumsiness and 12% grace
14% the world, 14% beyond
18% right, 12% wrong
infinity my love for her
infinity her love for me
100% Kay, 97% free.

Tony: "The maths don't add up... and neither do you."
Kay: "Did you just laugh out loud, Theodore?"

Theodore and I had spoken about marriage early on in our relationship and he proposed to me with a white gold set diamond ring. I had admired it in a jewellery shop just off Ecclesall Road and unbeknown to me, Theodore went back to buy it. We were so much in love. Or had Ashley been right: was I just in love with being in love? Theodore had agreed to move up to Sheffield, as I didn't want to move down south again, so he emailed a few agencies and they got him interviews with two top solicitor firms, in Leeds and Manchester. He was a very intelligent man, so was immediately snapped up by a company in Manchester. Theodore had trained and worked as a barrister in London after bar school, but had sold his wig for beer money years earlier. I had repeatedly told him not to rush into anything, as Manchester was a long commute from Sheffield every day. He would repeatedly say, "I just want to be with you."

The day he left Brighton, he queued behind Nick Cave, a hero of his, to get his ticket at the train station, and he was on a great high when he arrived. We were so happy to finally be together. The girls and Luke loved him, and although it was crowded, especially when Luke moved in permanently, we had some great times together. Theodore introduced me to my first ecstasy pill one sunny Saturday afternoon and I remember it being amazing. I was so loved up: I loved everyone and the world too amid the vibrant colours it produced within my head. No wonder that it's called the happy pill. From then on we took pills most weekends, but I never quite got back to where that experience had first taken me.

I remember it was Valentine's Day when Theodore took his first day off sick from his new job. He'd spent the whole day setting the table for a sumptuous dinner he had created, and Jenna helped him to light candles and run the bath, which had been sprinkled with rose petals, with a trail leading up to the bathroom. When I arrived home from work, I was amazed and felt so loved by the man I was to marry. The girls were sent out for the night and we spent a romantic night in.

This would never happen again during the rest of our time together, and as the year progressed, so would his depression. By March, he was signed off sick by his doctor and by May and our wedding day, he had left work completely. His workplace were extremely understanding considering that he hadn't been there long and they were very patient with him. I had to speak to his boss in the end to tell him that Theodore would not be coming back and to arrange a meeting for him to go and see him to finalise leaving arrangements. On the day he went to the station to catch that final train to Manchester, I left work for an hour to meet him on the platform to give him some moral support before he got on the train. He was a shell of a man and there was not much I could do to comfort him.

I asked him if he wanted to postpone our wedding, considering the strain he was under, and he categorically said no. The problem was that this was no public sector job like he'd had in Brighton. Every chargeable hour had to be accounted for, for except for a few comfort breaks. Time had become his enemy and had eventually broken his will. No more surfing the net in his lunch break when he was bored. It would take him about five hours to commute to and from the office. He had to go straight into work mode for the duration of the day, before coming all the way back again. I tried to make this transition as easy as possible and made him lovely lunches and dinner on his return, but nothing could ease his pain. He had made a mistake and taken the first job he was offered, then blamed me.

I shouldn't have married husband number two, but I went ahead with it because I feared it would send him further into depression if I didn't. One night, he flew off the handle about something and started throwing stuff around our bedroom. I ran upstairs to Jenna's room and demanded she phone the police as I heard the crashing continue downstairs. Something stopped me from wanting to involve them after all, and finally, when I went down to the room, he had left. Much of my stuff had been trashed, including many photos from my youth, which had had my face (and only my face) neatly cut out, thus ruining my photos forever. This would happen many more times to come (I learned to hide my photos and precious possessions when I feared a repeat performance) but on this occasion, I forgave him when we made up.

My second wedding day was nothing like the first. I had a dream before the wedding that my dress would be bright pink, and I found the material while walking through

Brighton station market one Sunday. It was a beautifully embroidered sari silk that I got for next to nothing. It was made into a skirt with a long train by a gay friend from work. I made the bouquets for me and my bridesmaids, Jenna and Fozia, out of bright pink gerberas. I also made a chocolate cake filled with Delia's rich chocolate mousse, while Fozia insisted she make the traditional fruit cake, which looked amazing. We had sent out homemade invitations and our guest list included some of our old friends from school, including Ian Hyland, Theodore's accomplice in tearing down my confidence all those years before, and David, who had got me into drumming.

The night before the wedding I stayed at home with Jenna, Fozia and Luke, while Theodore stayed in my old schoolfriend Claire's palatial marital home, and was pampered to within an inch of his life. I had to make the sausage sandwiches for breakfast for us all, while trying to get ready! We got down to the 'wedding cake', Sheffield's old registry office, in Jenna's car, to the sound of 'Pure Shores' by All Saints blasting out on repeat. All of our special friends were waiting for us outside, and unbeknown to me, my brother had secretly flown in from New Zealand, where he was working, and surprised me with Amy in his arms. I greeted my niece, before realising who was carrying her.

Second wedding day. Note Mike trying to surprise me with Amy in his arms.

It was a fabulous day, and as I said my vows for the second time that decade I believed it to be for life, again. I loved Theodore, and even took on his surname, much to Ashley's disappointment, as I hadn't done the same with his. I felt like I needed to shed some skin and a new name was in order. I thought I sounded quite rock and roll, but instead most people I introduced myself to thought I was Australian and called me Kayleen! We came down the aisle as a married couple to 'Nice Weather for Ducks' by Lemon Jelly, one of the most uplifting songs I've ever heard. Claire and her husband James drove us back to Ecclesall Road in style in their Range Rover, with a half bottle of champagne and two glasses stashed in the glove compartment for our enjoyment. We went on to a local wine bar for canapés, drinks, cakes and speeches, not necessarily in that order. We all made our speeches from the balcony at

Menzels, including Brian P Mitchell, who was Theodore's best man and who had prepared a very funny speech. Dad had kindly put a tab behind the bar for a free drink for people on arrival and everyone had a great time. I think our schoolfriends found it slightly amusing, and were bemused that Theodore and I had tied the knot, especially considering our sixth form years. Everyone piled back to our house for the evening do. I had set Theodore's decks up and we had a number of different DJs playing into the wee hours. We left the party still going strong and went to our hotel room in town to consummate our marriage. My mum kept saying throughout the day, "Kay, I think I prefer this wedding to the last one." It was so laid back and completely different from my very traditional one with Ashley.

All was well for a couple of days after the wedding; our friends stayed a bit longer and we were on honeymoon. I had lost my voice through all that talking you are expected to do at your wedding, including projecting my voice for my speech, and I felt rather delicate for days afterwards. We spent part of our honeymoon at my in-laws' in Morecambe, by the sea, as his parents were unable to attend our wedding due to illness. When we came back, however, Theodore started behaving in a manner not in keeping with being newly married. In fact, he was quite nasty, and I cried buckets before we'd even managed a week of nuptials.

It was to get worse though, and I would end up self-harming by slashing my wrists by the time things hit rock bottom. As Theodore no longer had a job, we were living off one income, which wasn't what we were used to, financially. We had never had to worry about money before due to Theodore's previously healthy salary. I took out a loan and my credit card was used to ensure that we still lived well. We had to be more creative, but we managed; always beyond our means though. I would come home most nights to find that he had that distant look in his eyes. Some nights he was worse than others, and he would rock gently back and forth, or I'd have to stick my hand down his throat to retrieve the anti-depressants he'd taken in an attempted overdose. My confidence was non-existent and he would use his clever tongue to cut me to the bone.

I hated myself back then, because he hated me and blamed me for everything, including moving up from his fabulous social life in Brighton and now being estranged from his son. Theodore gave his ex-wife quite a substantial amount of money for his upkeep, but later, when Theodore wasn't earning, she stopped him from visiting and it broke his heart.

I knew he had hit rock bottom when we were coming back from Brighton one Sunday after visiting friends; something which I had thought might pull him out of his misery. On the train back to Sheffield, he started shouting out random things as we passed trees and sheep and lampposts. All the people on the train looked on, thinking he was a bit mad, while I put on a brave face because I knew he had certainly lost it. The night I self-harmed was a sad night but it was my only control over such a situation. He hated me so why should I love myself? I just wanted to hurt myself, as the loathing remarks he repeatedly directed towards me were all I thought I deserved.

I went to work the day after with a bandage hiding my war wounds. I did show them to Margaret, our admin assistant, but no one else. If it wasn't for Margaret, I don't think I would have got through that period at work. She was also in a difficult relationship, and every day it was either me or her in floods of tears, comforting the other. Celeste, my boss, didn't make my life very easy and on occasions said that I should leave my personal life at home and made me fear losing my job and therefore the only income we had coming in. Months later, I spoke to human resources in a panic, explaining the situation with my husband. They were fabulous and helped enormously by alleviating my stress over my fears of being sacked.

To ever have a chance of moving our life on we had to get out of the shared house. Jenna was becoming more resentful of both couples and Fozia and Luke were planning on moving out together for similar reasons to us. Of course, it was I who started the property search with Theodore in tow during the viewing of the first property. It was above a shop called Acorn Antiques, and after the viewing I just wanted to cry, but it was all we could afford with only me working. I think we would have lasted a matter of weeks there before killing each other. You even had to come out of your secure flat door to use the bathroom, which was tiny anyway, with a small shower cubicle and a flapping curtain. The galley kitchen was more like a corridor with no cupboards and the bedroom fitted an ancient-looking double bed only, as there was no room for anything else. On the way home, Theodore said he was happy with it, while I was on the verge of tears, thinking I couldn't possibly live there.

A friend had given me her old landlord's number and I arranged to meet up for a viewing of a two bedroomed flat in Sharrow after work; without Theodore this time. As I pulled up outside I fell in love with the building. The flat was in a large block of Victorian houses set back off the tree-lined street, and had large front gardens. The rooms were spacious and the ceilings high; from our flat we even had access to the massive cellar for extra storage. The *pièce de résistance* was that the back door led on to a large private yard with a high wall and path linking the flats, and an overgrown hedgerow behind. I immediately saw the potential. I loved the flat, and although it would be a struggle until Theodore found another job, I felt compelled to take it immediately. Theodore went along with my choice but left it up to Mum and me to do the cleaning and to move all our stuff to the new place in several trips in my car.

I believed we could finally put our worries behind us, move ourselves forward and start our married life happily, in our new home together.

Jarvis, Raves & Reiki II

Cats are intelligent and definitely not stupid.
If we speak to them as equals and with empathy,
we develop deep friendships that last forever.
– Kay Rose-Hattrick

We were happy in the new place and Theodore soon secured a job in a call centre, which he quite enjoyed and where he met some nice people. There was no real pressure on him, but his wage afforded him some luxuries every month, namely all the cider he could drink! We also adopted a cat from the cats' home in nearby Broomhall. We found Spotty (so called because of his black and white coat) in the crap cats' room that was located downstairs. Upstairs, the friendly, preening cats were snapped up immediately by new families, but Spotty had been there for several months and so far nobody had wanted him. He shared a room with a three-legged cat, a blind cat and a cat who was even shyer than himself.

I was surprised at Theodore's choice, but went ahead with his decision and in the car going home, we decided to call him Jarvis, after the famous and much-admired Sheffielder, Mr Cocker, who had mentioned Broomhall in one of his songs. Jarvis had been a street cat but had adopted an old couple who fed him every day but who eventually got sick of him spraying everywhere to mark his territory. They took him to the cats' home to find a new home and to stop the powerful stench of tom-marking in their back yard! On his medical record that we were given from the cats' home was a written note: "Spotty is a very frightened cat and it will take him time to settle into his new surroundings."

When we got home, he ran under the dining table and no matter how much coaxing we attempted, he stayed under there for most of the night. I had a little chat with him later and

With Jarvis

said that I thought that we'd made a mistake by adopting him. I picked him up and brought him on the sofa with me and instead of flying back under the table, he curled up and went to sleep on my lap. It was only when I disturbed him to make dinner that he ran back under the table to his secure spot again. After dinner, I picked him up again and we returned to the sofa, and for the rest of the evening he relaxed and sprawled over me until we went to bed. That night, he jumped up on the bottom of the bed and that is where he slept from that moment on. Jarvis was certainly no mistake. From the moment of our chat, I knew that he understood me totally and that he had trusted me. Remember, communication goes far beyond words and I always knew exactly what Jarvis was thinking, with just one look!

Shortly after Jarvis joined us, we also got a new neighbour in the form of Poppy, who moved into the vacant flat above us. I could hear that someone had moved in and so left a welcome card and a pink gerbera at her front door. She later told me how she had cried on receiving this and knew that she had moved into the right place. Poppy was about five months pregnant and a soon-to-be single mum. We soon became close friends and she would often come down to our flat in the evening.

Poppy was an actress and graced our screen too, as within a few weeks of meeting her, she was in the idents (ads specifically made for the show) during *Emmerdale*. She also introduced us to her large social network and we often had barbecues in our back yard, which her balcony overlooked. The flat above Poppy was also now occupied by the lovely Salma, a student, and Stu, a relief teacher, and we all got on brilliantly. At Christmas time, we hosted dinner in all three flats. Poppy prepared the starter, Salma and Stu the turkey dinner with all the trimmings and Theodore and I hosted pudding and liqueurs, but we all helped cook it. What a wonderful energy our flats had, as we were all living harmoniously at the time. Theodore and I were always hosting parties; we adopted Poppy's crowd and we in turn introduced her to the people we knew, and sometimes they knew each other. They say Sheffield is the 'largest village in the world' and you're always guaranteed to see someone you know or recognise in town.

It was a happy time for Theodore and I; we loved our flat and our new cat Jarvis, and our social network was growing. So was our alcohol consumption and drug-taking. Our local, the Vine Inn, was where we did most of our socialising, and is where we met Merlin. He was trying to flog us an energy ball, which glowed when moved in a continuous arc, and which Theodore bought. What we really wanted was an eighth of weed and he provided that too, becoming our new supplier. He was different too, and understood my questioning of more spiritual approaches to life. Mad though, being an Aquarian, but definitely prophetic. More about Aquarians later.

The Vine had its fair share of misfits and most of the locals were on more than just alcohol, which added a further dimension to the proceedings. Sometimes you felt love in there and sometimes you had to tread on the proverbial eggshells, as comedowns can be quite nasty. From the outside, it's uninviting to passers-by as it stands alone, austere and rough-looking. Inside was a different story: lovely decor, a great beer garden and sunspot and generally a relaxed atmosphere given off by an eclectic mix of truth seekers, who had either opted out of the system altogether, or were desperate to get out of it, as I was. Unfortunately, the Vine is sadly no more , and is soon to become an Indian restaurant.

Merlin also introduced us to Wallace, a tall, kind, black man with long dreadlocks, a bandana and a gold front tooth, who resembled a swashbuckling pirate. He had a studio and played the bass and on hearing I was a drummer was keen to get his friend Andy, a guitarist, and me together to start a band. We were called CJ and Mary, but ask Andy why! We practised every week in Wallace's studio, playing one of Andy's own fantastic songs, time and time again, to get it right. Andy had secured us a gig at the Sharrow festival, our local community festival, and we only had to get together three songs to perform. It was at this point that I met Kerry.

I was asked to join a multi-agency communications group organised by the Young People's Directorate at Sheffield council, of which Kerry was the communications lead.

I was asked to join because my PCT had responsibility for children and young people in the city, and I was our communications lead. The group was attended by a mix of people from the voluntary and public sectors and schools, and its remit was communications for the city. To be honest, I was really nervous at these meetings. I was representing health and worried whether what came out of my mouth in the meetings was indeed the party line. I didn't have much confidence and was generally uncomfortable with myself and my abilities to perform. This group went on for years and we did some excellent city-wide work. Celeste seemed to think that this work was not a priority and I always had to justify my attendance to her. If there were any problems with this, Kerry would have to back me up.

After the first meeting, Kerry came over to me and started to chat about my role and the organisation and the remit for her job etc, as you do in these situations. The conversation then got on to her last job and I was impressed with what I heard. She had previously worked overseas, for Oxfam and a number of other charitable organisations, but had come back to her home town of Sheffield to settle down for a bit. She was a breath of fresh air for me as I wasn't used to her type at management level. She was a real person with a passion for her job, and it showed. She didn't speak in management talk either. I became more confident in myself, and after a couple of meetings we were firm friends. She even became the singer for CJ and Mary.

Although we were still practising the same songs repeatedly, it was so much fun with Kerry, and she changed the dynamic of the band for the better. Andy and Wallace loved her too. It was also an opportunity to catch up outside work, chatting about the daily doings and grumbles at two of the largest employers in the city: the council and the NHS. Over the years, Kerry gave me some very useful advice about my work with the union. She had herself been a union rep for Oxfam and other organisations overseas. We'd always have a laugh with the boys and a pint after practice and Kerry and I loved them both too. Gerry, a keyboard player, joined for a while and another guitarist, Martin, who told us we were rubbish, came for a couple of rehearsals. But Martin was right, we weren't that good, except for Andy, and we never played that gig. Despite our challenges on the musical side, we had a great camaraderie and those band practices gave me a chance to let off steam while hitting those skins.

Every other month, Theodore and I would head down to an underground techno rave beneath the Wicker Arches, and we would spend most of the night dancing or talking to people loved up on ecstasy, which was certainly our drug of choice at the time. We didn't know anyone when we first went there, but after several months we had become friends with a number of the locals, and I was reunited with Paul, my old work colleague from my HMV days. I saw Paul across the dancefloor. It was the first time we'd seen each other for over a decade, and we both stared at each other, trying to work out where we knew each other from. The penny dropped with us both fairly quickly and we became close friends after that.

Theodore and I even tried for a baby. Well, only once properly, on my most fertile day of the month. It was so functional, and I remember thinking, "I don't want a child of mine being conceived in such a matter-of-fact way." I didn't conceive anyway, thankfully. It's no wonder, as my body was being abused, albeit at weekends. Gosh, my life would be totally different now if we had been successful.

Margaret, our admin officer and my brick, sadly left and got a job outside the organisation. One day I enrolled the help of Ingrid, the temp employed by the admin office, who was mega-efficient and was always looking for things to do. I set her on a task that she undertook in our office and so I had an opportunity to talk to her for the first time. It seemed our lives had taken similar turns along the way, including divorce, living in London and reiki. She too had been attuned in Reiki I, and we spoke about this at length. Ingrid soon felt like a lifelong friend.

She temped for a couple of months, and during that time we built our friendship. After her contract had come to an end, I bumped into her on Ecclesall Road when I needed someone to turn to. Things weren't going well with Theodore and I ended up in tears in the coffee shop, crying on her shoulder. From that moment on, we connected and I knew her to be an angel sent to help. We still give each other support, even though she now lives overseas. She also introduced me to her reiki teacher and practitioner, Paul.

My reiki master at my first degree level said that we should feel right with our reiki master and shouldn't necessarily stick with the same one. I knew on first meeting that I wanted Paul to attune me further. I regularly went for reiki healing at his house in Woodhouse, and afterwards, we sat and chatted about spiritual things. I was unable to speak about such things with anyone, other than Ingrid, so it was a great release after such wonderful healing sessions. A topic which came up time after time was the end of the Mayan calendar, 21st December 2012. We discussed what we thought this date would bring and what it would mean to the universe.

I had been aware of this date for a number of years and it was always on the lips of any alternative spiritual seekers I met. I even spoke to a guy about it when Theodore and I were on holiday in Ibiza. We discussed that something was going to happen, as a matter of fact, but the date was so far in the future, we couldn't know what that would be.

I enrolled on the Reiki II attunement weekend not long after meeting Paul, and I went through another month-long detox before the weekend, to cleanse me of the impurities of everyday living. Over the two days, Paul taught us more about reiki energy and about the spiritual world around us, which resonated deep within me. By the end of the weekend, I had been attuned to Reiki II level and was again on a natural high, floating on all the positive energy the group had produced. The Reiki II attunement was very powerful and, although I was more open to the universal energy, I forgot to protect myself from any two-way energy exchange. It took me time to settle down and become in tune with its natural flow. I have been told that Reiki I opens you up about 25%, Reiki II by 50% and Reiki III fully. But by the time you are attuned as reiki master, you are much better able to protect yourself and others against destructive negative energy.

Our physical body comprises various levels of vibratory rates of energy. Within our physical body there exist numerous energy centres of yet higher frequencies than those previously acknowledged by science. These centres were long ago acknowledged by mystics in various parts of the world. The term chakra comes from the Sanskrit, meaning 'circle of movement'. My dictionary defines it as 'a centre of spiritual power in the human body' – or human battery, if you prefer. There are seven main chakras in your energy vortex, which should spin freely and equally depending on how balanced you are. Chakras spin in different directions, depending on whether you're male or female. The way to test this balance is by using a crystal on a chain or string and dousing each chakra to see how it is flowing. Reiki helps clear any blocked energy and enables it to flow freely again. I think it's so interesting that it shows the **Yin** (male) and the **Yang** (female) so visibly as opposites.

Take a look at the chart on the following page and you might be able to work out which chakra you need work most on.

It certainly makes sense to be balanced but our hectic daily lives are understandably likely to create imbalance, due to fears and anxieties over money, job, rent/mortgage, utility bills, car payments etc, poor diet, little time truly for yourself. We concentrate more on our physical and sexual desires than on our spiritual needs of intuition and self-awareness, which women tend to call their sixth sense. This leaves our lower chakras (base – sacral – solar plexus) over-stimulated and our higher, intuitive chakras (throat – third eye – crown), under-active and redundant. And the heart chakra, in the middle, is left not knowing whether it's coming or going!

Reiki II did take me to a higher level, but as I said, I failed to protect myself properly and I was left vulnerable.

Chakra	Colour	Position	Female rotational direction	In harmony	Out of harmony
Root (Base)	Red	Base of the spine	Anti-clockwise	Profound connection to nature, well grounded.	At odds with environment, fear, self-centred, violence, greed and anger.
Sacral	Orange	Just below belly button	Clockwise	A considerate, open, friendly, kind person who has no trouble sharing emotions and feelings with others.	Unstable in sexual and emotional matters. Cannot express feelings. Suppresses natural needs.
Solar plexus	Yellow	Between bottom of ribs and belly button	Anti-clockwise	Feeling of wholeness, inner calm, peace, tolerance and acceptance of others.	No trust in natural flow of things, need to dominate, great need for material security.
Heart	Green	Centre of chest	Clockwise	Feeling of wholeness, tolerance and acceptance of life and relationships. Self-love, laughter, happiness, joy and unconditional love.	The love you give is not sincere, you look for rewards. You cannot accept love from another. Weak immune system, unhappiness, conditional love.
Throat	Blue	Between inner collarbone	Anti-clockwise	Knows balance of expression, silence and speech. Trusts intuition.	Despite much talking cannot find expression, fearful of being judged and rejected. Afraid of silence.
Third eye	Indigo	Between the eyes	Clockwise	Awareness of spiritual side of being. Invites intuition and inner awareness into everyday life, connects to the universe.	Rejects spiritual aspects. Focus on intellect and science. Afraid of intuition.
Crown	Violet	Top and centre of head	Anti-clockwise	Living with the knowledge of unity. Knowing that the self reflects the divine.	Unable to let go of anxiety and fear, lack of vision.

ℕhs – The Battle at Orgreave

12

The media is as corrupt as the banks and politicians,
but we hate admitting that we've fallen for their lies for years too.
– Kay Rose-Hattrick

Whilst I was working for the National Health Service (NHS), it was the fourth largest employer in the world after the Chinese army, the Indian railway and Walmart. According to the BBC (2012), the United States Department of Defense sits at top place now, followed by the Chinese army. McDonalds', it seems, has knocked the NHS off fourth place and two other Chinese corporations have lowered the ranking of the Indian railway. I think this sort of says it all about where our world stands today.

Despite its still-large workforce, those who work or have worked for the NHS would no doubt agree that it used to be one big family. Orgreave was no different. We protected each other like family members and were there for each other during the great times, of which there were many, and the very bad, of which there were thankfully fewer. Many current NHS employees, I have been told, do not consider it to be like a family any more.

You didn't join the NHS if you were really money-motivated. It was more a vocation to do good, to put something back into the world, so you could sit back with your hot chocolate or a glass of wine at night in front of the TV and think you'd done something positive that day. Everyone was as important as the next person, as everyone had their position in the machine, and the cogs just wouldn't turn if someone was missing. Unfortunately, some people thought they were more important and they did harm.

Bullying was more commonplace than you'd expect in a public sector organisation. I certainly wouldn't tolerate it though, and I fought to change things, although most people were always lovely to me.

During my time at Orgreave, I was promoted to communications manager. I think they realised that their communications lead needed a management title to give the role some credibility. I was taken off an admin and clerical grade. I lost out on holidays and wasn't paid much more; certainly nothing close to my counterparts in the other trusts across the country.

Geranium continued to show her contempt for me, but I was not alone. She never welcomed her new employees or went on a walkabout to see how everyone was getting on, unlike the chief executives of the other Sheffield PCTs. In fact, new starters would ask me, "Who is that woman?" if they caught sight of her rushing up to her office from another outside meeting. I would reply in amazement, "That's the chief executive!" In fact, our chief executive had very little impact on my decision making. I had more autonomy than most during my time at Orgreave.

As a result, I was free to be as creative as I liked and with internal communications in my remit I worked hard to make everyone feel valued. We all looked after each other, despite it being frowned upon by some; people had lives and sometimes it was a struggle to stay focused solely on work. We are human beings, after all, and emotions don't just turn off because you've pulled into the work car park. You can't park your anxieties with your car and then pick them up again at 5 o'clock; it just doesn't work like that. Equally, I took work home with me a lot.

In those five years I attended a few weddings, even two in one day. I watched the gorgeous Natalie say her vows and partied on down with the lovely Michelle and other colleagues at her night do. I attended a funeral and supported other colleagues who had health problems or who had lost people close to them. In turn, they supported me. I helped with marriage breakups or relationship problems and was helped with my own. We looked after each other and news soon got around if more support was needed.

We had a great chairman though, and every week, without fail, he would provide goodies for the office staff. He was also very approachable and valued us all and told us so on a regular basis. He knew my feelings towards Geranium perfectly, but he just wanted to keep the peace. Her PA, 'Saint Joan' was the matriarch of the organisation; she was the soft, caring and smiling face of the chief exec's office and was the only person who could keep her in order. I moved offices when Gill, the complaints manager, was appointed and corporate affairs was born. Jayne, our PA, joined us some time later, filling the permanent position and looking after me, Gill and David. David shared the adjacent office with Celeste.

Jayne and I were like Gill's daughters, and she protected us like a little mother hen through all the ups and downs of our hectic lives. They were the best office buddies a girl could ask for and I loved them dearly. I met a lot of good friends there, including my smoking partner Brenda, whom I'd moan to about injustice while having a fag in her car. We still remain close and I have a lot to thank her for later in the story.

Part of my role was to edit our staff newsletter, which I also designed, wrote most of the articles for and produced using QuarkXPress, a specific design package I'd requested, and which produced a much more professional look than MS Publisher ever could. I had to photocopy numerous copies for the staff (there were about 500 employees in total) and it was also sent out to all bases and GP practices across south-east Sheffield. In the newsletter, I interviewed and featured as many people as I could and supported any project or charity event where possible. We were always up for a dress down Friday or a bun sale to raise money for red nose day or Children in Need etc. When birthday, wedding or maternity gifts were given I would lurk with my camera to get a shot for my newsletter. I covered lots of serious issues too, and promoted all the fantastic work that was done by our clinical staff outside HQ. It was so much fun; I loved my job. In fact, I felt so blessed that I had such a position and I knew that I was luckier than most.

I also had to deal with national press enquiries, as my remit included external communications. As press officer, I was the first point of contact for national journalists. Thankfully, not on a regular basis, as our PCT was not terribly controversial. But when I did get a press enquiry all other work had to stop and my day would be completely taken over, as I had to produce a statement in response. It was so nerve-racking at first. My degree was not in journalism or communications and so my knowledge was limited in this area, and some journalists gave me quite a hard time. You had to be so careful about what you said to them as they could twist your words or name you as a 'spokesperson' if you said too much.

Panorama was one of my great journalistic challenges. They covered teenage pregnancy in Sheffield, a subject for which our PCT was lead. I had to deal with their producer on a regular basis. He was an experienced journalist who understandably probed for information, wanting support from us to make the programme. Everyone went running scared (well, it was *Panorama*), and as first line contact I had to speak on our behalf. We didn't want to cooperate as much as he had hoped and I had to tell him so. It wasn't an easy conversation, but he totally understood that it was not my decision. He didn't shoot the messenger, but I was in the firing line on lots of occasions, and I didn't like it.

It was a different story with the local press, both radio and print. Although we had some reactive enquiries (for non-PR people, this means stories that could potentially be harmful to the organisation, which have to be 'reacted' to immediately, often with only an hour to respond), we regularly targeted them with good news stories (self explanatory: nice patient stories about the great service they'd received). Over the years, I made friends with Kate Lahive from the Sheffield *Star* and Andy Kershaw from Radio Sheffield, and good working partnerships were formed.

I had a few scraps with Dave Walsh from the *Star*, phoning for a story about issues that we would have preferred not to talk about. He was like a little feral dog sometimes; when he got his teeth into something, he'd not let it drop, but always with humour. The health reporter from the *Yorkshire Post*, however, was never terribly jovial! I learned how to deal with journalists, however fearsome, and tried to stay calm after their media enquiries. After I had left the NHS I met Dave in person at a friend's party, and we joked about those days when I revealed my anxiety over his calls.

Celeste, my manager, had a year off work for personal reasons and so our director took over the management of corporate affairs, and mainly left us alone to get on with our work. That year, I was able to produce our annual report without any interference from the top team. I had an idea for it not to be so achingly corporate, like most other statutory documents, with easy to understand articles and lots of fantastic visuals taken by the husband and wife team we employed, James and Nic. I entered the report into a national NHS annual report competition, unbeknown to anyone in our PCT, except for Gill and Jayne in our office. As I put it into the envelope I knew I was going to win; not through ego, just premonition, but I didn't tell Gill or Jayne that.

The report was shortlisted and I was invited down to London. When the winning entry flashed on the screen I was not surprised it was mine, but still totally delighted. I didn't win on my own though, as Brian, my designer, and my photographers, James and Nic, made up a fabulous team. A Sheffield colleague named Sue, along with Claire from Barnsley, were also shortlisted, but I had pipped them to the post because, as I had intended, it wasn't corporate, like most reports generally are.

My designer, Brian, had accompanied us down to the awards ceremony, as he had two shortlisted reports in the competition. On the train back from London, I spoke about my dream to set up my own events company, something that had been developing in my mind for a number of months. Everyone was encouraging, especially Brian. When I first approached him to do some work for our PCT, he was working as a graphic designer for the hospital trust. He knew more than most about NHS internal politics and, although it was daunting for him, he finally took the leap to set up by himself. He still maintains, nearly nine years later, that it was the best decision he ever made.

We spent some of the journey back to Sheffield brainstorming some names. Brian's suggestion of Showtime stuck, and my events company was initiated. Brian had so much belief in me that he even bought me the domain name for my birthday, and designed a holding page. I was serious about this new company and had so many hopes for it, as I could organise events standing on my head and was confident in my abilities to achieve success. It would also mean my own escape from NHS politics.

Following the win, I got emails from chief executives and directors across Sheffield congratulating me, but only cursory thanks from my own chief exec, through her PA. During this period I was also nominated for a staff award, which I also won, but Geranium presented it to me through clenched teeth at the AGM. I must say, when Celeste returned from her time off she did congratulate me on both achievements and was genuinely happy for me. She wasn't all bad really; she'd always give credit where it was due and was very thoughtful with presents at Christmas and birthdays. But her return meant that my reins were back on, as she insisted on micromanaging me again.

Everyone thinks they know how to communicate. Organisations tend to communicate on a level far above that of their workforce. They use management terms that essentially mean nothing, but which sound impressive to the ignorant or plain speakers like me. I refused to be corporate and promoted plain English in all my communications, except the dreaded *Team Brief* I produced after every board meeting.

I found the *Team Brief* such a challenge, and it would be my downfall at the end of my NHS career. I, like most of the other employees, was confused by the corporate messages, thinking they were too complicated to understand, and way beyond my comprehension. I had to wade through the board papers to make a readable version for the staff, which seriously hurt my head. I would go through items that were received in the monthly board meeting and nothing seemed to make sense, despite several re-reads. I know my grammar was not beyond reproach and not all of my work executed to perfection, but some of the papers from senior management were severely shocking. Every month I'd churn another one out, which no one read, anyway. They were so achingly dull, although I did try my best to sex them up!

I felt regularly undermined and not taken seriously as a communications professional. This was clearly shown when Celeste took communication matters into her own hands one day. She decided that we needed to issue a press release following a rather 'average' patient survey. As press officer, I warned against it, but thankfully didn't have time to write it myself as I was on my way out to a meeting. Against my advice, she went ahead with it anyway, knowing best, but she still kept my name on the release. That afternoon I met up with Sue and Alison, the other communication managers in town, for our monthly meeting, and I burst into tears in front of them, through sheer frustration. The other Sheffield PCTs had thought better about drawing attention to such average results. The article was printed, but the local paper had picked up on the below average parts of the survey and slated us. I didn't say a word, but made sure a copy of the article was put on her desk so that perhaps next time she would listen to me. I was furious with Celeste's decision, and that my professional opinion had once again been undermined, and that she had kept my name on the release, despite my warnings.

In 2005, Agenda for Change was introduced by the government. It was a complete overhaul of the pay structure across the NHS, which I think we all initially embraced, thinking that pay would no longer be up to the individual trusts to determine. The pay structure hadn't changed much since the NHS was established in 1948, and it was badly in need of updating. But like most government reforms, it was cobbled together hurriedly by people who didn't have a clue and who hadn't thought it through completely, probably in some pub in Whitehall. Anyone working in the NHS now knows the flaws of the Agenda for Change process only too well. The theory was equal pay for equal work, regardless of area of specialism, but of course this was going to be open to interpretation. Being a positive soul, I thought that it would result in me being paid equal to my other colleagues in communications across the region and even the country. I filled in the long form outlining my job and responsibilities without any real knowledge of the process. Celeste refused to let me be an assessor and go on the training for it, saying I had too much to do.

We all went for our job-matching panel interview and waited for the results with bated breath. When the letter containing the results of the decision came to my home address, I was outraged. I had been matched to a librarian on a grade 5: two grades lower than most of my colleagues in the region. This is no offence to librarians, of course.

Band 1	Not applicable in our organisation, for example domestic support workers
Band 2 – 4	Administration and supervisory
Band 5 – 7	Supervisory, junior and middle managers
Band 8a – 8d	Senior management
Band 9	Very senior management

When I voiced my indignation at the outcome to Celeste, all she could say was, "Oh, aren't you happy with the decision, then?" No, I bloody was not. I think she got an 8c.

Over the following months, after many reapplications, it transpired that if you knew what to put on the form and said the right things in the interview you could guarantee a higher grade. The people who were party to the training were all successful, as they made the process work for them. Some employees were definitely paid above their level of responsibility, but most would be underpaid, as I was. Why should I accept a grade that was clearly much lower than that of my communication colleagues in other trusts, including in Sheffield, when my responsibilities matched and in some cases exceeded those of my peers? It would take at least another year to fight this decision and I still only went up one grade, but by this time we'd had a complete restructure, and my role had changed anyway. It was my interim manager at the time, Jane, backed by my director, who instigated this upgrade and ensured my pay was much fairer.

After the Agenda for Change outcome I realised that I couldn't let things go without a fight. When an email came round looking for a UNISON rep for our trust, I had to respond. No one wanted the job and the post had been empty for some time after the previous holder had left the PCT. I rallied my support, and without any obstacles I was embraced as a steward, even by Celeste, who was a member herself. My trade union days had started and my father grumpily said that my career would never progress now.

He was right. I would NOT rise to the higher echelons of management, but I WOULD fight injustice by representing those who had the same shit dealt to them as I had. As a union rep, you do have to put your head above the parapet, backed only by people when it suited them, and who could remain anonymous. Sarah didn't care either: bright, beautiful and talented, she too became an ambassador for the cause.

Sarah worked for public health but was interested in communications and public relations, and approached me to be her mentor. She would help me on many of my projects, adding that creativity that was otherwise quashed in her substantive role. She also expressed her interest in union work, and also became a steward. Her manager didn't like our regular meetings, but she couldn't stop us, as mentoring was encouraged. However, she could make it difficult for us on occasions.

UNISON did have its flaws: quite a few actually, but it was a voice management still had to listen to. Our branch secretary was Sue Highton, an Aries all right, and we shared the same birthday. She was quite a formidable woman and I certainly wouldn't have messed with her, which was quite reassuring. She could put Quentin Horrocks, our HR director, in his place. Obviously, after the Agenda for Change process there were a lot of people who, like me, were rather pissed off and demanding fair pay. How can a person go into work every day and know that their counterpart, who does a very similar job to them, is getting paid considerably more? You don't just put up and shut up, but as representatives of the union, we had more to lose. My union work became increasingly demanding as more claims of unfair pay became the order of the day.

It was obviously not just going on in south-east Sheffield, but across the city and the country. Reps from the other unions fought the cause too. We'd meet regularly and attend the monthly staff consultative committee with a chief executive from one of the Sheffield PCTs, and Quentin was always present. The chief execs should have taken it in turn, but I don't think Geranium ever attended. They generally left it up to the chief executive of the west, Simon, who was a fair person anyway. My comrades and I were approached by many disgruntled people wanting us to fight their case over their Agenda for Change decision.

We were more prepared in the appeal process. If you happened to miss out certain management words you were penalised and downgraded on that basis. A decision could hinge on using such key words as 'analytical', 'complex' and 'autonomy' etc. You had to know what to say, and this time most of us were briefed as we prepared to fight for our jobs and dignity.

No wonder I had done so badly, considering I am crap at interviews. I thought they might mistake passion for points! I remember stupidly saying, "I really love my job," not "I manage a heavy workload and carry heavy objects." It was another tick-box exercise, like the management bingo people played in tedious meetings. Key words were ticked off and your grade decided by how many you'd accrued. No wonder Celeste didn't want me to go on the training: I'd have caused havoc if I'd known at the beginning!

I did love my job though, and I thought I was the luckiest person around. Perhaps my colleagues nationally had more money than me but I had almost complete autonomy. Geranium always kept her distance as long as I was producing. I enrolled on a pilot course titled Professional Development for Healthcare Communicators, which was organised and funded by the Department of Health. I didn't meet the criteria, I didn't hold a communications qualification and I was on a low grade, but I desperately needed some decent training, and communication training was very expensive. I spoke to the organisers personally and wrote a long letter outlining my desire to be accepted onto the course, even although I was only a band 5. Others in my organisation were being funded for courses but I knew I needed to fight to get on this one. The Department of Health agreed and allowed me to enrol.

Every month for nine months I travelled to the hotel on the outskirts of Birmingham where the two day course was held, mixing with colleagues all sharing similar issues; sharing and developing ideas and learning from professionals brought in by the Chartered Institute of Public Relations (CIPR), including our tutor, who was excellent. He brought in speakers from all areas of communications, including the revolutionary Andy Green, whose presentation 'You're never more than 12ft from a great idea' encouraged creativity and left me inspired and wanting more. He was a partner in a highly reputable communications firm in Huddersfield, which he started from a shed in his garden. He was also a regular CIPR speaker and would command a considerable amount of money for his time and knowledge.

I shared the journeys with Helen from the teaching hospital, and we'd take it in turns to drive. Fiona, the communications manager from Rotherham, was also a participant and I was glad I had them for moral support, because I must say I did feel out of my depth at first. I still felt rather stupid and refrained from much course discussion. In a small group I was fine, but was still worried about sounding as 'articulate as a lorry' in front of larger audiences. I gained so much confidence on this course and grew considerably as an effective communications professional. Following the nine-month course, I remember finally seeing the light one day.

It happened during a communications conference put on in Leeds by the Department of Health. One of the speakers had been a fellow student on the course. She did her presentation, and what I observed was that although she said stuff which sounded impressive in management terms, it really didn't have any content whatsoever. I realised then that the reason I didn't have a clue what people said in meetings was not because I was stupid. It was because of their inability to communicate clearly; using their management training knowledge to suppress the rest of the workforce, keeping us vulnerable. I said to Alison afterwards, "What did she say exactly? It made no sense," and she agreed with me totally. This observation again built my confidence, as I was no longer scared of asking people in meetings for clarification.

Every year, we put on staff awards and every year they became bigger and better. I'd persuaded the powers that be to move them from the stuffy annual general meeting to our staff conference, which was a more appropriate setting. James, Nic and I went out to film all those who had been nominated at their bases, making everyone feel special. We spent hours in my bedroom after work recording the voiceover, as we had no funds for a professional actor. We played this on the day of the awards, and in true Oscars style, the winner was announced and their name flashed up on a large screen. Each winner got a trophy and a certificate, and I'd bought gold balloons for them all too.

The staff conference was part of the Improving Working Lives (IWL) scheme set up by the Department of Health; another box-ticking exercise designed to improve the working lives of staff. This was certainly not the case for the IWL committee, as it proved a lot of hard work on top of their day jobs, especially for Rachel, the lead. To combat this extra stress, I practised my reiki on Rachel during lunch hours.

We did a good job though, and the staff conference was a tribute to this. Andy Green was asked to speak, and he did a fantastic presentation, stimulating some creative thought in the audience, which everyone seemed to enjoy. Staff also had an opportunity to experience a bit of pampering. We offered taster sessions in alternative therapies, including reiki, back massage, yoga and Indian head massage, to name but a few. Celeste tried to take over that day, of course, until I announced, "I don't want to sound rude, but I am managing this event." She left me alone but continued to make her presence known by taking over the reception desk and telling Debbie, whom I'd put in charge, how to run it. Debbie was responsible for running training courses as part of her role and she knew her job inside out, but Celeste just couldn't help herself, thinking she knew best. Andy was so impressed with the event that he even asked Geranium to thank me during her own presentation, which I missed. It wasn't that personal anyway, as she failed to thank me face to face again. I was used to it by now.

Following the event I sent the following email to all staff at south-east Sheffield PCT, which originates from Bevan's dream for the NHS, and which was adapted by Theodore.

It was a thank you to all our staff, but our chief executive was incapable of expressing anything close to this sentiment.

> *A Britain without an NHS would not be a Britain I understand. The NHS is a nation's dream that we will be cared for from the cradle to the grave, irrespective of means. And now it's no longer a dream, it's an expectation, because you and those who came before you work for that dream, and this is our opportunity to say thank you to some of those people who made that dream a nation's expectation.*

I wrote the following version years later, and which is probably closer to the truth these days:

> *Britain is ever-faster becoming a nation without an NHS and this would not be a Britain I understand. The NHS was a nation's dream that we would be cared for from the cradle to the grave, irrespective of means. And now it's no longer a dream, it's now heading towards the history books.*

Around this time, the following email was doing the rounds, presumably across the whole of the NHS. I picked it up, like anyone else working in the fourth largest employer in the world, and it certainly resonated within me. I kept it to remind me of a few things; that humour is so important, and that I was not alone!

> *Last night as I lay sleeping*
> *I died or so it seemed*
> *Then I went to heaven*
> *But only in my dream*
> *Up there St Peter met me*
> *Standing at the Pearly Gates*
> *He said, "I must check your record*
> *Please stand here and wait"*
>
> *He turned and said, "Your record*
> *Is covered with terrible flaws,*
> *On earth I see you rallied*
> *For losing every cause*
> *I see that you drank alcohol*
> *And smoked and used drugs too,*
> *Fact is, you've done everything*
> *A good person should never do.*

We can't have people like you up here
Your life was full of sin"
Then he read the last of my record
Took my hand and said, "Come in"
He led me to the big boss and said
"Take her in and treat her well
She used to work for the NHS
She has done her time in hell"

AMEN!
(Author unknown)

JULY 2005 – APRIL 2006

ᴬTTEMPTED MURDER,

IBIZA & SHOWTIME

*1**3***

I was overcome by a greater force than just myself,
and on seeing that knife, I danced into it, without fear,
just knowing that it was my destiny.
Theodore was arrested for attempted murder.

– Kay Rose-Hattrick

heodore was slipping back into a depression, and as a result, our home life was deteriorating. Although we did still have our moments of fun, generally drug or alcohol-induced, Theodore and I were fighting more. I had booked the week off and Theodore hated this, as he still had to go to work. On the first day of my leave, I cleaned the house from top to bottom and as a result seriously knackered my back, to the point that the next day, I could barely stand up straight. I still got up with Theodore in the morning to make him a drink and his lunch, but he sneered at my pain, thinking that I was putting it on.

Whilst he was at work that day I asked God for a sign, any sign, to give me hope for our future. I felt that I had lost my spirituality and spent most of the day trying to reconnect by meditation and some reiki self-healing. Nothing seemed to calm my mind and I was left feeling empty and alone. I visited some spiritual sites on the internet and these didn't inspire me either.

Theodore came in from work that night, still as grumpy, and we had another argument, which culminated in me throwing my drink over him, and so he went to the kitchen and pulled a knife on me. He said later that it was supposed to defuse the situation, but when I saw the blade, something came over me and for a second, everything turned into slow motion as I 'danced into the knife.' It was the only way I can describe it, as it was so graceful, and so that's what I put on my police statement. Afterwards, I ran into the bathroom to inspect the damage and blood was gushing out of the wound on my forehead, which was quite deep. I grabbed a towel and, knowing this was definitely not a plaster job, calmly asked Theodore to call the ambulance. Which he did, but it certainly wasn't calmly.

The first to arrive on the scene was a lone police officer who, despite being in the middle of a scene from *The Texas Chainsaw Massacre*, asked me for my name, address and date of birth for the first time of many that evening. He was pushed aside by the paramedics, who dealt with the situation like the professionals they were. Whilst I was rushed to hospital in the back of an ambulance, Theodore was taken to the police station and arrested for attempted murder.

The hospital staff were fantastic, but I had to wait outside the room where they were going to do my stitches until it became vacant and my doctor was available.

Picture the scene: Kay holding a dressing to her forehead to keep pressure on the wound. Blood on her clothes, her face, her hair, sitting on a chair all alone. Reliving the previous one and a half hours in her mind, with disbelief at this surreal outcome. Unwilling for anyone else to be brought into her misery; waiting for the obvious pain from the stitches and wondering when Theodore would arrive.

Enter stage left PC Plod who introduced himself, before the conversation went like this:

PC Plod:	"What's your name, address and date of birth?"
Kay:	"I've already given it to your colleague!"
PC Plod:	"I need it again." His pencil sits poised over his notebook.
Kay:	Dutifully provides this information again and then asks, "Where's my husband?"
PC Plod:	"He's been arrested for attempted murder."
Kay:	Laughs out loud.
PC Plod:	"I need your clothes for evidence."
Kay:	"What, now?"
PC Plod:	"Yes."

I was left in shock and disbelief that Theodore was banged up for trying to kill me and would not be by my side when I needed him. This police officer was now telling me he needed my clothes for evidence, but I was adamant they wouldn't gain entry and rifle through my things to find an outfit, even though they still had my keys. And where was Jarvis the cat in all this? Dd he go outside or stay in during the kerfuffle? I didn't want my baby disturbed by strange people in uniforms making sarky comments about the situation, while going through his mummy's stuff.

An arrangement was made with PC Plod that his colleagues would come with my keys, pick me up after the stitches were done and take me back home, so they could have the clothes they needed as evidence.

After PC Plod left, I was whisked into the now vacant sterile room by a very pretty nurse. My handsome doctor was on the phone to one of the top plastic surgeons in town, requesting advice before he started the sutures, because of the position of the wound on my forehead. He did a wonderful job, all without the use of anaesthetics, as they apparently wouldn't have been effective anyway. All the while, the pretty nurse held my hand and distracted me from the pain.

I ended up with 35 stitches in my forehead, was given an 'Are you the victim of domestic violence?' leaflet and was discharged, but had to wait for a further two hours next to the busy drugs cart until a nurse took pity on me and suggested I wait in the nurses' area until the police arrived. I was finally taken back to the flat by the police, who wanted my clothes for evidence and who took my statement, starting with my name, address and date of birth.

Before I did anything, I went to put the hot water on for a bath, as I had blood caked everywhere and understandably, wanted to wash. One of the police officers told me on two occasions that I didn't want a bath and should go straight to bed after they left. Since when is that your decision, mate? Whilst his female colleague took my statement in illegible English, he checked out our CD collection, interjecting throughout my story with comments like, "I don't believe that."

Everything I told them was the truth, but those police officers were simply not able to comprehend that I would want to 'dance into the knife' of my own accord. After they left, I had a long soak, realising I had just had a lesson in how the police can behave, even towards the so-called victim. Theodore was kept in for most of the night but because he was a lawyer and knew his rights, he was treated far better than I was and was let out of the cells, with the charges being dropped a few hours later.

After what happened we did start to get along better and for a while it was good again. I went to Chris, a local hairdresser, to have a fringe cut to hide the stitches and scar. I lied to him about how I got them. How would you explain how you got 35 stitches across your forehead? I told Chris the truth about what really happened some time later. I decided that I was going to stop lying about anything after that incident. Not even a white lie. Try it yourself, but it is quite hard at first! 'Dancing into the knife' was no lie though.

Married life meandered on, and we had our good moments with fewer arguments, but all the sharp knives were thrown out, just in case. Theodore had expressed an interest in doing some standup comedy and so I got him his first gig at the Last Laugh comedy club, hosted by Toby Foster of Radio Sheffield and Peter Kay's *Phoenix Nights* fame. He went down very well and of course was very funny. A lot of his material included taking the piss out of the wife and my 'A' level results, but I saw the funny side, and was very proud of him that night. Over the next few months, I tried to get him more slots at other standup nights across the city, as he was too nervous to secure the gigs himself. I was told honestly by one of the organisers that unless Theodore phoned him directly, he would not feel confident in putting him on stage, and so his comedy career came to an abrupt end.

I took Theodore on a two week holiday to Ibiza to cheer him up, on the recommendation of James and Nic, who said there was more to the island than just the parties. We booked the flight only, with me envisaging an adventure, but disaster would be nearer the truth. On the first night in Ibiza Town, Theodore threw his wedding ring out of the window of our guesthouse and from then on, the holiday spiralled further towards a living nightmare. It rained every day. After a couple of nights in the old town, we travelled across the island to San Antonio, looking for at least a little action, as outdoors adventure was limited due to the weather.

One saving grace was that every day we were on that island, as the sun was setting, the clouds would clear and the sun would shine on our bodies, if only for a few moments, before she disappeared behind the horizon. The sky became an amazing collage of swirling colours and incredible cloud formations. The sunsets made it all worthwhile and I could definitely feel, and could almost hear, the buzz of the energy still in the air from the partygoers who had flocked there in their thousands over the previous few months, looking for fun. The season was well and truly over as we sat on the Sunset Strip, almost completely alone, with a spliff we'd managed to buy from the local bar.

Said bar also provided the wine and two glasses that we'd pick up on the way to the beach every day to watch the sun go down. It had become a ritual, and the only thing to look forward to during the day. Over the first week, the bars started to close for the season and it became quite depressing as the rain continued relentlessly, the partygoers having long since departed. Theodore was becoming very anxious, well, mental actually, and it was hell. In the end, we cut our losses and booked another flight back to the UK on my credit card, after only one week.

Once back in the UK, we got stuck in Manchester late at night as they'd cancelled the trains and had only put on limited bus services. Of course, none were going even remotely near Sheffield. Nigel, a friend and an angel, who had been looking after Jarvis, magnanimously agreed to drive all that way in the middle of the night to pick us up. What an amazing star. He must have known it would have been the icing on the cake if we'd got stuck in Manchester overnight until the trains to Sheffield had started running again. I think I can safely say that that holiday was the worst of my life. It certainly didn't improve Theodore's mood.

Also that summer, a Chinese guy called Roy had just moved into our friend's house opposite our flat, and an unlikely friendship was forged. Roy had a clothes shop in the

Forum, a trendy complex in the city centre, where he sold beautiful gowns and Chinese dresses. One night, while I was a bit tipsy and he was sober, as he didn't drink, I agreed to put on a fashion show to help him sell some more dresses in the run-up to Christmas. When I was sober, he reminded me of my promise and I knew I couldn't get out of it. If I make a promise I always stick to it, so I have to be careful what I do promise, especially when I've had a couple of glasses.

The venue was my parents' local pub, the George and Dragon, thanks to Norma the landlady. We enlisted the help of several friends to be models, including my sister Trace, Poppy from upstairs, Joanne, a friend of Jenna's we had adopted and myself. I knew how to do the model walk after I'd enrolled in a local model agency following my 'O' levels.

Dad had paid for me to go on the 'style for life' course at the agency, which was located in an area known locally as Heeley Bottom, and so Theodore had always jokingly referred to it as the 'Heeley Bottom Finishing School'. As there had been no takers for this course that month I had instead been enrolled on the modelling course. I loved and hated this course at the same time. I loved it because I learned new skills, like how to put on makeup for fashion and photography shots, how to do the walk, which I think is useful for any young girl to learn as it aids with posture and makes you walk sexily if it's not overtly contrived, and how to walk in heels, although I never mastered this skill! The final performance was a fashion show that we helped choreograph and set to music, picking our outfits and doing our own makeup.

What I hated were some of the vacuous and vain fellow students, who thought they were rather gorgeous. We all had photos done as part of our portfolio and we had to cake on the makeup and wear stupid hats in unnatural posses, which I felt very uncomfortable doing. It certainly gave me valuable skills to take me into adult life, though. I suppose organising a fashion show was not such a massive undertaking considering I had done the training.

The event was a great success, although the free advert I had secured in the Sheffield *Star* didn't generate any punters. That night, Roy sold loads of dresses and gave me one as thanks. He went to live in Canada but returned to the UK to do the Christmas markets, coming back to Sheffield to see Poppy and I, claiming we were his only friends. I put on a party to sell his beautiful pashminas and Chinese cushions and his sales were good. I have still got all my Chinese cushions, which were a thank you for my help; Roy was always so generous.

My first Showtime event, however, came as a result of Poppy's dating quest. She came down one night after attending a speed dating event, which she moaned about at length, claiming we could do better. So, with little persuasion and another glass of wine I agreed. We wanted to make it different and so we plugged it as 'alternative speed dating'. We found a perfect venue in the cellar bar at Abbeydale Picture House and we started to organise the event. I asked my friend Ju Ji, not quite small enough to be considered a dwarf, but teeny anyway, and quite a character with his Stetson hat and a bugle, to time the three minutes of conversation before the participants had to move. Ju Ji had been a DJ called the Mighty Atom back in the 60s and had worked for Peter Stringfellow back in the day. His image was used on the publicity, which James and Nic, my photographers from work, kindly professionally designed for us.

Along with some free editorial in the *Star*, this attracted our punters, as well as friends who were keen to meet that special person. Almost immediately after the newspaper went on sale I received my first phone call from John, a habitual speed dater, who had been to every speed dating event in Sheffield and the surrounding area and was keen to attend this one too. I'd roped in Theodore and Brian P Mitchell, our friend from school who was a comedy writer, who came up from Brighton especially for the event. I'd asked friends to provide equipment and their DJing skills, as that night was also my 36th birthday and I wanted the party to continue into the night.

We made everyone wear a name badge with their star sign on, for compatibility reasons, and each round was different as we had compiled a list of questions. Instead of just talking for three minutes, as the usual speed dating dictates, the hosts asked questions such as "What would you choose as your last meal?" and "Who would you want to meet, dead or alive?" and we had teamwork rounds for the couples. Whoever made the most romantic sentence from the love hearts sweets we had put on each table won a bottle of cava. Brian and Theodore were hilarious that night and made an amazing comedy duo. Everyone had a great time and some relationships were formed for a short time, including for Brian the compere himself. Merlin had bought two tickets for him and a mate, but didn't turn up. Brian and some fairly good-looking bloke, whom I think we pulled off the street, had to make up the numbers for the men. All ten girls were present of course, including my sister Trace and Kerry from the band. You can always rely on the women!

Poppy and I did feel a little like Cilla Black; my sister paired off with my car mechanic friend and other friendships were made that night. Everyone stayed on for my birthday party and the bar was filled with invited friends and their plus ones/fives. Theodore went home early that night. He had threatened to pull out as compere in the run-up to the event, which added to my anxiety, but thankfully, Brian had reassured me that he would persuade him to change his mind or would go solo. Theodore was usually so thoughtful and generous with presents but that day I had one, unwrapped, thrown onto my lap.

After the event I got a phone call from John, the habitual speed dater. Although not successful himself he said it was the best speed dating event he had ever been to and urged me to put on more. We never did, though I still have some great speed dating ideas.

We didn't make much money as we kept the price low, but we learned a lot from the experience, and making a packet hadn't been the primary aim anyway.

My relationsip with Theodore went on a downward spiral after the event, as the following diary entry reflects:

I wanted to write something down to then reflect later, perhaps following this weekend, of how I am this very minute.

I am terribly sad about what has become of us. Our happier moments probably far surpass any couple I know through joy and intensity and of being truly and deeply and madly in love. This said, our darkest do equally. Bible black, with just despair, distrust and destruction for company.

As such, I cannot continue on this path together, for my own sake. I am weary of feeling hurt and betrayed by a man who claims to love me more than life. Who has the ability, or rather did, to make me feel so bad I just wanted to hurt myself because I believed him when he said I was 'rubbish', because I loved him. How can anyone claiming to love you want to destroy your whole core and leave your soul vulnerable to the attack of jackals?

This is not going to change. You've just got to be true to yourself and admit that splitting up is the only way forward. Just like I did when I left Ashley. It did seem so much more straightforward then with so much more to give up, and I still did it. This time though, I want him to go. I'm buggered if he gets everything when all he has done is sit on his arse. He may be beautifully active in his pretty little head. Oh, he's so clever. Bully for him.

He hates me calling him evil, but as far as I'm concerned how can anyone with a kind heart say the things he does to me and strip me of all my shaky self-confidence? He does it to hurt me, the only way he knows how, and has done since the first day I set eyes on him. Maybe I bring out the worst in him, but he's certainly not all sweetness and light.

He blames so much on me and yes, I guess I may provoke him to some extent; he really does have a totally irrational nature. He would just love to destroy me. It's almost like by hurting me it makes him feel better 'cos he's got someone to blame for his own shortcomings.

This talk about him slipping down into depression is possibly an attention seeking exercise or a cry for help, who knows. I don't claim to know anything, remember! I do search my mind for the things he says I do and if I am in the wrong I say that I am sorry, but most of time, I'm not really sure what I have done.

There is no point in carrying on like this as it makes me so sad.

I didn't send this next email, to my friend Joanne, and which was written at about the same time, because everyone had heard how upset I'd become. What would be the point of continuing to moan while staying in this toxic relationship?

Hi Jo

T and I are once again at loggerheads. He starts behaving all strangely and then says that I should be looking after him as he's been going through a depressive mood. What do you reckon I do, anyway? He comes in, sits in his chair and doesn't move for the next five hours. I'm not sure I can cope much longer, because I'm not feeling so bright lately. I think it's the weather, work and relationship all combined and I'm feeling quite low, but I've got to be perky for him all the time.

If he does go into depression again then I cannot stick by him again because I will not be able to cope myself. I'm not sure what he wants from me any more. I'm not happy. I don't have a physical relationship with him; even the baby thing lasted one night and then he didn't want to know.

I'm scared even to have a day off work as he gets so bitter, even though I'm usually working round the house or doing something for him. I've got some vouchers from my awards and I said I was going to spend some of them on Saturday. He was silent and couldn't even be happy for me. He started saying again last night that he sacrificed everything for me and it was my fault again that he'd had a breakdown. I can't hear that anymore, I'm weary. I can't think of putting up with this life for another 30-odd years. I need to stop this now or never. I know I keep going on about this but I'm sick of feeling sad.

I have no one to turn to as they've heard it all before, and who wants to hear about me complaining again? I'll just keep it bottled up as much as I can and one day I will end it, I'm sure of it.

The day I left Theodore came about two weeks after the speed dating event, on Maundy Thursday 2006. Something inside just snapped and it was time to end this destructive relationship once and for all. We had been married for three years. I was attending a UNISON stewards' residential course that week and was back for the Easter holidays. That fateful night, he hosted his regular bridge night at our house and I went on our NHS communications night out, so was in a fairly jolly mood. When I returned and his bridge friends had gone home, we started to argue again. This time, it culminated in me throwing some clothes into my rucksack and phoning my band to rescue me, and finally leaving him for good. I had hit the point of no return.

Raphey, Reiki III & Sudden Death

14

> *Death makes angels of us all.*
> – Kay Rose-Hattrick

Wallace, Andy and his then girlfriend Mandy, aka 'the band', answered my call by turning up in a black cab, enabling me to have the courage to finally leave Theodore and that unhealthy relationship. They took me straight to a party and I sat in the corner of the room sobbing uncontrollably, hugging my rucksack. Shaun, then an acquaintance and now a friend, came over to me several times to ask if I was OK. But his third attempt was his last after I screamed, "Just FUCK OFF!" Why didn't they just take me somewhere quiet? A party was just the wrong place to be in in such a state. Instead, Wallace took me to a quieter room and started to kiss me. I couldn't believe that he'd take advantage of someone so vulnerable, especially with him being my friend too. He took me back to his house, where I would stay for a few nights, finally succumbing to his embrace.

The next day was Good Friday, and I remember it being a fantastically sunny day, certainly in the league of a summer's day. Theodore had sent me a text that morning saying that we should meet up later in the Vine to sort out this "unholy mess". I sat in a seat by the door with the sun streaming in through the windows, nursing a pint and crying uncontrollably with Prince's *Purple Rain*, a particular favourite of mine, playing on the jukebox. This is the moment I met Raphey. He still tells the story of when he felt compelled to look round the room, his focus finally becoming fixed on the crying girl in the corner. He got up from his seat, strode purposely over to where I was sitting and without any introduction asked, "What star sign are you, doll?" "Aries," I responded, thinking, "What the fuck?" His response was simply, "You're mine!"

From that moment on Raphey and I were inseparable. He too was an Aries and as obsessed with astrology as Poppy from upstairs, so I had no chance! Raphey is such a character, a very funny and flamboyant man, and he makes everyone feel ultra special if he makes a beeline for you. And it doesn't matter who you are, if you're having a bad day, he'll make you smile with his camp banter, even under such circumstances as I was in. But he has a strange aversion to Pisceans for some reason. He was certainly my angel that day.

I explained to Raphey what had happened the night before and leading up to that point. One of the locals told me that Theodore had already been and gone, so Raphey dialled his number, humorously requesting his presence, pronto, saying I was waiting for him and in a bit of a state. Theodore arrived and was venomous; he had such contempt for me written all over his face, and especially obvious in his barbed words. I knew right there and then I did not want to go back to him ever again. Later that night, I ended up breaking my vows and sleeping with Wallace to officially end my marriage to someone I had grown to hate.

After the weekend, I went to stay at Mum and Dad's, but I was determined that Theodore was not going to keep the flat. Why should I leave? He'd never lifted a finger to move in, decorate, clean, anything. So after two weeks at my parents', I moved back into the flat until Theodore sorted out his living arrangements, and it was hell. He was so nasty to me I don't know what I'd have done without Raphey and his vibrant energy and humour.

During this period, Richard Jackson (RIP) died, a friend of Poppy's. I had spent a bonding night with Richard, another Aries, while he worked on Poppy's kitchen. It was a sad blow for everyone but he had kept his terminal cancer a secret until he finally left this physical realm. Theodore tried to rekindle our relationship when we attended his funeral together and was very attentive. It was too late: I had given myself to another man and as far as I was concerned, our marriage vows were now a sham. I was also not going to go back to what we'd had. I think I'd given it as good a go as I could, without going back down that slippery slope to self-hatred.

Richard's landlord, Webby, now had a room free, which was just round the corner. I actually helped Theodore pack and move his belongings the short distance to his new accommodation. At first, we remained friends, him still convinced there was some hope of a reunion, until he caught Wallace round at the flat one evening without the bandanna covering his dreadlocks. He later said that he knew we were an item then, as Wallace never went out without his dreads being covered and it was a sure sign that he was far more comfortable than just a friend. After that, we didn't communicate for some time.

It was during this time that I was attuned by Paul to the next level, Reiki III. I went with Alison, the communication manager for North Sheffield PCT, who had been looking for a new reiki master. It was a very enlightening and powerful couple of days, and by the time Sunday evening had arrived, Alison and I had become fully attuned reiki master practitioners. We would have to give attunements ourselves to be fully fledged. After this, Alison and I would send healing energy across the city to each other from Orgreave to Firth Park, where she was based, and back again, neutralising any negative energies affecting us.

About a month after Theodore left, Raphey decided he was moving into my spare room as he had become bored with his flat! Debbie from the landlord's office requested a letter so that Theodore could be taken off the tenancy agreement. He did send the letter, but Debbie said she couldn't accept it as he had written, "...I am moving out as she is now shacking up with a raving homosexual and a geriatric Rastafarian." He was barbed, and although Wallace may have been in his fifties, he looked younger than I did.

That summer, the world saw another abhorrent terrorist attack, but this time closer to home, in London. In fact, I would have been able to see the bus from outside my window when I worked for BTEC, next door to the BMA. We watched the devastation on TV at work and I was in shock, like the rest of the country and the world. But it wouldn't be long before I questioned the truth surrounding that day.

That summer I also met Tony, who would become husband number three ("Oh no, not another one," I hear you cry!) at the Sharrow festival, a community festival I helped organise for three years. The first time I had attended the event was with Theodore, and I thought, "What a great festival." I knew through my experience of organising events that a lot of hard work had gone into this one behind the scenes. I decided to offer my services and attended the committee meetings every month. After the first year, I was put in charge of the stallholders, when the previous volunteer decided to leave. It was a big commitment and took up a lot of my spare time, especially in the run-up to the event, when my phone would continuously ring with late bookings and queries.

At my first working festival, I spotted Theodore coming onsite with sparks of hatred pulsing out of his every orifice. I looked around quickly, hoping to find a hiding place, because I didn't want any confrontation, and I spotted a guy in the middle of a sea of faces who was wearing a funny prayer hat and who had a kind, serene face. He looked quite safe, so I made a beeline for him and asked him to hide me from my estranged husband.

I sat down and we chatted until the coast was clear and I could get on with my stewarding. Tony was a Sufi (a mystical Muslim) who chose to live a very simple life in the Sufi centre, situated just round the corner from the festival venue. He attended prayer, helped cook the communal meals and looked after the chickens. I could tell immediately that he was pure-hearted, with little ego. When the coast was clear, I left my sanctuary in the middle of the field. "What a beautiful man," I thought, even telling a few people I stepped over as they picnicked and watched the bands: "I've just met an angel!" Later on in the day I saw him again, and we chatted some more and exchanged mobile numbers, although we would not contact each other until we met again at Merlin's, almost four months later.

Not long after the Sharrow festival, my whole foundations were blown apart when I received a phone call from Nick, a close friend from London, saying that Ashley had suddenly died. I was devastated by the news. I left work immediately, crying inconsolably all the way home, where Raphey and Poppy found me in my room, watching our wedding video time and time again, working myself up to the point of frenzy.

For the next few days, I walked around in a daze because I loved that man dearly, despite our breakup. My brother had only been with him two weeks before and he had asked after me. We had even started contacting each other via email at work, about NHS issues and *Resident Evil*, which we had played when we had been together. It was banal conversation but we were communicating again. He'd not been very happy when he found out that I'd changed my name, having insisted I kept Hattersley during our marriage together. I'd always said that I sounded too much like a furniture polish: "Stay bright with K-bright," of course, but with Theodore's name, he pointed out, I was very K-leen!

The day after Ashley's death, I went a bit crazy and focused on the Buddha mask that we'd bought in Vietnam, which became alive in my mind, and I remember lying on the sofa having some kind of fit. I needed a smoke, so phoned Merlin, who agreed I could go over. I let myself into his flat, as the door was always open, and went upstairs to find him mixing records. I got a mere nod as I walked in, though I was clearly in a bit of a state. He just kept playing record after record without so much as a word, while I just rocked on the spot like a deranged lunatic, until he announced, "If I'd thought you were this bad then I wouldn't have invited you round."

I couldn't believe a so-called friend could treat me like this during my hour of need. I sent a text to Theodore letting him know the news, and after weeks of refusing to talk to me, he was there for me 100%. It was Ashley's death that brought us together again. He even took that afternoon off, and for a while we were inseparable again, and spent a lot of time talking about Ashley and our marriage together, and what I had wanted to say to him. I was aware Ashley knew it all anyway now, as it was evident that his spirit was close by. I took great comfort in this, especially when my second husband channelled my first husband through him. Theodore announced Ashley wanted to say something. The words came from Ashley, not Theodore, and we both felt his presence profoundly that day.

This period also saw the sale of our flats to individual buyers. The whole building was originally nurses' accommodation when it was built in the 1870s, and now over twenty flats were to be sold by Mert, our landlord, following the sad death of his wife. Even though it stated clearly in the auction brochure that these flats were 'outside viewing only', loads of prospective buyers tried to peek a look inside anyway, especially as my flat was an end terrace with easy access. This too added to the stress. None of them were concerned that this was my home, only that it was a potential cash cow. I'd put a massive notice on the washing line as you walked in my yard, saying, "PLEASE DO NOT ENTER! RESPECT MY PRIVACY." Even that didn't stop them. One bloke, who caught me in a towel, even asked me out for dinner, which I flatly refused!

The message came through my brother that I would not be welcome at Ashley's funeral. The news devastated me, but it was clear that my in-laws blamed me in some part for his untimely death. The cause of death was sudden death syndrome, which is like an adult cot death. He was found dead, alone, at his parents' house. I sent his mum a letter expressing my heartfelt sympathy for the passing of her dear son, whom I did love, but our lives were not meant to continue on the same path together. Despite the hurt I felt at not being able to say my final farewell at his graveside, I respected their wishes and stayed away.

So while my own brother carried Ashley's coffin to his grave down in east London, I went alone to have my own special service in the stone circle in the cemetery in Sharrow. I lit candles and incense, buried my engagement ring in the ground and read out passages from books he'd given me, including the diary of our travels in south-east Asia. I'd kept my phone on, only to ensure that I spent the whole of the actual service in contemplation of our life together. I cried and felt supreme sadness that I couldn't be with my brother, sharing my grief with others who had loved him too.

My phone bleeped, alerting me to a message, and to be truthful, I was annoyed that a mundane message should disturb my reflective sadness. It was my brother, who reported that Ashley was "now in the ground and at peace." Ashley did visit me that day; he flittered from his own funeral to my small ceremony with his new-found wings and it was comforting. I left him with an album by his favourite band, New Order, donated by Theodore. I spoke to my brother later to see how things had gone and he passed me on to Nick, who had first contacted me about his death. Nick couldn't believe I was asked not to attend. Ashley's father had cruelly said, "Why did you tell her?" after Nick told him I'd been informed of his death. What had I done wrong exactly? I loved that man, but he had put his family and friends before me and I'd had to leave.

That night, a group of us were out the back having our own wake for Ashley, when a couple came up to the back yard, staring at the house and through us as if we were invisible. It was the final straw, and I went mad at them, the others quickly explaining the situation. They didn't seem to understand, and were cold as ice, and rude to boot. This was my home and would remain so, despite me being just a renter. I did let a couple of women take a look around the flat at a later date, as I was concerned about who my new landlord/lady would be after an encounter with a group of men. They drove, with darkened windows, up to the top of the short, dead-end road at the side of the property, next to the entrance to our back yard. Four men got out and one asked for the landlord's number, aiming to do a deal directly. He said that if I didn't hand it over, he could make it difficult for me if he became my new landlord! This bully did indeed buy the flats, and he continued to bully me throughout our contract. But the women even brought me a bottle of wine as thanks.

Raphey brought the sunshine back into my life, as long as the sunshine lasted. He suffered from a mood disorder and SAD, so while sunny days made him hyper, long winter days made him crawl so far within himself I'm surprised he managed to remain bright enough for work. Raphey worked in human resources, so we were able to empathise with each other professionally. He also gave me some good advice over the years, both personally and with my UNISON steward's hat on. He would, however, take the piss out of fat cat union reps and threaten to tear up the monthly steward magazines I got through the post, to my horror.

With Raphey came his friends, who were lovely guys, mostly gay, who would often visit. My favourite was Mick, but we got off to an interesting start when he came round to vet the flat before Raphey moved in. I'm a bit of a clutter monkey and Mick very much a minimalist. Without so much of an introduction he started on my clothes on the washing line, before moving on to my precious belongings inside, saying only, "Mine!" if he liked the item or "Get rid!" if he didn't. He left as quickly as he'd arrived, claiming he was now "bored!", and I was left alone in hysterics, and shock, at what had just occurred. Raphey's friends were like that, flamboyant and funny as fuck; not all of them as camp as Christmas though.

Raphey and Poppy both got me into my slight obsession with star signs. I'm more interested in the bigger picture now and am aware that we are made up of all of the elements, if we're lucky, to balance us. Whatever you think about star signs, Poppy and Raphey could guess correctly at least nine out of ten times. It was their party trick, I suppose, and over time I started to be able to recognise the traits of the signs too. I was always very good at spotting an Aquarian. My own sign, Aries, became easy too. As the pattern emerged I seemed to surround myself with certain signs, always lots of fellow fire signs, and Geminis and Virgos. My mother is a Gemini and it seems that every mother figure I've ever had has been a Gemini; but I seem to have a lot of Virgo bosses! I always start with the element of that person, which I usually guess right, and then you've only got to guess out of three! My interpretation of the star signs I've met, and their unique quirks, follows on the next page.

Key: **Cardinal** – on a hinge, forever turning. **Fixed** – Unchanging. **Mutable** – subject to change.

Aries – Cardinal Fire – Leader of the Zodiac

Aries jump into projects enthusiastically but can lose momentum if not supported. Can be quite formidable and sometimes scary.

Taurus – Fixed Earth – 2nd house of the Zodiac

A Taurian wants to please everyone, but takes rejection badly. They are dependable and can be very creative when left to their own devices.

Gemini – Mutable Air – 3rd house of the Zodiac

Geminis love to be spontaneous and are completely free spirits. They have wonderful motherly energy, but there can be a darker side to their twin.

Cancer – Cardinal Water – 4th house of the Zodiac

Cancerians are home lovers foremost. They can be very emotionally challenged and can sulk for days, but are creative and passionate.

Leo – Fixed Fire – 5th house of the Zodiac

Leos are very dramatic and like to be the centre of attention most of the time. They are mostly very charismatic and fun to be around.

Virgo – Mutable Earth – 6th house of the Zodiac

Virgos strive for 'perfection', but can be quite anal as everything has to be done their way, which is the 'only way'. They are good organisers and especially good with finer details. Great for editing books!

Libra – Cardinal Air – 7th house of the Zodiac

Librans can often be found weighing everything up and as a result few decisions are made. When they are balanced though they are dynamic. They have many creative thoughts and ideas.

Scorpio – Fixed Water – 8th house of the Zodiac

Charismatic and charming and good lovers, I'm told. They are very faithful when they trust you. But just don't mess with one!

Sagittarius – Mutable Fire – 9th house of the Zodiac

Are all very sweet and dependable but can be prone to moods as they turn their burner on and off. Can also be very good lovers (and I haven't been told this time), charming and charismatic like their Scorpio cousins.

Capricorn – Cardinal Fire – 10th house of the Zodiac

Fixed in their ways but will reach their goal no matter what, however long it takes. Stubborn but dependable with a good sense of humour.

Aquarius – Fixed Air – 11th house of the Zodiac

Overall just a bit mad, but full of amazing ideas, but which don't necessarily all come to fruition.

Pisces – Mutable Water – 12th house of the Zodiac

Highly creative, but often emotionally challenged. They comprise all of the above signs and hopefully all the best bits. They have unfortunately got a bit of a reputation for lying.

Does any of this ring true with you? Remember, we are all made up of different signs, depending on where or when we were born. My Moon is in Scorpio and my Mars is in Taurus and I even have some Virgo in me, and of course my ascendant is Cancer. This combined makes me who I am, with a delicate balance of fire, water, air and earth. But don't listen to me. Your best bet is reading *Sun Signs* by the late Linda Goodman, for a more professional approach.

Our first summer together had been fairly mental, but Raphey did a downwards flip into the abyss as we moved into autumn. As the nights drew in, I called for his friends' assistance in looking after him and keeping him cheerful, but they made it clear that he was "all mine!" and that I needed a medal. They were used to this pattern in him, but I wasn't. Thank goodness for Poppy, otherwise I'd have jumped off the proverbial cliff edge with him. I'd already done that with Theodore and didn't want a repeat performance.

He'd struggle out of bed every morning and then into work. By the time he came home, every bit of energy had been sucked out of him and it was straight to bed from about 7pm. Some nights, he didn't eat and when he did it would be what I'd prepared for him. He would lose the will to live, only barely managing to exist, until the spring sun would finally fill up his banks again and his battery would be fully charged with, alas, no regulator! I did love him though, and still do.

Raphey's mood did have a massive affect on me, as had Theodore's depression. Poppy took over the burden for me, when she'd pop down to see if he was OK, and at least I could have a laugh. Theodore, too, was a blessing when it came to dealing with Raphey, until Theodore trashed my room and stopped talking to me again.

At the time, Theodore had started dating an old friend of his called Geena, and on this occasion, she was coming to Sheffield for the weekend. Poppy and another mad Aquarian friend, Ian, were charged with decorating his lovenest for her imminent arrival, while I made sure that his bedlinen was washed and dried. Theodore was playing bridge that night, so it must have been a Thursday. I had left his clean washing with his keys in the bag outside my back door and remember putting the keys into the bag, in slow motion, almost pre-empting what would occur later.

I was out with Wallace that night, and on the way back to his house, I received a call from a very irate Theodore, screaming down the phone, "Where are my keys?" I told him to calm down and that they were in the bag with his washing. Raphey said that he then locked himself into my room and just started trashing it, he was so angry. He kept saying that I'd done this to try and jeopardise his relationship with Geena. I obviously had not; it's just not in my nature, it was pure projection. By the time he had left in the morning, lamps had been broken and live wires exposed, he had smashed glass in pictures, ripped out my face in my photos again and had broken a very special glazed plate that Ashley had bought me in Lyme Regis. He found the keys in the yard the following morning, where he had tipped all his clean linen, and obviously the keys, the night before. Needless to say, we did not speak again for some time. What a twat! He hated me calling him evil but these moments were. But he still preferred to play the blame game rather than accept the truth.

Salma and Stu had moved out some time before, and so we had some new neighbours occupy their old flat in September 2006. Jemma was a drum and bass DJ and Cloe was a disciplinarian. By day, Cloe worked as an NHS temp and by night, she smacked rich men with her massive collection of whips. Thankfully, this was not done in their flat, but she did once put a serious business proposal to us. She asked if she could tie up one of her clients in our large cellar underneath the flat for a few days, and she would pop down every so often to whip him. She said she would pay us well, but the thought of someone tied up underneath the floorboards, while we were trying to watch EastEnders on a night, was too much for us to comprehend and so we said absolutely not straight away!

Her clients were generally very well off and held top jobs in a number of different professions, but their thrill was being beaten by Cloe so that their bottom was literally red raw after a good session. No sex ever took place and she didn't even dress that provocatively; mainly as a headmistress or gym mistress, and with no leather in sight. They were both good girls though, and we spent a lot of time together at first.

That Christmas I paired up with Jenny, a friend from work, to put on a Christmas cabaret at the Lantern theatre, just at the end of our road. It's a lovely theatre that holds no more than a hundred people, and was built by one of the Sheffield steel cutlers for his daughter at the end of the 19th century, so that she wouldn't run off to London to be an actress, something which was still considered akin to prostitution in polite society. It was Jenny's baby really, as she pulled all the acts together. I insisted that I only have a small speaking part in one of the sketches, but it was great fun. Jemma and Cloe were fabulous that night, and dressed up as Santa's little helpers supporting several of the acts, including the incredibly flamboyant and talented David Markus. He was fabulous, and performed all of his own showpieces with a different spectacular, glitzy outfit. All proceeds went to the homeless in Sheffield and it was a very successful night. Even Mum and Dad turned up, and Poppy and Raphey, but once again, Wallace was not there to support me.

I spent that Christmas with Wallace, Jemma, Cloe and her sister. It was a good day, but I felt a bit used by everyone, as I ended up funding the whole meal. Although I was still friends with Jemma and Cloe, I became more distant as I felt unable to take on their problems as well as my own. I wrote a diary in the first few months of 2007; it had been a Christmas present from Jemma and Cloe, and this entry, written on 6th February, gives an indication as to where my head was at the time. I was searching for something and someone to make my future clearer and to support me through my spiritual growth to the next level. Reading back, it's almost like a message coming from elsewhere that I had to get down on paper.

What's the point in questioning it, it's all just meant to be.

Just ride it and don't take it too seriously.

It's simple, take one day as it comes,

do your best, never lie, no matter what,

start meditation at work,

don't take shit from anyone and for anyone.

Keep your humour above all and your sense of fun.

Don't be disheartened, you are making a difference.

Try and get something done every day towards moving away from the matrix. You're not mad.

You'll get strength from others who also know the truth. They will come soon. You know already.

They will learn with you together and you'll have the ability and opportunity to overcome the

barriers to that truth. Embrace life, people, energy, but keep protected from the dark light present

in everyone's physical being, tormented by themselves.

Wallace and I were still hanging on throughout this time, not that you'd really know as Merlin tended to monopolise him. It was the usual thing for Wallace to turn up for food and sex at the end of the night, but I wouldn't see him otherwise. I could have told him I was cooking for 8pm but I'd generally have to phone him at 10pm to see where he was. He was definitely on 'Jamaican time', as they say. Most of the time, he was at Merlin's, who would grab the phone off him and tell me childishly that, "Wallace is my friend too." I eventually ended it on Valentine's night. Cruel on such a night, you may think, but the result of the pattern throughout our relationship. The final nail in the coffin came when I'd prepared a lovely romantic meal for two and even bought him some red roses. After numerous calls, he eventually turned up after 10pm. That was the last straw.

He didn't give up, but, despite some flowers being left on my doorstep, I wouldn't budge in my decision. I decided to write a dumping rap. Jemma and I spent one night writing and then performing it live on tape to backing tracks we had both picked. It only took us one take but we were happy with our first time results. Wallace had the option of taking the tape home with him in the knowledge that I was serious this time and that our relationship was finally over. He chose not to take it. I don't know; I think if it had been me, I would have been quite intrigued to hear it, especially if someone had gone to that much effort to dump me. Wouldn't you?

About this time I met a guy called Ray at the Vine. He seemed to come from nowhere and then he was gone. Whilst he was in our lives, he introduced me and most of the Vine to the 'conspiracy theories' that 9/11 and the London bombings were both inside jobs. He did this by literally flooding the Vine with copies of Alex Jones' controversial documentaries that exposed, with seemingly credible evidence, the truth about the US and UK governments' part in this terror. One to watch is *TerrorStorm*, which is available free on YouTube. It's even more terrifying that they were both allegedly set up from within than to think that terrorists were to blame. These attacks are commonly known as 'false flag' and there have been many such examples in history.

The start of the Vietnam war was blamed on the Tonkin incident, when American destroyer Maddox was supposedly attacked twice by three North Vietnamese torpedo boats in 1964 in the Gulf of Tonkin. It never happened, but got the backing of a nation, for a while at least, to justify the war, and is considered a 'false flag'. These attacks are initiated by the governments themselves, who then blame the so-called terrorists or enemy. By putting the fear of God into their citizens, they will then back any measures to protect themselves. This has resulted in more cameras, more restriction and of course an excuse for a war; Orwell's vision of Britain was beginning to feel more real to me. In fact, on the twelfth anniversary of 9/11, a national survey by the polling firm YouGov revealed that one in two Americans have doubts about the government's account of 9/11. Ray always believed he was being watched, and he left Sheffield a short time later, but we all kept the films to pass on to others who were starting to see the real and scary truth of the world we lived in.

I was introduced to Paganism by an old friend of Poppy's. Nick was a solitary hedgewitch (not part of a coven, choosing to practise alone or in small groups). Over the period of a year, I went to his flat for each sabbat, and we would perform the ancient rituals. He would represent the god Woden and I the goddess Freya. He would make beautiful headdresses of ivy and flowers for us to wear. The altar would be set up and decorated with garlands and offerings appropriate to the time of the year. They were such magical ceremonies and I spent every one at his flat, with the exception of the summer solstice. I had learned so much from Nick and I was determined to observe all eight sabbats, which have mostly been adopted by the Christians, including winter solstice/Yule (Christmas), Lammas (harvest festival), Samhain (Halloween) and Beltane (May Day).

On 21st June, the summer solstice, I was down in Brighton at the UNISON conference and was obliged to perform the ceremony on my own in the hotel room. I set up my altar, and even made myself a headdress with red roses beforehand at the house of Jane, my old work colleague from London. As I left her flat to go and do my practice, I walked along Brighton front and was surprised but reassured to see that I was not alone. A couple of covens along the beach were in mid-flow, also observing the solstice.

There is always something sinister attached to Paganism, as most people are programmed to believe. True, there is a dark side to everything, but I only practised the good, white stuff. A spell is only a prayer or a wish and candle magic is still performed at every birthday, when the candles are blown out on a cake and a wish is made. Always be careful what you wish for, as any spell will come back to you threefold. You would be a fool to wish harm on anyone.

Since ancient times, indigenous peoples across the world have celebrated nature's natural cycle. The Romans named these people Pagans, meaning land-dwellers. Ancient Britons lived harmoniously with nature and the elements, worshipping the god and goddess. The divine couple, seen as lovers and equals, were said to have created the cosmos. Paganism celebrates the harmony of yin and yang, with the feminine and masculine energies complementing each other perfectly. No longer was I calling to a male god, I was calling to the goddess too!

The Witchcraft Act of 1542 was the first to declare witchcraft a felony, punishable by death. Twenty years later, Queen Elizabeth I lessened the punishment to imprisonment, except when it caused harm to others, in which cases the death penalty still applied. The Witchcraft Act was only repealed in 1951. A hedgewitch was traditionally a wise woman or man who knew which plants and herbs could help with certain ailments. Unfortunately, a lot of that knowledge has now been lost forever.

Wicca (modern witchcraft) was introduced by Gerald Gardner in the early 1950s, and its origin is open to many interpretations. I prefer to remain attached to my ancient roots, and practise as a solitary witch, acknowledging the cycle of life, as my ancestors would have done. As with any practice or religion, covens are not always as equal as they make out and hierarchies may exist to keep the 'congregation' in check.

Theodore and I became friends again. I can't remember exactly now, but I think Poppy got him to apologise to me. Whilst we were estranged, he had written a play in which I was one of the characters. He laughingly joked that I would need a libel lawyer, as he had been quite cruel about me. Ironic really, as perhaps with this publication, he will now need said services, though all that's been said is the truth. Sticks and stones may cripple me but no amount of words from him could hurt me any more. He taught me a lot, and I'm eternally grateful to him for that. I became my own wordsmith, and the 'articulate as a lorry' girl could finally become a woman, with her own weaponry!

Theodore and I were out having a drink in the Vine one afternoon when we bumped into Gerry, the ex-keyboard player from the band. I don't really know what happened, but that afternoon I ended up starting a relationship with another band member. What's the matter with me?

Shortly afterwards, Jemma and Cloe moved out, after a fairly volatile few months.

In brief: apparently Cloe had given Jemma her rent money, but she hadn't given it to the landlord, and of course Nazeem was on their cases big time. Behind with their rent, Cloe went mad, prompting Jemma to take a large amount of ketamine as she was so down on herself. That night, she came downstairs and Raphey and I promptly got her to hospital, after speaking to a friend about ketamine overdoses. After that, Cloe did a disappearing act and Jemma moved up to Scotland, to her uncle's house, never to be seen again. I still think about both of them though, and one day I hope to see them again.

When you enter into any relationship, it's so new and electric that you see just perfection in the bonding, and it gives out the energy that could keep you going for months. It's when you start seeing the major cracks that you wake up to the harsh reality. Gerry started showing his true nature quite early on, but not before I lent him over a grand from my backdated Agenda for Change pay, so he could move into the flat vacated by Jemma and Cloe. His two adorable kids were round every weekend and they used to hang out with Poppy or me. I certainly put up with him for longer because of his children, but I soon got to realise I was being well and truly used. They have grown into fine young ladies now and I am delighted to still be in contact with them.

The first time I experienced Gerry's nasty side was when I called him after 6pm, to ask if I was going to see him that night, and indeed just to make casual contact as couples who are dating generally do. He was working, but his manner was so abrupt I was left in shock. I hadn't known he was going to be working and it was after six. He could have said assertively, "Kay, I'm working, so I can't talk. I'll call you later." That would have taken up less time than the rant I got down the phone instead. He was truly venomous, and afterwards I can remember thinking, "Did that really happen?" but also being totally apologetic that I'd disturbed him and hadn't mindread the situation!

For a moment, I thought in my Aries way, "I'm not going to stand for that, it was totally uncalled for," to "Oh, you should have been more in tune with him and not called him at that time." What was I thinking? The realisation of how stupid I was at the time really is tough to understand, as is why I put up with it for so long. On reflection, he knew how far to push the boundaries with me and what he could get away with.

He became even nastier, and in the end I just didn't want his energy near me, as it actually scared me, which is why his mere name still sends shivers up my spine. His name has been changed here to protect the identity of his kids, and because I cringe when I even write it! He finally left the upstairs flat, owing me a lot of money, but I just wanted him out. It was difficult to admit that I'd opened up so much to him, leaving me vulnerable and exposed. Love is surely blind. I still berate myself for not learning the lessons earlier, so I didn't have to go through that period of my life. But everything happens for a reason.

The lessons learned here were:

1   Not to believe everything someone tells me because I think everyone thinks like me and doesn't lie.
2   To go along with my gut instincts or sixth sense straight away.
3   To look at a person straight in the eyes to know the truth. Remember very few people are able to lie convincingly with their eyes.
4   Don't put up with irrational behaviour without sound justification!

My relationship with him certainly shook me up. I decided to take a vow of chastity, and wore a small padlock on a long chain as a symbol. I was to keep it around my neck for the next ten weeks. It was Wallace who supported me through this experience as a friend. He remains my friend to date and we still chat regularly, when we bump into each other locally.

The gayzebo

The second summer I spent with Raphey was a complete washout, literally. Sheffield experienced its worst flooding since the Great Sheffield flood of 1864. Because we hadn't seen the sun for weeks, except for the one day of the Sharrow festival, for which the sun always shines, I decided necessary action had to be taken. That was the erection of a gazebo in the back yard. One night, on the way home from the pub, Raphey and Poppy purloined an unwanted, shabby red sofa that had been left on a pavement, and the *gayzebo*, as Raphey affectionately named it, was created. I did a *Changing Rooms* on it one day, with the help of our neighbour Phil, who had been round the previous night to complain about the noise, and whom we had befriended. Phil had complained a year earlier too, and had left a note on the door, but it took another year for us to finally meet him face to face, on the day before he moved out.

Phil helped me collect some carpet from a skip on the road, which was a perfect fit. We then filled it with rugs, throws and lots of candles, to Raphey's great amusement, and with Theodore and Poppy watching us from the balcony above. The *gayzebo* became an extension of our living room, and we had great parties out in the yard, despite the weather. Raphey would build a bonfire to keep us all warm in the summer freeze. We even slept out there on occasions.

At the end of the summer, changes were afoot. Merlin introduced me to Mirage, who was staying with him due to her homeless state. They also had a thing for a short time. I invited her round to dinner and was bewitched by her demeanour, beauty and grace.

She wore a feather in her hair, spoke softly and was very tactile. I really thought I was gay for about half an hour, until I realised that I really wouldn't know what to do with her bits; but I was still taken with her charm and softness. A week after meeting her, she turned up on our doorstep one night, crying uncontrollably, saying that Merlin had kicked her out and was currently throwing all her stuff out of his front door, adamant she was out. I immediately jumped into my car to help retrieve her stuff from the side of the public passageway. There was nothing else to do but to bring her back to ours.

She was accompanied by her friend Titan, dressed in a multicoloured tutu, who came to help settle her in. I was fuming at Merlin for his treatment of her, and wouldn't really understand his behaviour until some weeks later, when I too was in a similar position and wanted her out for good. She was in a bit of a state and soon fell asleep, while Titan and I chatted on. He was very intriguing, and someone definitely out of the ordinary, with his strange but unique dress sense.

For the next few weeks, Mirage was welcomed into our home and Raphey and I made her feel special. She had no money at all, so I stocked the fridge with food she had said she liked, but she contributed by doing the housework or cooking. Raphey was happy because she had lots of shiny things, which soon became part of the decor. Everything was fine for a while. She was the perfect house guest and we all got on well, at least until Raphey moved out and I started a relationship with Tony.

When Mirage first moved in, Tony, the guy I'd met at the Sharrow festival the previous year, and who I had thought was an angel, accompanied her everywhere – or rather, he took her everywhere in his car. I thought he was more like a little lapdog than anything else and I knew they'd had a thing too, which was confirmed when she told me, "Tony is a very sexual person, you know."

Months before, I had seen Tony at Merlin's and he had given me a lift back home. I rolled us a spliff while he played me his own song, 'The Lady of the Lake', on my guitar; neither of us realising it was written for me until we became a couple. We sat on the bed after his rendition and I was completely moved by such a beautiful song, written by this obviously gentle and very spiritual man. That moment, we came dangerously close to kissing, but both of us were restrained. He was a Sagittarius, another fire sign, and Poppy and Raphey obviously approved. Although he did ask me out for a drink, I declined because I was still involved with Gerry and it would make things far too complicated. Being a gentleman, he honoured my word and stopped the chase. I texted him when I was single again to meet at Peace in the Park, another fabulous community festival in Sheffield, but I only saw him for a few minutes and spent most of the day with Theodore.

Out of my control, Tony became a fixture at our house, and at the end of August enter stage right his ten year old daughter, Neneh. She had just moved down from Goole to Sheffield to live with him full time and so she was always by his side when they visited Mirage. The first time I met Neneh, she looked like a little ragamuffin, with clothes that were obviously hand-me-downs; just that bit big for her and already well-worn by one or both of the half-sisters she had inherited them from. She was a character, like Tony, and a sweet young thing who obviously loved her dad dearly.

Just before Mirage moved in, Raphey had met a guy called Danny and had fallen in love with him big time. My relationship with Raphey was becoming more volatile, and on one occasion, he got so angry with me that he kicked a doorframe and couldn't walk for a week. It was late summer, and he was of course in his hyper mood. All he wanted to do was to shack up with Danny and spend the rest of his life with him.

One day, Neneh wanted to bake a cake, so Tony brought her over to ask if she could borrow some weighing scales. Raphey gave her my scales and I was of course happy to oblige. When he told her that she could keep them I was fuming. I waited until they had left to berate him. For a start, they were my weighing scales, which I used often, and they were not his to give away. Unfortunately, or should I say fortunately, they heard me shout at Raphey through the closed door and so Tony made sure that the weighing scales were returned a couple of days later. This is when my world changed overnight, and all our lives would never be the same again.

Author's note:

Kay read Tony the bit about him and asked, "What do you think? Is it accurate? What would you change?"

Tony announces, laughing, "I wish I'd kept the scales!"

Nhs – Orgreave – Don Valley 15

I read the newspapers avidly,
It is my one form of continuous fiction.
– Aneurin Bevan, founder of the NHS

At work, the government were doing their usual and making radical changes to a policy they had thought was the answer five years before. It was announced, following consultation of course (not that it made a difference), that the four PCTs in Sheffield would now merge, as would other PCTs across the country. It had taken us all this time to develop new frontline ways of working, and now the government were going to spend millions again to change it in time for the election. They called this process Commissioning a Patient-Led NHS. Don't they come up with some cracking titles? The acronym was CPLNHS, quite a mouthful, but then the NHS acronym is famous. Celeste left again, on secondment to manage this process, and we were put in the capable hands of Jane.

Whatever guise it's under, the NHS is not a government office or department; it's a separate organisation at arms' length from the Department of Health (DoH), who never communicated with us effectively, anyway. The South Yorkshire Strategic Health Authority (SYSHA) was the buffer between the NHS and the DoH. We had to inform the SYSHA about whatever we did, including press releases, and they would inform the DoH. We had little direct contact with the DoH's huge communications department, except through our monthly regional meetings, where we were asked to give comments on their national health campaigns. They spent hours on these, spending lots of money on developing them, but they were rarely brought to completion. I suppose they must have spent the rest of their time spinning favourable stories for the government. Public health campaigns were usually in our remit, with little or no budget to promote them, and with only our creative input to generate their success instead.

The only time we were contacted by the DoH directly was either for MPs' questions or if a minister was coming to the city. As part of my job, I had to organise the communications for those ministerial visits. On two separate occasions, the MPs Rosie Winterton and Caroline Flint MP visited Sheffield. Both were health ministers at the time.

On the first occasion, I didn't have a clue what I should be doing, but MPs have so many communications and press people looking after them to continually spin their existence, I just sent the press release to our local media and hoped they'd bite. MPs are notoriously media hungry and if they don't have at least Radio Sheffield present they'll start going a bit prima donna. My contact at Radio Sheffield, Andy Kershaw 01 (as there are two working for the BBC) was a tough nut to crack. If it wasn't enough that an MP was coming to visit a Sheffield pharmacy, what else was interesting? They thought they were special enough though, and Rosie's press officer called me on their way from London saying, "Kay, help, I've forgotten the camera. Can you bring yours, as Rosie likes a lot of pictures taking of her?" I did, and took lots of photos, although I don't think I could persuade Andy at the Beeb that it was 'interesting' enough. But Rosie at least had her pictures and the visit was covered by the Sheffield *Star* anyway.

The second visit was by Caroline Flint, who visited the Centre for HIV and Sexual Health. She was very attractive, and definitely had presence, oozing self-confidence. But it always seemed clear to me that politicians didn't really care about the NHS, or indeed have any empathy with its staff.

As we went around the room, everyone introduced themselves. When it got to my turn I said, "Hi, I'm Kay, the communications manager." She responded, "Oh, you're the spin doctor?" What I wanted to say was, "Yo bitch, I don't do no spin," and although furious, I didn't show it to the member of the government, and just nodded politely. Thankfully, Radio Hallam turned up with a microphone, which fed her need for a media rush on that occasion. She did redeem herself slightly when she fearlessly encountered a mouse on the stairs in the old building. "Oh, I feel like I'm in the Houses of Parliament," she giggled, as she stepped daintily aside. But then again, she had to deal with Blair on a regular basis so, I assume, a mouse was nothing to her.

When we finally knew our destiny, that the PCTs would merge, Sheffield was put on 'turnaround'. This meant that we had collectively overspent and were under strict observation from the people commissioned by the DoH to streamline finances. It was at this time that I was forced into telling a lie. I vowed I would never lie for the NHS again, but on this occasion I received a phone call from Radio 5 Live and so I had to deal with it. Understandably, all the chief executives were reluctant to speak on live radio and discuss why Sheffield had overspent by millions. They asked me to make up a lame excuse for why they were all unavailable to enter into debate, because of short notice and outstanding commitments. Not because they were worried about putting themselves in the firing line.

That night, I cried all the way home, and during the journey, I phoned Dad from my mobile.

Kay: "I've just had to tell a lie, Dad," and I told him what had happened. Remember, I'd vowed not to tell a lie since the 'dancing into the knife' incident.

Dad: "Sometimes you've got to do what you've got to do, Kay."

Kay: "But Dad, I vowed not to tell a lie and I felt pressured into telling one for them… it's not fair; I should not be put in such a position."

Dad: "Life's not fair, Kay."

After I had said goodbye, I cried even more, thinking, "Why isn't life fair, and why shouldn't it be?" with the ignorance and innocence of a child questioning the harsh reality of life.

Turnaround was serious, of course, and it meant no more spending. Jackie, our assistant director of finance, told us not to spend anything, and we all pulled together as a team to adhere to this. I even had to get my brother to take some photographs free of charge for our annual report, and at a cost to him. He did take a cracking front cover though, and I thanked him in the report itself. Geranium had other ideas though, and wanted to go out in a blaze of glory. She told me she wanted a DVD making of all the best bits of the PCT, to be shown at the very last AGM of her career in PCT-land. I heard her demand money from our director of finance. Of course, he couldn't say no to her; no one was allowed to do that, and I dutifully made the video.

I had to really use my reputation and friendships made over the years to encourage people to be part of the show. This was particularly true with the gorgeous Steve, director of the Centre for HIV and Sexual Health, who had become a good friend and confidante, and who actually believed in my abilities. He said that he'd only be part of the video for me and definitely not for Geranium. You know, the only thing the DVD proved was that it was the people who made the NHS, despite having the head honcho think it was her management of the organisation.

James and Nic were once again my partners in crime, interviewing a wide range of staff in the many bases we occupied, as well as at Orgreave. We made a great film, and when I showed it to Geranium on the morning of the AGM, she cried. I'd never seen her sensitive side before and my heart went out to her. So much so that I insisted we go out and buy her flowers from my sponsored awards money and present them to her at the end of the meeting.

As well as the official staff awards, my sidekick Sarah came up with the fabulous idea for the Little Miss and Mr Men fun awards, initially discouraged by management, who thought it might cause offence. We eventually persuaded them it was not contentious and received loads of entries: the staff loved it. I applied for a small amount of funding, from an approved pharmaceutical company, to pay for the prizes: a copy of the appropriate book for each category, which included Mr and Miss Chatterbox, Giggles, Tidy, Messy and Happy, as well as a certificate. I was overwhelmed: shocked, to be honest, and a bit embarrassed when I heard my own name being read out on stage by our comedy host for the fun awards that day. Behind my back, Sarah had commissioned the following poem, written by a colleague, Jill, and which was printed on my certificate:

Little Miss Splendid

She dances, she's amazing – she is very 'leen'
Kay's such a free spirit, our communications queen
We'd like to reward her for all that she's done
She's worked like a Trojan but always with fun
Her laugh is infectious, her demeanour is calm!
She's magnificent, she's splendid and everything warm.

Out of the three awards I won, this is the one I am most proud of, and I was deeply touched by my colleagues, who were all in on it. I felt so valued by them all. In my mind, this was far more important than being valued by Geranium.

We also put on a garden fete of sorts. Gill and Jayne organised the stalls, which included a tombola, guess the name of the rat, guess how many sweets in the jar and a book stall. It raised money for the Multiple Sclerosis Society, as a very respected member of staff had been forced to retire early that year due to this debilitating illness.

For Geranium's last presentation, she requested only a few slides during her speech (for a change). Usually, I'd have to produce huge amounts of them from her scribbled notes, generally handed to me on the day of the AGM itself. I always arrived late to the meeting, after making sense of endless A4 pages and turning them into the slick presentation that the chief executive expected. On this occasion, I was only required to produce slides of each of the annual report covers we'd produced, as she spoke about the achievements of the PCT through the years. James, Nic and I sat backstage doing the technical stuff, listening to Geranium speak as though it was her personal success alone. She had received an OBE for her work, after all!

She was a right old cow that day, and for the last time showed her true colours. I almost wished I hadn't bought her those flowers. She walked off without even thanking me or the others for the hard work we'd so obviously put into the last time we were all together. Our chairman made up for her; he always did, and he thanked everyone personally. I still went back to base that afternoon fuming at her insensitive behaviour – but for the last time. Thankfully, that woman was no longer in control of me as I had booked the following week off work. Our new chief executive would then take over the helm of a much bigger ship than hers: he had all four PCTs. It was October 2006.

The weekend before my leave ended, I climbed up our ancient, wooden stepladders to reach the high cupboard where I stored our vinyl, as Jemma and Cloe were having a party upstairs. Without warning, the records fell on top of me and I fell onto the table, dislocating my shoulder on impact, so that it stuck out of the socket. I was off work for nearly a month; sore though it was, I was in no rush to get back to a new and much stricter regime. Alison said not to rush back as things were changing rapidly.

Our new chief executive was Pan Dora, a very charming and personable man and such an extreme contrast to the last one. He was also charmed with the name 'The Chopper', due to his previous track record in cutting jobs, and so there was an immediate threat of this happening in Sheffield. In fact, in our first face-to-face meeting with him, he looked around the table at Alison, Sue and I, all in communications posts for three of the PCTs, saying, "You'll not all keep your comms roles, you know." In the end, it was Alison and I who filled the two communications posts, but my job was junior to Alison's because of banding. I went from a manager to an officer, and she became my boss overnight. I was actually very grateful that Alison would now bear the brunt of Celeste's micromanagement for a change. Sue had to go through a very long period of uncertainty, not knowing whether she would have a job at all. She was not alone.

When I had my first conversation with Pan, I was sitting at my dining table on the phone to his office, asking him some probing questions about himself and what our future held; and more importantly, his star sign and his favourite band. Pan, a Leo, loved the attention, or so I was told by his communications lead. He actually changed his favourite band before publication of the article in our newsletter, that I still had the remit for. I think he did so to help create the image he wanted to portray to his staff and to improve his immediate appeal. Maybe I'm just a little cynical.

A few months after we merged, Gill, Jane and I had to leave our base in Orgreave and move up to Don Valley House, leaving David to fend for himself, wash up his cup and make his own coffee. I had been at Orgreave for five years and I left the building for the last time grudgingly and in tears, clutching my waste bin containing the last of my personal possessions, as the removal men had taken everything else. I knew our glorious days were over and that this was not going to be a pleasant ride.

KAY ROSE-HATTRICK

Don Valley House is situated just beyond the Wicker Arches and close to the motorway network, which was obviously why this building was picked to be the interim HQ, as Pan and some of his directors lived out of the city. We shared the fifth floor with Pan and his directors. Everyone else stayed put in their various bases until we were all moved en masse to a new building nearly a year later.

The summer of 2007 brought some of the worst flooding in Sheffield since Victorian times. Following the floods I wrote this, and featured it in the staff newsletter.

I was once told of the Great Flood of Sheffield, which caused devastation to the great people when the Dale Dyke Dam burst its banks back in 1864. I was shocked by the photos taken of the aftermath and the huge death count of 250 people who lost their lives as they were swept away by the power of the water; channelling its fury through Loxley Valley then Hillsborough and all the way down to the Wicker and beyond. It became the worst dam burst disaster in British history. I never thought I would ever experience a catastrophe in my home town and in my lifetime. I was wrong.

That Monday in June started in pretty much the same way, but the rain came and came and actually the water had collected on the flat roof above my head at Don Valley. I only knew this when the roof collapsed over my desk and a torrent of water spread over computers and electrical equipment and five of us were rushing to try to ensure that everything was unplugged and moved out of the way. Little did I know that this was the start of things to come.

The river Don burst its banks, as we all learned later, and Don Valley House became an island, with water surrounding it as if a lake; only accessible by tractors and helicopters. I was lucky; I escaped to a meeting in town while all this took place. My colleagues were not as lucky and many had to be rescued by a tractor and trailer, the driver altruistically saving anyone who would risk its lack of Health and Safety 2007 checks, but most people's only feasible way of getting closer to home, or so I have been told.

I have spoken to a lot of people about their individual experiences since then and they are told with passion, anguish, a sense of humour, that beautiful Yorkshire resilience and not-seen-since WWII togetherness.

I had no idea what was really occurring until my flatmate called me from the other side of town, to say, "I can't get home tonight." I replied, "What do you mean, you can't get home?" His reply urged me to flick over from Film 4 to Sky News to find out for myself. Well, would you believe it? I saw a boat on the road I had left a few hours previously, my colleagues being rescued by a tractor and helicopters rescuing people too. This Great Flood of 2007 killed two people in Sheffield this time; it brought the city to a standstill but its citizens together and made us think you just don't know what's round the corner. Our hearts went out to the people in neighbouring towns and villages who have lost their all.

The moral of this story was to 'listen to Orgreave', who had viewed the river Don getting higher and higher thanks to the online council cameras. They had informed the director in charge in plenty of time to evacuate and other colleagues at Don Valley pleaded with him to send them home, but when the Don eventually burst its banks it was too late. Many of my colleagues had their cars completely ruined by the floodwater, but Pan's 'business as usual' attitude prevailed every time. Incidentally, he had left the office hours earlier.

After the flood, all the Don Valley lot were evacuated to the picturesque Fulwood House, which had housed the old Sheffield South West PCT and other central services, including IT and human resources. I'd never worked there before and always wanted to, but I had visited often for meetings. It's a delightful mock Tudor manor house with breathtaking country views and a wonderful garden where staff can enjoy their lunch on summer afternoons. At Orgreave we'd had nothing: I had to go behind the building for a fag and sit on the piece of grass by the bins. At Don Valley, we didn't even have that. Claire and I, the only two smokers, were pushed out of the car park onto the road when the smoking ban was introduced to all NHS premises and grounds. Even the views from the fifth floor at Don Valley House were hardly breathtaking, merely depressingly industrial.

At Fulwood, a nasty concrete tower block had been built as an annexe to this grand house in the 1970s, although you couldn't see it when you looked out of the window in one of the grand meeting rooms. On the walls in the original house, old pictures hung, capturing the time this house had been a private residence. The boardroom had been the billiard room, and on viewing an old photograph and the room as it stood now, the only difference was that the billiard table had been replaced by a large board table instead. The energy of the room remained and I'd often drift off, thinking of who had lived there and how their lives had been so different to mine. Claire has recently informed me that it was built by a GP, whose sons were killed in WWII. After his own death from natural causes, his wife allowed it to be used as a hospital annexe. It was officially sold to the NHS some years later. Claire also told me that Fulwood House was supposed to be haunted and that staff had reported some strange happenings over the years.

Although we were evacuated to the tower block side, it was linked by a corridor to the old building, which even had a canteen on the top floor. At Orgreave, we had a burger van and at Don Valley, we had the pie man call every day, but a canteen: wow! It was quite a treat, and it gave people the opportunity to have a break from their work, not eating at their desks and working through like a lot of bases did.

Unfortunately, the week after the floods, Alison was on holiday and I was left to hold the fort. I was summoned, as were all key players in such an emergency situation, to a briefing meeting twice a day. I was then required to go and write a briefing for all members of staff and other community services by noon that day. Actually, Pan was quite nice during that week, although I was petrified of messing up. Thankfully, all press enquiries were being handled by 'bronze command', based at the Town Hall, as Sheffield council had dozens more communications staff than we did.

Needless to say, under that amount of pressure, I was so glad when Alison came back and I could hand over the reins again, although the emergency had passed and the floodwaters had subsided by then. The flood caused complete devastation for many people living in Sheffield and the surrounding area, but it showed beautifully the population's ability for comradeship in such an adverse situation.

It was horrible going back to Don Valley after being in the countryside, and the place stank from the stale flood water. Although we all wanted to stay at Fulwood House, which I'm told was more cost effective anyway (and there was room for us), most of the directors lived outside Sheffield, and as Don Valley was easier for them to access, we all had to go back. It still continued to rain though, and not long after, the roof fell on me again. Despite protests about 'duty of care' and 'health and safety', the security guard had said it was OK so nothing else was done about it. That was until it fell down for a third time, when thankfully, I was not in the building. Alison felt its force on this occasion and someone more qualified than the security guard investigated the roof.

I must give the security guards a mention though, because they got me through working at Don Valley. Every morning, I would go through my small ritual. When I could see the building ahead of me, standing very tall and austere, so uninviting we called it Death Valley, I started building up speed, and by the time I passed the building I had clocked up 40 miles an hour. I was then able to slow down for the turning to the car park at the back of the building. I used to chant, "I feel the need, the need for speed" as I sped by, and it gave me a bit of power and control; at least enough to get out of the car and walk over to the foyer. On entering the building, the 1970s reception/foyer, with its plastic plants, was the first thing you saw. Walking past the security guard's office, there was always a, "Morning Kay, how are you today?" Whichever security guard was on that day greeted me with such joy that it gave me enough energy to climb the stairs on good days or to use the lift, if my reserves were low. By the time I walked past the directors' offices on the fifth floor, I was struggling to get to my desk and start working with all engines steaming.

There were only three smokers and then one gave up. It was left to Claire and I to escape together on the long journey from the fifth floor for a cigarette. It took too long to get to the car park (and after the ban, outside the car park) for a mid-morning or mid-afternoon smoke. To make up for this we would chain smoke two at lunch to keep us topped up until home time. Of course, we were caught on several occasions by important people, ie the chief executive, chairman and directors etc. We didn't actually care who caught us as we were on our designated lunch hour and outside the building; they didn't own us for those few precious moments and we made sure they knew it too. If I hadn't actually left the building for those fags I would have jumped off it!

Claire, a Cancerian, added a little insanity to the mix at Don Valley and it was much needed. She was fun, and gave some life and humour to the everyday, mundane routine. We had met when we both attended a course run by a women's entrepreneurial organisation that I think was called Successful Women in Business, and which had given me fresh inspiration for setting up my events company. There were a few places allocated to the NHS and Claire, Linda and I, each from different PCTs, became quite close. The other students on this twelve week course were from HSBC and Rotherham council. We attended one afternoon a week and we all learned a lot from the programme, which included a laughter workshop, professional dressing, the best colour to wear with our complexion, plus lots of mentoring. I later joined their mentoring programme for women setting up in business and attended other events they had organised for women in my position, who were aiming to become self-employed. There was even a testimonial from me, as the director of Showtime, on one of their banner signs. I'd just not had the courage to jump and set up on my own so far.

Claire was now the PA to the delightful Melanie, director of finance, who was another Aries. Melanie hated me going on about star signs, but Hazel, another director, quizzed me about the compatibility and traits of hers and other signs. Hazel and I would have some heart to hearts about my management issues too, and she'd listen, but it was difficult for her to do anything.

As each of the five director posts were filled, I wrote an article for the staff newsletter about their lives: what made them tick, what they did in their spare time etc, to build up a picture of each of them. Of course, I also included what they were going to achieve in their new role. But I'd always find out their star sign for my own compatibility test. I was quite impressed with the rock and roll credentials of the other two male directors: one had been a session keyboard player for the Waterboys and the other a drummer for Alison Moyet's band before she became famous. I knew more about our new team than most, with such direct daily contact and my probing questions for my articles. We became so isolated from the rest of the PCT, who were mostly still in their old bases, and Death Valley became my prison.

We did have a few lighter moments. A funny thing happened one Friday evening. Claire and I were on the great weekend exodus, and we stormed through the director's corridor with the door of freedom so close in our sights. Melanie was the only director still present, as she so often worked late, and she caught Claire to discuss some work. If you spent time chatting with Melanie she came to life and her smile lit up her pretty face. I teasingly used to play with her to get a reaction, respectfully of course, and which was generally, "Oh, Kay!" and a giggle. On this occasion, I don't know what possessed me but I went straight up to her, told her not to work late, gave her a cuddle and kissed her goodbye. I think she just needed that cuddle: she had a tough job, but was well respected by her staff. She immediately went crimson, looked shocked then burst into a great big smile and giggled. Claire was dismissed forthwith for the weekend though, so it did the trick, and our entrapment was at an end.

Melanie also went to Sheffield Girls' High School, like myself, and her mother was my sister's form tutor, so we had a mutual bond with that. I think this is why I never felt intimidated by her, unlike I was of Dr W. Before the merger, Dr W had been the director of public health for North Sheffield PCT, and had secured the job for the whole city. Alison originally came from the same PCT and was used to his humour. The first time I approached him about a press release, however, I felt cut down to bare bones with his reaction. I said, "Sorry to disturb you." After several awkward minutes, he responded with, "You already have," without even looking up from his screen. I got used to his sense of humour eventually and I'd give him as much back, and he liked that. A Scorpio, and very in tune with his emotional side, he even guessed that I was in love straight away. It was in the kitchen on Monday morning after the weekend I had fallen in love with Tony. He just looked at me as I was making coffee in the kitchen and announced, "You're in love!" A very intuitive man, Dr W. It must have been that Cheshire cat grin!

It was a shame that not all management were so human. Others either wouldn't or couldn't empathise, namely Celeste. Her management style was only effective in getting people's backs up. Unfortunately, she didn't command respect and so had to use her management card to show who was in charge. Alison started to get pulled down by this energy and every time she came back from a one to one with Celeste, she would start snapping at me. Both were Virgos with similar understandings about structural working, but Celeste was belligerent to boot.

When Alison said she was handing in her notice to set up on her own, I felt a bit let down that she would no longer be there to protect me, but I also knew that I would do the same if a position arose. She was also saying, "Shove it! I am capable of being my own boss." Alison had so much more experience than me and had more confidence in setting up on her own.

Alison had given three months' notice and, because of the merger, I was the only person in the trust eligible to go for her job, which I had made quite clear I didn't want. I didn't want all that responsibility for not much more money. The process of CPLNHS was very rigid for some, but flexible for others, and it did throw up many unfair anomalies. Oh, that sounds familiar! Every time Alison was called into Celeste's office, she was given a huge pile of work; too much for us both to handle. We knew that Celeste was under an enormous amount of pressure, but it was the way she dealt with situations that was the issue. She was a vulnerable chick in a sea of sharks, but unfortunately she tried to emulate the sharks in their behaviour, and it just didn't work.

Alison's vacant post should have gone out to advert straight away, but Celeste had insisted that we wait for the end of the process, which was only a month or so away. Alison left and I was to hold the fort until a replacement could be found, and was given some agency help. The agency produced most of our good news stories, but the reactive press enquiries still remained well and truly in my remit, and I felt a slave to the press phone, with good reason.

There were only two other people who could cover my press officer duties if I wanted to take any holiday. I almost had to beg them, otherwise Celeste would refuse to sign off my leave. Understandable, as it's not a nice job; never knowing what will be thrown at you from one day to the next by either the local or national papers. Our chief executive was making some quite radical moves; Sheffield was in the red and under more scrutiny than most, so press enquiries were frequent. These enquiries were on top of everything else, including internal communications and inheriting Alison's large pile of work from Celeste every week. In most other trusts similar in size to Sheffield, or smaller, the communications department would usually be three-strong. In Sheffield there was just me. I didn't know what to do with the amount of work I had, but knowing there was a light at the end of the tunnel and that we would soon have a replacement, I battled on.

I was still an active shop steward, and attended the monthly joint staff consultative committee (JSCC), to ensure that the management behaved fairly with its staff, especially during the merger. There was a lot of unrest among staff during this time. Sometimes, four people were competing for half the number of posts in the new organisation, while others would have their colleagues managing them, which sometimes caused difficulties.

Because I was under so much pressure from my day job, my steward's role was compromised, and of course, I had to prioritise. Unfortunately, there were only four active stewards for the PCT at the time and Sarah at Orgreave, who had been my mentee, was still relatively new. Not only were there still disgruntled people from the Agenda for Change pay restructure process demanding a rebanding; the CPLNHS also had its victims. Everyone wanted support from the union at this time, to ensure they were fairly treated. As my daily workload increased, Sandra, an experienced steward who was still based at Fulwood, bore the brunt. We couldn't persuade anyone else to support us in our quest for more union representatives, but they all wanted our support to fight their battles.

Sometimes I found it difficult remembering which hat I was wearing: internal communications officer or steward's. These roles were beautifully symbiotic and meant I was also responsible for ensuring that staff were truthfully informed about what was going on throughout the changes. Well, that was if I was told about it, and not lied to. I was also in a position to question the chief executive, should I want to, although I never did challenge him in those union/management meetings. I preferred to do that at other, probably less appropriate times; sometimes in the kitchen, as was generally my approach with all those more senior to me.

I liked working for Pan though; he was certainly a different kettle of fish than I had been used to with Geranium, and I felt as though I could approach him about issues. I was still a well and truly flogged workhorse though. Not only were we isolated from the rest of the organisation at Don Valley, I was now alone and unable to bounce ideas off anyone in a professional sense. Instead of managing my workload, I just touched the surface and everything was put on the back burner when I got a reactive media enquiry. It was about this time that a friend and colleague, Denzil, went into hospital one day for tests and never came out again.

Denzil Hart (RIP) was our webmaster and we had known each other for years, working very closely together over that period. He started feeling poorly and when they admitted him, it was because they had found a brain tumour. Overnight, the strong, tall, capable man became a shell of his former self. The last time I went to see him he couldn't really communicate any more, and not long after he left this world. It put everything into perspective. A man in his early 40s could be living a full life one day, and the next day it was over. Was all this chaos at work really worth getting stressed about? The newsletter was renamed *Perspective* through a staff poll, and the first edition was dedicated to his memory.

Unfortunately, I had already started getting heart palpitations, only mildly at first, but they became more frequent as the pressure on me intensified. I was not coping with Alison's workload as well as my own, and most days I was tied to my desk with yet another press enquiry, so that the work in my in-tray just kept getting higher and higher.

To add to this pressure, I received a phone call from Alice, who was now in charge of our website since Denzil had passed away. She was keen to alert me to the fact that Alison's job had not been put on the NHS Employers website with all the other jobs at this stage of the CPLNHS process. We were in the same department now, but she was still based at Fulwood House, which is where I was that day. I went straight down to human resources to ask some questions. As I walked into the offices, I saw, stuck to the walls, the colour coded remnants of jobs left after the restructure. I found Alison's job still stuck to the wall, highlighted in yellow. When I asked what that meant, the HR assistant told me that the job was on hold for another couple of months. "Why?" I asked her in total shock, but she didn't know. I felt like I'd been smacked in the mouth. I was now looking at another five to six months (after job adverts and notice periods) continuing with this heavy workload on my own, as I had done for months already. Why hadn't they told me, and did they not expect me to find out? I was understandably outraged.

The following Monday, back at Don Valley, I requested a meeting with Celeste. When I asked her outright, she just laughed in my face. It was the laughter of someone embarrassed to have just been found out and her default reaction was to laugh out loud. I had backed her into a corner and I wanted to know the truth. She had no choice but to tell me their plans for the restructure. Alison's replacement would now be a grade higher and the post renamed head of communications.

I knew that this change to the communications department made sense, but I couldn't believe that after so long holding the fort, I was not party to such information, which directly affected me and only me. I finally had a breakdown at work and was signed off by my GP with work-related stress. I had collapsed at my colleague's desk, in tears and shaking uncontrollably, saying I couldn't go on. I couldn't behave like a sycophantic robot as they would have liked. I was taken into the staffroom to calm down, but I was like a little frightened rabbit, knowing that this place had finally got the better of me. Even in this state, I was summoned to Celeste's office to hand over, as it was clear I was no longer fit for work. My work was spread between several people and the agency was stepped up to cover all press enquiries.

My GP initially signed me off for a month, which turned into three before I was able to return. The news that the post had been filled by an old colleague of mine, from another PCT in South Yorkshire, and whom I liked and respected, was disclosed to me on my return. Her name was Leena Peters, and it was only her imminent arrival that kept me going for the next couple of months. Thank heavens for Leena though; I had told her the score in our first meeting and she empathised with my situation. I was good at my job but I just couldn't perform under this regime and without support. The day Leena arrived, I drove home feeling that a great weight had been lifted from my shoulders, as she now took the brunt of it. She quickly realised what Celeste was like, but was strong enough to fight her, and had Pan on her side as she had worked for him for a number of years before.

Leena, like Tony, was also a Sagittarius from Goole. She was even in the same class as Tony's cousin at school. After Tony, she was an important person in my life, as she dictated my day. Leena and I worked well together and she gave me the space to concentrate on my own projects, encouraging me to be as creative as I wanted. She shielded me from Celeste and inspired me to be my best. I wrote a piece about her in the newsletter, and in the interview I asked her what qualities she admired in a person. She answered:

"Honesty, I hate liars," [Pauses] "Definitely compassion and empathy… altruism… yes, being selfless. Enjoy life and be positive… hold on, let's see what Plato has to say… hmmm… yes, I agree." She looks up from her laptop and smiles: "You can do what you want to do and be what you want to be."

What a role model! I went overnight from one kind of management to the other extreme, where there were no conditions, including on our friendship. At long last, my work and home life were in unison and both were happy.

KAY ROSE-HATTRICK

2ND SEPTEMBER 2007 – 3RD MAY 2008

HUSBAND NO. 3 – TONY

Only after the last tree has been cut down,
Only after the last river has been poisoned,
Only after the last fish has been caught,
Only then will you find that money cannot be eaten.
– Cree Indian prophecy

he day before Raphey moved out, Tony and Neneh returned the weighing scales. Raphey, Theodore, Mirage and I were going to a party down at our friend Bert's studio, and Poppy agreed to sit for Neneh so that Tony could come along too. Before we went to the party, we all had a couple of glasses of wine. Tony wasn't used to drinking so after a couple more he was well and truly pissed and I avoided him at all costs. He's annoying when he's pissed, but then a lot of people are. After a fabulous party and when the sun came up in a cloudless sky, I started up a conversation with a beautiful and very spiritual man called Gandhi. By then, Tony had sobered up and was quite humble, and he asked me not to leave without him. The rest of our group had already gone to their beds some time earlier and so the three of us went back to my flat and continued to chat until the buses had started to run again and Gandhi was able to get home to his wife. Gandhi also read my cards, which had shown work as my 'challenge' and warned me that I wouldn't win against it.

We exchanged numbers and Gandhi left to catch his bus home. Both deciding some sleep was in order, Tony went to lie down on the sofa, and I went into my room and got in beside Theodore, who was asleep on my bed. Theodore and I often shared a bed but it was purely as mates. We did try making love once, after our split, and I knew we would never be lovers again. I genuinely thought he felt this way too. Sometimes, when it got late, he'd crash over and I would hug him as I had as his wife. He said he felt protected when I spooned him. We slept for a few hours and then we were all awoken one by one by Neneh.

First Mirage, with whom she was sharing her bed, then Tony, who was on the sofa, then Theodore and I

Tony tried to kip in Mirage's bed for a bit, but Neneh was in there playing, so he asked if he could lie down on my bed; probably his hangover kicking in. He stood in front of me with a towel round his waist, showing his body to me in its full glory for the first time. I was quite taken aback, as he was really rather ripped and fit and tanned underneath the loose clothes he always wore. I also have a thing about tattoos, and Tony's body is covered in them. I remember thinking, "Phewy, he's gorgeous!" and I wanted him there and then. I still maintain to this day that I don't know what came over me. About ten minutes later, I followed him into my room and blatantly asked him if I could get under the covers with him. He says he was rather taken aback but agreed to my request. I then asked him if he minded if I took off my clothes. STOP! That's enough! Now, this isn't *Fifty Shades of Grey* you know! I had never been so brazen in my life, but I wasn't in control of my own thoughts or actions. However, I was also perfectly aware, as though it was all part of a play written and rehearsed before. It felt so right; as though our union was meant to be. Theodore walked in on us post-coitus and his fuming face said it all.

I can't really remember what time Tony and Neneh left, but I was asleep on the sofa. I remember Tony covering me with a blanket, which I thought was so sweet and such a caring thing to do. I awoke later to the sounds of Raphey trying to move furniture and prepare for his leaving do that night. He'd not been at home much over the past few weeks, choosing to spend every available minute with his new beau. Theodore came round for the party, seemingly jovial, until it became obvious to him that Tony and I were now an item. He kicked a large hole in the bathroom wall and left. He refused to speak to me from that moment on. I think he always thought there was still a chance of us getting back together, despite both of us having other relationships. He must have seen then what Dr W had seen later, and known that there was no chance now. Not that there ever had been in my mind.

The following day, Tony and I had a very open chat about his past. He'd had a life far removed from my relatively middle class upbringing. He was completely honest with me and I immediately fell in love with him for having turned his life around so profoundly. He had supreme understanding of where his life had been and where his life was taking him. His journey was about to take another turn. He articulately deconstructed and analysed the lessons he had learned during his misspent youth. He spoke eloquently about his future with a wisdom and an inner understanding of something much higher than us both. I heard the words come out of my mouth, "I love you, Tony," and although he tells me he was taken aback, he knew that there was something very special between us too. I believe my diary entry of a few months before predicted the arrival of my soul partner, and I was sure I had finally found someone who truly understood me and could set me free.

Our relationship didn't go down well with Mirage either, even though she had moved on to other lovers. She had the audacity to say that she didn't like Tony coming round. Bear in mind that she was living rent-free in my flat. I gave her some space for a few days and went to stay with Tony, who was now living across the road from the Sufi centre, following its closure. On the Thursday, I went back to a flat which was different. It was devoid of any energy, like a vacuum, and I felt as if I was in a strange house. Even Jarvis sat on the sofa under the *gayzebo* in the yard and refused to go inside. I went up to Poppy's and she felt the weirdness too, saying that it wasn't the same without me: the energy had completely changed.

For weeks, I had been taking Mirage into work, as it was on the way to Don Valley House, and every morning she would start an argument. She didn't pay any rent, and once Raphey had moved out, and when we started talking about money, she was quite adamant that she wasn't going to pay as much as he had. She used to phone all her mates from my landline (unbeknown to me until I got the bill), yet she still felt able to dictate who I saw.

I decided that enough was enough and finally asked her to leave, as I didn't think it was working. She left within the hour, thank goodness, and moved in with another friend. She lasted a week or so there, then went on to someone else's house; that was the pattern. She was like a cuckoo; she would slowly take over your house with her shiny possessions. Like me, people were only happy to help because she enveloped them with her beauty and charm. She showed her true colours once she got what she wanted. I was bloody well taken in again, but saw the light later than most, of course.

After Mirage moved out, and over the next few weeks, Tony, Neneh and I got closer and they would come over most nights. Neneh now had access to a much bigger room than she was used to in Vincent Road. I'm not entirely sure how long it was before they moved in with me and officially gave notice to Graham, their landlord.

I had been introduced to Graham by Merlin a few years previously at the Peace in the Park festival. He and his then wife, Anwen, were organising a festival called Fairyland, which Tony and Neneh were attending and which Tony was helping out with. I was intrigued, and paid my money before I'd even asked for the time off work. I had plenty of holiday left as it was always a struggle to get cover, but I really wanted/needed to attend this festival. Celeste refused to let me go until I had secured cover. I remember thinking, "You are not going to stop me from going," but I had to almost beg my two colleagues who were the only ones able to cover for me. One of them did relent, so I was able to attend.

Tony went on site early, as he was helping to set up, and Neneh and I arrived a day later. The event took place in Edale, Derbyshire, and the surroundings were breathtaking. The field is owned by the local farmer, Roy, and his wife, Gwen, and there is a magic to the place. It sits snuggling the river Noe, and is surrounded and protected by large hills on all sides, including the famous Jacob's Ladder, which is at the start of the Pennine Way. I knew very few people at the event but everyone was so friendly, I settled in comfortably. Graham's large canvas dome was at the centre of the activity that weekend and everyone camped in a ring around it. I didn't know what to expect, as it was the first festival I had ever attended, but the intention of the event was to call on the Fairy people in a structured ceremony, led by a head druid and very practised spiritual teacher.

Although I never saw the fairies myself, other people did, and I certainly felt a presence that was not human. I took lots of photos, and one in particular of Anwen playing the flute was full of orbs; distinctive circular white lights, which when zoomed in on, had faces too. You may think I'm a bit odd, but I bet you've also taken pictures with unexplained white, perfectly circular objects in them. Just take a closer look and you might be amazed. Can anyone give a scientific explanation for this, please?

Here I felt among people who understood me for the first time, including Leigha, who had also attuned me in Reiki III. It was here I met the community who would become part of my life. Most people said that Tony and I looked as though we'd been together much longer than only two weeks, and that we behaved like a family, but then again we felt like a family.

It was at Fairyland that Tony carved me my own magic wand, and I felt enveloped in a safe and protective energy, the likes of which I had not experienced for a long time. I could talk to him about everything I'd been keeping quiet about with others around me for fear of being thought of as a nut job. He understood me totally.

The time away in Edale bonded us tightly and it wasn't long before we settled into a family life properly. Neneh had started her new school, which was round the corner, and we went out shopping, buying her some new clothes so that she fitted in and didn't look as though she lived solely in oversized hand-me-downs. First impressions always count. She settled into her new life in Sheffield quickly, but she hadn't counted on having a stepmum so soon!

Tony taught me a lot, and he also introduced me to my Mayan sign. You can download a Mayan calendar from the internet. You will be asked for your date of birth and your sign will be worked out for you. Alternatively, you can work it out from the calendar, called the Tzolkin, but good luck. The Tzolkin is an elaborately complicated, but beautiful work of art and science combined. I won't even start to explain how it works here, in just a short paragraph. If you're interested, check it out for yourself.

What I can say simply is that there are 20 totems in total: five red, five white, five blue and five yellow and there are 13 tones.

Red

Dragon	Nurture	Being	Birth
Serpent	Survive	Instinct	Life force
Moon	Purify	Flow	Universal water
Skywalker	Explore	Wakefulness	Space
Earth	Evolve	Synchronicity	Navigation

White

Wind	Communicate	Breath	Spirit
Worldbridger	Equalise	Opportunity	Death
Dog	Love	Loyalty	Heart
Wizard	Enchant	Receptivity	Timelessness
Mirror	Reflect	Order	Endlessness

Blue

Night	Dream	Intuition	Abundance
Hand	Know	Healing	Accomplishment
Monkey	Play	Illusion	Magic
Eagle	Create	Mind	Vision
Storm	Catalyse	Energy	Self-generation

Yellow

Seed	Target	Awareness	Flowering
Star	Beautify	Art	Elegance
Human	Influence	Wisdom	Free will
Warrior	Question	Fearlessness	Intelligence
Sun	Enlighten	Life	Universal fire

Out of the above you could also have one of the following 13 tones:

Magnetic – Purpose	*Lunar* – Challenge	*Electric* – Service
Self-existing – Form	*Overtone* – Radiance	*Rhythmic* – Equality
Resonant – Attunement	*Galactic* – Integrity	*Solar* – Intention
Planetary – Manifestation	*Spectral* – Liberation	*Crystal* – Cooperation
Cosmic – Presence		

As you can see, there are many more combinations than the astrological chart. What sign you are is supposed to indicate your purpose in life. Each combination has a short affirmation. As a White Spectral Worldbridger mine is:

> *I dissolve in order to equalise releasing opportunity.*
> *I seal the store of death with spectral tone of liberation.*
> *I am guided by my own power doubled.*

I take my role as Worldbridger very seriously these days, as according to the Mayans, my purpose of being is all about Death and Liberation! Of course, death means change.

Tony also reintroduced me to David Icke. When I first came across the sports presenter it was on *Wogan*, when I was 21. I walked into the lounge, where Dad was watching it, and asked innocently, "Why are they laughing at him, Dad?" He responded with, "He thinks he's the son of God, a born again!" As I listened to what David had to say, it didn't seem preposterous to me. What he said was that we're all part of the divine energy and that the world was being controlled by a few elite families. This made sense to me back then, and has stayed with me ever since.

Seventeen years later, David had found out so much more! Tony went to listen to a talk he gave in Goole and it got me interested in what he had to say. Since then, I have watched hours of interviews with this man. I think people are waking up to the fact that he wasn't talking bollocks and, as he continues to expose the real truth about this world, it is starting to ring true with many people now. Since being ridiculed on national TV, he now has a very strong following and sells out Wembley. His new TV show, *The People's Voice*, is definitely worth a watch. Although he continues to be publicly discredited by some, he stands resolute, and thankfully won't be put off. Interestingly, it was Betty Shine who also got him started on his spiritual journey, just as she had got me started on mine. Tony also introduced me to Stuart Wilde (RIP) who sadly died recently. Stuart once said, "Some people think the world will end. I've often wondered when it might get started." This wise and enlightened man helped me to figure out my role in life.

When we got together, Tony gave me a rose quartz crystal in the shape of a heart, and every morning he would charge it up with his energy, so that it would give me the strength I needed to get through the day. Rose quartz is the stone of unconditional love and infinite peace. It is the most important crystal for the heart chakra, teaching the true essence of love. It purifies and opens the heart at all levels, and brings deep inner healing and self-love. It was really hot after Tony had charged it and I usually wore it in my bra to keep it close. I did feel the energy and it gave me the boost I needed, especially before Leena, my new boss, had rescued me.

Raphey was still popping round to the flat. On one occasion, he had let himself in and was waiting for me when I arrived home from work. He had pre-empted that I would shout at him as he'd also brought round one of his new boyfriend's friends, but she held a silver tray on which a freshly poured gin and tonic was placed, and so I couldn't really chastise him. Pea, as she would become later, was in her late teens, wise beyond her years and having major issues with life and how she fitted into this world. Our way of thinking made sense to her, and she went from being a 'chav' to a 'hippie' almost overnight, with little encouragement. She was going through quite a turbulent time and having major rows with her mother, as most teenagers do. She just needed a bit of space to find herself, so Tony and I adopted her and she spent a lot of time at our house. We looked after her, making sure she ate, and I'd buy her little presents to treat her. Neneh loved her too and they were inseparable for a time. She eventually moved into the recently vacated Vincent Road rooms at the same time as Jimbob, whom we had met at the Fairyland festival.

Tony and I had fallen deeply in love and spoke about marriage early on in the relationship. He proposed to me one night in the Vine, on one knee, with a beautiful dolphin stone ring, and we made plans to be handfasted in May. A handfasting is a traditional Pagan wedding. It is not legally binding, but still endorsed by God, and so seemed to us to be a perfect way of committing to each other.

I asked Pea to be my chief bridesmaid, and she was an absolute star, due to her efficiency and organisational skills, which are essential when putting on a big wedding. I started to panic about how big the event was getting and Graham, who was helping organise it, reassured me on many occasions that it would not get 'out of hand'. He told me everything would be done on-budget. My bank pretty much threw a loan at me and so I was able to put aside financial worries, with a little extra to play with. I was no longer bogged down with work-related stress and, with Leena at the helm, I was able to spend more time preparing for my forthcoming nuptials. I also booked two weeks of holiday without even having to beg, for a change.

We even got an announcement of our marriage on Radio 6 before the big day. The weekend before the wedding, Nemone, the radio presenter, had asked her listeners what they were up to that day. I sent a text back to say I was writing my vows for my imminent Pagan handfasting, and she was obviously quite interested, due to it being a little different. She read it out on national radio, a bit like our banns being read out in church, I suppose.

The backdrop for the handfasting was Edale. With help from our friends, it looked like a scene from Shakespeare's *A Midsummer Night's Dream* as we walked into the sacred circle to say our vows. Neneh was my flower girl, and she spread rose petals, which I'd been drying out for years, over our path after we'd said our vows as a handfasted couple. Pea and Kat were my bridesmaids, and like myself, were dressed in green for the occasion. My dress was made by the lovely Aries Jenny, a larger than life Jamaican, who was still putting the finishing touches to it before the ceremony. Time obeyed its own rules that day. Pagans accept that a plan doesn't always pan out, so we were a little late saying our vows, scheduled for 3.33pm. Well, what time do you think I'd get married?

The nuptials tent

Tony and I kept very much apart that day, as tradition dictates, and for the first time I felt like a pampered bride. Whilst Tony worked so hard with the others to ensure that the marquee and dome were fit for a wedding, I kept indoors under canvas, enjoying breakfast in bed and courting guests who came for the day. Many of our guests, including colleagues from work, had never attended a handfasting before. Tony and our friends had done us proud. As I stood with my bridesmaids on the incline by my tent, looking down at the scene and waiting for my cue of 'Teardrop' by Massive Attack on the sound system before joining my betrothed in the circle, surrounded by our family and friends, I felt like Titania, the Queen of the Fairies!

The dome, the setting for the ceremony, was beautifully decorated with ivy and coloured material, as was the altar table. That had been the responsibility of Nick, the hedgewitch, as the Elder. He had skilfully laid out everything needed for such a ceremony. We had asked Eliza and Graham to perform the ritual and represent the God and Goddess. Eliza, whom I had first met at the Fairyland festival, was a practised Pagan and Graham had experienced handfasting first-hand at his own.

KAY ROSE-HATTRICK

The players:

- ❀ The flower girl – **Neneh**
- ❀ The bride and groom – **Kay & Tony**
- ❀ The High Priestess and High Priest – **Eliza & Graham**
- ❀ The Elder – **Nick**
- ❀ The Maiden – **Jo**
- ❀ The Temple Summoner – **Jamal**
- ❀ The Quarters
    - ❀ **Jimbob:** Air/Blue/East
    - ❀ **Mike:** Fire/Red/South
    - ❀ **Fiona:** Earth/Brown/North
    - ❀ **Lianne:** Water/Green/West
- ❀ The drummer – **Bert**
- ❀ The witnesses – **Anita & Martin**
- ❀ The bridesmaids – **Pea, Amy & Kat**

They had all dressed theatrically for the occasion, adding to the dramatic effect. It was early May and the weather was very changeable, with a high wind. But as we said our vows to each other, the wind dropped and the sun poked through the clouds, illuminating all below.

The Pagan handfasting would be recognisable to all who have attended a Christian wedding, as it's very similar. I should know: I've attended many weddings, including my own church wedding. The well-known term 'tying the knot', which we all understand to mean to get married, comes from the Pagan ceremony. We chose a shamanic handfasting, which includes a traditional communion of sharing bread and wine, along with the words, "May you never hunger," and "May you never thirst." This was instead of the Christian body and blood of Christ, and which I think makes much more sense in this day and age. We then exchanged rings, which we bought for £12.50 each on the Moor the week before. The exchanging of rings is used by Christians in their wedding ceremony, but as Tony slipped on my ring I said instead, "With this token, Tony, I give you a reminder of our love and our vision for the future, a symbol of our union together. Will you join with me?" I think these particular words are much more expressive than "With this ring I thee wed," and are much more a positive symbol of the union and less of a command.

Handfasting usually lasts for a year and a day, but Tony and I chose to commit to each other not just for a lifetime, but for an eternity! Usually, you would renew your vows after a year and a day to fully commit to that person, if still so desired. So it's quite a sensible arrangement really.

The wedding kiss

The actual 'fasting' took place when our wrists were bound together with red, green and gold plaited cords:

the **red** cord signifying *love and passion;*
the **green** signifying the *heart and nature of all things;*
the **gold** cord signifying the *divine light.*

Each guest was then invited to tie a knot in the cord, which signified a blessing or good luck wish from them; to us, it indicated the tender bondage of our mutual commitment. This cord was not unbound until 24 hours after the ceremony. Tony and I were tied together for this whole period, including joint trips to the compost loos!

As with all weddings, we said our vows to each other. We wrote them ourselves, and these were mine to Tony:

With you Tony, I feel free and protected and am myself for the first time this lifetime. To have found
you again, after so long apart, makes me feel certain we are here for a reason. Let us unite and go
forth to spread the word of love. For love is all we have to give.

Tony Rose-Hattrick, I love you with all my heart, despite judgement from others. We know the truth and the truth is us. Let us build our family and light the world.

Bless our guests, witnessing this union, and join us in celebration with love in their hearts and give thanks to the divine for making this be.

The judgement from others was referring to my father, who chose not to be there on the day. As did my brother, who chose to visit Ashley's (my first husband's) parents that weekend. He didn't even decline his invitation to watch his sister marry for the third time: his decision was passed on by my sister. It was Christelle, a beautiful French Leo, who performed the traditional father's role of giving me away.

Third wedding day, with Neneh

At the end of the ceremony, we jumped over a broom (from a broom bush; not the sweeping variety!), which symbolised leaping together into our new life as one. This tradition was not kept on by the Christians for some reason, but the broom appears throughout the centuries, in wedding rituals from a number of different cultures worldwide.

The first time that we signed our new names, Rose-Hattrick, was on our wedding certificate that day, in front of our witnesses, Martin and Anita. Hattrick is a combination of my maiden name, Hattersley, and Tony's surname, Trickett. What was I going to do this time, as in my previous marriages I had both not changed my name and then had changed my name! I knew I wasn't going to be a Trickett! The combination was perfect: Hattrick, as Neneh made us three. It became Rose-Hattrick because Neneh didn't want to be called Hattrick, and so instead chose Rose, which we obligingly added.

It was a wonderful ceremony, and our rehearsal the week before had ensured it went without mishaps. Random walkers, together with the crowd that had formed in the campsite on the other side of the river, stopped to view this uncommon sight. My third wedding almost perfectly mirrored my childhood image of my wedding day, wearing flowers in my hair and walking barefoot down the aisle.

Merlin had chosen not to be part of the ceremony, but, as head chef that weekend, he really excelled himself, preparing a fabulous buffet spread in the marquee. Some of my closest friends from work camped out, including Brenda, my old smoking partner, Sally, Linda and her husband. They all clearly had a ball. Linda took some beautiful photographs and really captured the essence of the day, the talented lady that she is. Tony's dad Mike, who is a professional photographer, took some corkers too. But unfortunately, the only moving images that we have of our handfasting is a short blast of Bongo Bert on the drums.

My mum really enjoyed herself, and my friends Jo and Kerry really looked after her throughout the day. She didn't want to go as she watched Lianne perform some of her bellydancing routines. Mum had started forgetting things beyond normal old age, and we knew that the onslaught of Alzheimer's was now upon us. The important thing is that, beyond anything, my mum was still there to support me, whatever I did. That pure, unconditional love continued to pulsate through her veins.

Neneh left in my sister's car for Berry Hill, where I knew she would be warm and safe, although Pea had already been put on babysitting duty that night. After much begging by Amy, my niece, who had become great mates with my officially new stepdaughter, I finally relented, and so they left together. I had wanted Amy to be my bridesmaid but Trace and Roger, her partner, had got lost, so were too late for her to take part in the ceremony. Distracted by the high spirits of the event, we said it was OK and they trundled off excitedly, before the chill started to really embrace that 3rd May. We regretted our decision later.

The celebrations continued well into the night and some of the campers, who had watched the service earlier, came over to join in the party. It turned into a mini-festival in the end, with many people seeming to arrive from the city for the event. Some of them were people whom we'd never even met before, but who were 'a friend of a friend', and a few were excellent musicians. We were given a couple of ecstasy pills, which we took, as we toasted our wedding with cava. I knew my sister had clocked this, as her mood became quite aggressive.

The party was rocking though, and we even had Jeanette and Kay, both experienced flautists, playing in the sophistication of the marquee. The dome had been transformed into a nightclub, after the musicians had handed over to the DJs. The DJs who wouldn't stop. I apologise to everyone in Edale that weekend who had to endure the music going on until 5am. That was when I sent a message via Alex to "turn the fucking music off NOW or else!" Poor Roy the farmer got it in the neck from the locals the next day, and we made sure this would never happen again.

The following day, we woke up in our nuptial tent just over the hill from the main party. Once again, it had been decorated by our friends to resemble a Bedouin tent, and the flower arch from the ceremony had been placed in front of it. We hadn't yet cut the cake (chocolate this time) that Fozia had made, but unfortunately, Luke and her were unable to attend. Our friends had set up a table in the marquee, with the cake and all our presents, but we first had to leave the site and pick Neneh up from my parents' house.

When we arrived at Berry Hill there was a massive row, as Dad had obviously heard about the ectasy pill via Trace. He said that Neneh was going to stay with them for another night, threatening to call the police if we protested any further. We went back onto that field without her, carrying very heavy moods, and I cried pretty much continuously all that night. This was supposed to be our special time, and Dad, in his own wisdom, remained in control, dictating our moves. When we got back, our cake had already been cut, by a guest who was hungry, and so that special moment was lost forever.

Despite the time of the year, we enjoyed a heatwave the following week and we spent our honeymoon camped down by the river in our nuptial tent. Neneh was finally collected from Berry Hill and went back to Sheffield for the week, as Jo had agreed to look after her and Jarvis, the cat. Other guests stayed for the first part of the week, but after all the anxiety of the past few weeks we were keen to start our honeymoon on our own. We had to ask the final guest, whom we hadn't even met before, if he could perhaps leave us on our own. But it didn't go down very well with him: I'm sure he'd have stayed all week if we hadn't had had a word with him. Some people do have a problem empathising with a situation sometimes!

We were completely alone there, except for the occasional visit from Roy the farmer on his three-wheeler, who came to see if we were OK. We spent the week as true Pagans: land-dwellers, sometimes skyclad, cooking on an open fire. Roy said that this was now our spot, and it has been ever since. It was bliss, and we were so loth to rush back to the city to start our married life together. I could have stayed there forever, but unfortunately I had to get back to work. On returning to Sheffield, we were welcomed home by our friends, who had gathered round a fire that they had built in the back garden of Airy Fairy,

Anwen's cafe and gift shop. They had been amazing. We certainly couldn't have done it without them. It has been said that "friends are the new family." My biological family seemed to be slipping ever further away.

Nhs – Don Valley – Darnall

17

No problems, just solutions.

– Pan Dora

When I went back to work, Leena was there, fearlessly protecting me and encouraging me to be creative, while giving me her full support. I loved my job again, and I concentrated on internal communications, except when Leena was off. We were keen to be finally moving to our new base at 722 in Darnall, as the whole organisation would now be united. This excited the Don Valley girls a lot more than most, as we would be with our colleagues again, in one big family. As internal communications officer, I was determined to make that move as smooth as possible for those being ripped from their long-term bases for the first time. As I had been through it a year earlier, I knew how traumatic it could be.

That summer, Leena also made a commitment to her long-time partner, and Tony and I were invited to the service in Wales, where they also had a weekend house. It was on the day of the Sharrow festival, but Pea had agreed to take over from me, and I gratefully handed over the site plan to her. I knew she was very capable after helping me organise the handfasting.

It was to be my last year of volunteering, as it was consuming a lot of my spare time, especially as the date drew closer. In all the paperwork I sent out, it was underlined in **bold**: "I am a volunteer and this is not my full time job!" (I think people thought I sat in a Sharrow festival office all day, waiting for phone calls from potential stall holders.)

"Please only call me after 5pm or at weekends." But this didn't stop them, and they called throughout the day, despite my pleas. Pan was at my desk one day and, as if on cue, a Sharrow festival call came through. I realised that I couldn't give it the attention it needed, and so the following year I handed over the responsibility to Mark.

In Leena's absence, I was in the press seat when the PCT was criticised for spending money on a travel coordinator, who was on secondment from a travel company for a couple of days a week. Tom became a good mate, but we had to justify his existence to Dave Walsh from the Sheffield *Star* one day.

Because of Leena's absence, Celeste decided to take control again, and under her micromanagement I was left feeling like a junior admin worker. I wrote a letter to human resources to formally complain about her. Although I spoke to several people about this letter, including one of the directors and my interim manager, Jane, I never sent it. I was fully supported by Leena on her return. Although things would never actually be the same again following her nuptials.

Her guests included Pan and his wife Brigitta, as well as another director and her partner and an assistant director with his family. Before I met Brigitta, I could only picture a Cherie Blair character: confident, high-flying and emotionally challenged, like Pan. She was nothing like I'd imagine Mrs Blair to be like, but was instead quite bohemian, a good laugh and easy to talk to. As the wine flowed, she became loose-tongued, and when we said we were going outside for a smoke she joined Tony and me. We sat down on a grassy patch by the country road, just down from the house and with breathtaking views in the brilliant sunshine. We asked her if she minded if we lit the spliff we had brought, and she didn't. And while we smoked, she relaxed a bit more and started chatting very openly about Pan and their life. I think she just needed to download it all to strangers and she must have felt comfortable with us, the spliff-smoking hippies that we were.

I will not disclose any of our conversation, as I respected our heart to heart. Needless to say, when Pan came out into the garden and realised she had 'spilled some beans', he was none too pleased. I now knew everything about our chief executive, and mainly the bits he didn't want people to know about, especially those in a lowly band 6. I was no stranger to Pan though. If his wife really felt like that, then what chance did his employees have?

This affected our relationship from that moment on, and although I never mentioned the chat I had had with his wife, I could never look at him with the same level of respect as I had done. In his weekly staff meetings, I could only hear Brigitta's words. One day, I reproached him about one of his unpopular decisions, saying, "Pan, you're not winning any friends around here." He replied, "I don't have many friends." I was far too gobby, and he knew it, but I wouldn't sit by and watch his treatment of the staff without a fight.

I was no longer a union steward: the pressure had been too much. I had to be realistic and put myself and my family first, as I had so little extra to give at this stage. I was still approached by people who had nowhere else to turn and I always helped where I could. People would also open up to me in my capacity as internal communications officer, or as a friend or colleague, and I was amazed by the people whom they identified as bullies.

Examples of bullying or harassing behaviour could include:

* Spreading malicious rumours
* Unfair treatment
* Picking on someone
* Regularly undermining a competent worker
* Denying someone training or promotion opportunities

You would think 'butter wouldn't melt' with some of them, but through their own insecurities, these bullies controlled people, making very unpleasant working conditions that could even result in illness for the member(s) of staff affected. Nothing much was ever done about accusations and the victim often remained under the management of the person they were accusing of treating them unfairly. I know that this happens universally, in every profession, but I did expect more from the good old NHS, who you would like to think would always be decent employers.

It's interesting that the bully is usually a vulnerable person too: it's just their position within the hierarchy of the office that enables them to get away with it repeatedly. They are very often the victim themselves, and so reflect the bullying back to those in more junior positions. This way, they retain some form of control themselves.

Work continued. For the 60th Anniversary of the NHS, Leena arranged for us to don NHS T-shirts and spend the afternoon on Fargate with one of our favourite doctors, the gorgeous Professor Ian Philp CBE. He was the professor in charge of health and ageing for the city and had been a regular on a national TV show about ageing. His brief for the day was to guess both the actual and biological ages of the people we stopped. It was all filmed by James and Nic and was later uploaded to YouTube by Alice. We were one of the first trusts to use social networking to encourage good health. It was here that I had a conversation with an American lady, who was very vocal in praising the NHS, and Sheffield specifically. But she clearly points out the inequalities of the American healthcare system and the strengths of the UK's.

> *It's a basic human right because people in America die without health insurance. I think people in England are great, but they don't appreciate the NHS. They don't know what it's like to have a child who's got a fever and you can't take him to the doctor because it's food or health insurance. You*

sit there holding your child all night long because you don't know whether you can afford to go to the doctor. You know if you had a heart attack they would send you to a different hospital. People in America perceive that free healthcare means you wait much longer for an appointment, when in fact, I only wait two days for an appointment with my GP in the UK. In America, it's six weeks with health insurance.

We have to remember that our healthcare is second to none. The American situation is a horror story I hope we never emulate in this country, but I fear it's coming our way, considering the abolition of PCTs in 2013 and a new way of working, yet again.

That day a young, pretty, long-haired blonde girl who was working in one of the phone shops approached me while we were filming. She had just graduated from university and was looking for a job more in keeping with her communications degree. As luck would have it, we had an opening for an assistant, and Laura started shortly after that. Laura was a Leo, another fire sign. We became a great communications team, and with all the fire signs represented in Leena, myself and Laura, were a force to be reckoned with! Laura was fabulous and I took her under my wing like a younger sister. She was great at her job too. She helped me with internal communications and Leena with the external stuff. We had so much fun developing the quarterly staff newsletter, which was now being professionally printed by a company in Worksop, who were able to place adverts in it which then paid for the design and print.

Not only did we cover the usual corporate stories, we also had regular features. These included Professor Ian Philp with his tips on how to live longer, Richard from the library with his quirky 'From Behind the Shelves' and a themed photography competition, 'Snapshot', which encouraged staff to send in their JPEGs. The winning photo was then used as the front cover of the following issue. One of the directors was a keen photographer and wrote the editorial for the piece. He was also on the judging panel, along with my old pal Brian Parkinson, who still did much of the design work for the trust. Matt, the designer of *Perspective* was the third judge. We got some fabulous cover shots, and the competition was held in high regard by many staff.

'Minute Moments' was also a staff favourite. Departments who wanted to take part put forward three members of staff, and I sent them four questions to answer. It should have only taken a minute. Have a quick go yourselves. I'm sure that it will transport you back to somewhere interesting, or make you think a little about your ideal place or dinner guest!

"What was your first job?", "What was the first record you ever bought?", "Where in the world would you most like to be now?" and "If you could invite someone to dinner, past or present, who would it be?"

Our department was never featured, of course, but these would have been my quick answers: "Babysitting", "'Hit Me With Your Rhythm Stick' by Ian Dury", "Somewhere hot and exotic, with soft, icing-sugar beaches and clear blue waters, with incredible people selling barbecued fish that they'd caught that day" and "I think it would be the Dalai Lama actually: he fascinates me."

These questions often teased out some interesting facts about people and there was no shortage of departments wanting to take part. The newsletter also included social events, fashion and quizzes that had decent prizes. My editorial team were great. They were as excited as I was as we discussed possible editorial content, including 'Steph's Super Saving Tips'; something that we all raved about. Sarah and Emma, from the Orgreave days, were also part of the group, and Emma corrected all my grammatical mistakes before we pushed the button for Matt, the designer, to send it to the printers. These were always nerve-racking times, as if things were incorrect, either factually or grammatically, we would come to know about it. People did point out our mistakes, so we endeavoured to make as few as possible! Of course, the newsletter did cover serious stories, and mainly promoted corporate messages, but we were able to inject some fun into the remainder.

It was a staff newsletter for the workforce and I wanted it to be a fun read, as well as informative. Leena rarely changed anything and the go-ahead from Pan was always forthcoming. People commented on how they looked forward to it, and the readership was over 2,000. Every Friday, we also did a weekly roundup for staff, which included all our weekly local and national news coverage, any 'stop press' news plus a 'what's on?' guide. I made sure that it was not so dull and corporate, but still contained all the information staff needed to know. Alice also got Laura and I blogging. Once Alice had showed us how, we regularly updated our internal page with more informal staff news. People were generally happy with the internal communications structure, as my staff survey showed.

Laura was also encouraged to blossom and she always achieved anything we set her, exceeding expectations. In our new premises in Darnall, every meeting room was named after a famous Sheffielder. It was Celeste's idea to involve staff, getting them to choose the names. She had some really good ideas sometimes. Once the names had been chosen, I asked Laura to see if she could get something from some of the chosen Sheffield stars to hang on the walls.

She got a framed photo and room message from Michael Palin saying, "Welcome to my room!", some historical stuff from Thorntons and even got Joe Scarborough, one of Sheffield's highly acclaimed artists, to come in person to present his room with one of his prints. We both tried with Jarvis Cocker but to no avail. The Cocker Room always had such a ring to it! I asked David, my old office mate from Orgreave, if he could help, as he had known Jarvis in his youth; in fact, he still did. Instead, he gave me a photocopied picture of the famous Sheffielder, when he was in his late teens, at a party they must have attended together. It was too small to frame and not appropriate to put on his wall; only probably good for some childish taunting about his quiff if we ever meet face to face. And yes, I've still got it!

Unfortunately, I was still tasked to produce the *Team Brief* every month. Do you remember my plight with *Team Briefs*? I still always left it to the last minute, because it continued to cause me a lot of grief. I had to go through all the unbelievably boring board papers and turn them into an easy and informative read. It was a very daunting task considering how dry some of the papers were. Many, written by top managers, weren't always clear, whether it be the grammar or readability of the original document. If I couldn't understand the paper, how could I expect a staff member to? I knew no one read it. They would attend their meetings duly clutching a paper copy of the *Team Brief*, but not really taking it in, unless it directly affected them. If it did, it would be translated into proper speak by their manager, anyway. This would eventually be my downfall, despite all my other work being beyond reproach.

Leena wanted to expand the communications department and proposed two new staff members: a press officer at band 7 and another at band 6, working more with the community. This latter post appealed to me more, and so I applied for it. The day of the interview came and I felt sick all day. Interviews always do this to me. I work myself up into a frenzy and am then unable to perform, especially if my interview slot is one of the last of the day.

I had tried to get out of the NHS before; most recently to Sheffield Hallam University's communications department, where my old colleague and fellow annual report shortlist contender Claire was now in charge. I had written a great presentation and had even practised it on Raphey, Theodore and Poppy the night before my interview, and they had been impressed. The presentation itself went well; it was the dreaded interview afterwards that let me down yet again. I literally froze and lost the power of speech, and was unable to give any intelligent responses to their questions. At the time, I had taken it as a sign that I shouldn't jump the sinking ship!

This interview panel consisted of Leena, another colleague who I liked and a woman Leena had asked to be a panel member because of her work in communications for a private company. She looked as though she'd eaten a wasp, and her demeanour really threw me that day. The then health correspondent from the Sheffield *Star*, who had become a good friend over the years, also applied for the job and she said the same thing about that panel member. Needless to say, the phone call from Leena that came later that night, as I shopped in Tesco, did not have a positive outcome.

What did that say about me, exactly? I didn't get the job because, although they knew I could do it, I was unable to demonstrate this in the interview. This had prevented me from securing it, even on the same band that I was currently on. Leena debriefed me the next day, but I declined feedback from the private sector bod. I knew what my performance had been like, and I didn't need a woman who knew neither me nor the NHS to criticise me. It was a blow, but I did recover pretty quickly, knowing that everything happens for a reason. That day I had even pulled my daily 'cosmic ordering' cards, which read: "What you think you need isn't necessarily what you **do** need." Looking at things positively, it would mean I could keep my 'baby', my newsletter, anyway.

The band 7 press officer joined the team shortly after and I knew things had changed in the department when, during a media enquiry, I heard her say, "Should we lie to them?" Leena said no of course, but she was a new breed of NHS communications professional, straight from the private sector, where manipulating the truth seemed de rigueur.

Things started to go wrong when Leena was away on a course in London. It was *Team Brief* time and as she was not around I had gone straight to Pan to get it authorised. Oh, he was all sweetness and light with me in the corridor later, even saying that he'd spoken to Leena about changes, with a smile on his face. That was to be the last time I spoke to him. It transpired that he had pulled Leena out of her breakfast, making an urgent phone call to complain about me and that month's *Team Brief*.

In my defence, I had gone through the monthly board papers and had duplicated a story that had read to me as two different items. Even the names of the new directives were different in both pieces, as most things are when they arrive new in the boardroom and when a working name has not been chosen at that point. Some of the grammar was incorrect as well, but it had been taken directly out of the board papers anyway, and a final re-read would have picked up any mistakes. I'd had to catch him when I could as he was out of the building for the rest of the week. I'd told him that it was not in a finished state.

After Leena returned I received a formal letter concerning my performance. I asked an old schoolfriend who worked in human resources whether it would remain on my record and the answer was affirmative and indefinite. It was like another massive punch to the head. I was also told not to approach Pan in the future. In the past, there had been no choice as I had been the only person covering communications, but now it was strictly forbidden. I had put everything into that organisation and every night, I would take all the shit home with me to my family, who had to put up with the stress that had accumulated during the day.

To make matters worse, there was the change to the one to ones that we had every month with Leena. In the past, they had been an informal chat, but now they would be formally documented with clear black and white objectives to achieve. Apparently, I was to be the first. I felt under pressure, especially as I believed the change was made to manage my performance even further. In my first (and last) new-style meeting, I declared that I was too sensitive for this job, but Leena reassured me that being sensitive was a good thing! There was also the imminent arrival of the new girl, who had been successful at interview, at band 6. With the expansion of the communications department, as our numbers grew, my boss grew more distant from the team, mostly hot-desking in empty desks in other departments, and her role became more corporate.

I felt that I was hitting my head against that proverbial brick wall in every respect. Nothing I did seemed to make a difference to staff and how they were heard. Now I felt I was being personally persecuted, with nowhere to run.

Christmas of that year was tough for me. I was going through another breakdown and I knew the time would come for me to say, "I can't go on any more!" Most mornings, Tony would give me a pep talk and charge up my heart crystal, which would enable me to get out the door and into my car. My journey to work was accompanied by very loud music from no preferred radio station, just one which played a decent tune. When I pulled off the Parkway at the Darnall turnoff I felt sick, my heart palpitations growing with every inch I crawled closer to 722 and my eight hours of torture.

Again I have to mention the security guards here who gave me that much-needed bolt of energy when they greeted me every day. Nice fellas they were, and once again hurrah for security guards. We must remember that everyone is important. We sometimes forget how much influence people do have, especially security guards, when it comes to getting things done. They didn't much like Celeste, or any of her team in corporate services, but they would do owt for me!

Every morning in the run-up to Christmas, my heart palpitations increased, and one morning, when Tony was not around and I went about my daily ablutions alone, I had my worst attack yet. I sat down on the sofa, almost overwhelmed by the amount of missed and half-beats my heart seemed to be taking, and it scared me rigid. I knew then that it was time to take this matter to my GP and, once I had regained enough composure and my heart was calmer, I called my surgery and made an appointment.

I was due to have Christmas off and work through New Year. During the holidays, I went to see the doctor who had originally signed me off the previous year. She immediately signed a sick note, starting New Year's Eve, and with the words, "I'm surprised you went back after last time" echoing in my ears. After Christmas, I went back for those few days and spent that quiet time, when the phones don't ring and there is not much activity going on, sorting out almost a decade's worth of accumulated stuff. I made sure that all my loose ends were tied, everything was in order in work terms, and that anyone could easily take over at the helm in my absence.

I saved any files that I didn't want to lose and copied them to my flash stick, before the delete button was pressed and all my work over the years was forever deleted from the hard drive. The one saving grace was that Leena would still be on leave and I wouldn't have to confront her knowing that I was planning to take extended sick leave. It was never really Leena's fault, merely the organisation that she represented that finally broke me.

In any office, and certainly the ones I'd been part of in the past, the time between Christmas and New Year was an easy time. It was certainly a time for colleagues to recount their stories about parties, presents, friends and family. In 722 this was not encouraged, and despite still being in the middle of the festivities, the place remained solemn and quiet. No joy was present; chocolate, biscuits and other unwanted Christmas goodies were instead shared silently by colleagues.

As I said goodnight to the skeleton crew on New Year's Eve, I genuinely thought that it was my last day. That night, Raphey had other plans for me. He told me that I had to go back into work at the start of January, otherwise I would have not been back a full year after my last sickness. With his human resources hat on he said that I had to go back for that one day to ensure that I would have my full quota of sickness cover back. Otherwise, he said, there would be "complications". He ripped up my sick note, saying that it was for my own good, and I nearly ripped his head off!

So that was it: I had to go back to work and get another sick note to replace the one he had destroyed. Leena was back that day and it was business as usual. Although I don't think I did one bit of work; I just sat and ripped off every single nail I had left. Luckily, I had one half-day of annual leave left and I asked Leena if I could take it that afternoon. The following day I had a counselling session; something that Leena had encouraged after I was unsuccessful in the interview. During these many weeks of counselling, I had been able to see rationally and came to realise that I needed to put my health first, and do something radical. After counselling, I booked an appointment with another doctor as my GP was now on holiday. I explained the situation to the GP and she had no problem re-issuing another sick note for a month. She even prescribed Valium, I was in such a state.

I walked out of the doctor's and made the phone call to Leena to say that I had been signed off sick for a month with work-related stress. I couldn't stop crying and was hardly able to string a sentence together. I apologised to her for signing off sick and leaving them in the lurch, but stressed that I was extremely worried about my health, and that this had been a decision that had not been taken lightly.

I walked home from the doctor's in floods of tears, and Tony was there for me. I took some of my prescribed Valium, as I couldn't sit still and my mind had almost reached explosion point. I was worried about the future, worried about work, worried about my health, worried that if I didn't act soon, I would try something stupid. I couldn't see any other way out, to be honest. Until I had regained enough control to make the decision to visit my GP, I thought I would never get out alive, even if I was just a shell.

I wrote the following letter of resignation pretty much straight away, but I didn't send it. I knew I could never go back. My GP couldn't believe that I had returned to this situation. I knew it would only be a matter of time before I had to face the truth, and that my employer would soon become my ex-employer.

Ironically, the NHS had made me ill.

Letter of resignation (not sent) – January 2009

Dear Leena,

It is after much thought and with much certainty that I write this formal letter of resignation to you. My contract states three months of notice to be given and therefore, I anticipate my last working day to be Friday, 3rd April 2009.

I am unable to continue to work for this organisation, after giving eight years of my heart, soul and passion working for the NHS. I have been unhappy for some time and as you know I suffered a 'breakdown' that was not recognised or addressed in any way, after being deceived and treated like a number rather than a human being with emotional needs. I think it is also important for you to know that I think Pan's style of management is questionable, and quite clearly filters down the organisation, manifesting itself in the stress levels of his management team and their ultimate treatment of their staff. I was clearly caught up in this when I was physically, mentally and emotionally unable to continue to function, without support from the organisation and my line manager.

Since you have managed me, things have got considerably better and for some time, I was able to express myself in my role creatively, and, I believe, actually make a difference in the way staff thought about the organisation and to their feeling of being valued. It has been tough trying to motivate them and convince them that their voices are being heard, because of the way the senior management team have continued to reinforce the message that individuality and the ability to feed back concerns to line managers or above is clearly discouraged.

The recent letter I received from you about it not being 'appropriate' to approach Pan directly exposes, beyond question, that his so called 'open door policy' only relates to his 'top team'. It was clearly 'appropriate' a year ago, when I was the only communications person in the organisation! Is he worried that I might actually speak the truth, and does he not want to hear this truth, which resonates in most of the staff he refuses to engage with? When was the last time he did the rounds and say "hi" to his important workforce? Does this not just show how important he thinks his workforce is? This is commented on by staff on a regular basis, very few of whom feel valued by this organisation.

It is with this in mind that I write my letter of resignation. I hope that this may have some impact on the way staff are heard in the future, and not just via the Joint Staff Consultative Committee, to which, in my opinion, Pan only pays lip service to.

This health service has made me ill and I am too battle-weary to continue to fight for the truth. I do wish you all the very best in your future careers and please heed my warning. On several occasions, I have heard Pan's voice coming from your lips. You say that you're not the bad guy in all of this, but you do represent the bad guys. Does this mean that you endorse their behaviour? You do some fantastic work and I hope you continue to do this from the heart, which will ensure it is right.

KAY ROSE-HATTRICK

Thank you for everything, I have learned a great deal from you, and hopefully you from me, but it's time to leave. My family and health are much more important than NHS Sheffield, and I choose them, not the organisation!

Yours kindly

Kay Rose-Hattrick

Internal Communications Officer – NHS Sheffield

CC:
Quentin Horrocks – Head of HR,
Pan Dora – Chief Executive,
Sue Highton – President of UNISON

I'm so glad I didn't send it!

Sickness, Drugs & Miscarriage 18

 To lose a miracle is to know that one has occurred.

– Kay Rose-Hattrick

eing off sick was horrible. My head was so screwed up with worry and anxiety and I really didn't know what my future held. I didn't trust the organisation, so I was very wary about what moves they would make. What I wanted to do was go to sleep for a very long time. The only people I spoke to for advice were my UNISON steward, Sandra, and Sue, who was by this time president of UNISON. When I was finally summoned to a meeting with Leena and an HR representative, I was still very raw. Leena admitted that she was very surprised that I had been suffering from work-related stress and wondered why I hadn't gone to her earlier. I said that she had not been around to talk to very often, and that some of the situation had been compounded by her, anyway.

At one point during the meeting she tried to blame my state of mind on Tony. I clearly pointed out that if it hadn't been for Tony providing the support I needed, I would have been signed off sick much earlier. Organisations like to point the blame away from themselves and cover their backs, making you feel incapable and solely accountable for the state of your mental health. They are the very last people to admit faults in their treatment of people and to see the consequences of those actions. The meeting ended with me agreeing to go and see occupational health. Following their assessment, another meeting would then be convened.

It took a while for my appointment to come through. The consultant I eventually saw was the doctor who had heard my story a year earlier, and who actually remembered my treatment by the organisation back then. Occupational health are there to assess whether you are fit to return to work, and if not, to work with you until they are satisfied you are ready and can agree a start-back date with your manager. The consultant wrote back to Leena saying that I was clearly not ready to return yet and that she would be in touch with me to organise another meeting at a later date. Reading between the lines, it said to leave me alone until then. That was the institution telling the institution to back off.

I didn't see or speak to anyone at work at that time, with the exception of my union reps and Sarah. I was told later by colleagues that my sickness was kept very quiet. I think people are worried about contacting you anyway, sometimes not knowing what to say, especially when it's not a physical illness. However, Sarah, the lovely Aries I had mentored many years previously, was there for me throughout my year off and was a great support. Thanks, Coxy!

On my birthday, my dad confronted me over the phone about my use of drugs. For a number of years he'd known that I smoked weed, but it was ketamine he was concerned about. He had heard from a 'reliable' source, namely my brother, that I had been using the horse tranquilliser for recreational purposes. Apparently, Theodore had called Mike to tell him, because he was worried about me. What? Theodore worried about me? Maybe he had an ulterior motive of dropping me in it with my family. But not worried. He didn't even look at me again after Tony and I had got together. I never believed that story somehow, and it hurt me not knowing what the truth really was. I was told that I would always be welcome, but Tony, whom he blamed for my drug use, was not. It had in fact been Merlin who had introduced me to the drug when I was with Theodore, and we occasionally bought some for the weekend. I was by no means addicted and actually I felt that it helped me, by transporting me far away from my head into a different zone, giving me a little peace away from the nightmare that my life had become.

According to Wikipedia:

> Ketamine has been shown to be effective in treating depression in patients with bipolar disorder who have not responded to antidepressants. In persons with major depressive disorder, it produces a rapid antidepressant effect, acting within two hours as opposed to the several weeks taken by typical antidepressants to work.
>
> Ketamine is a 'core' medicine in the World Health Organization's 'Essential Drugs List', a list of minimum medical needs for a basic healthcare system.
>
> Patients have reported vivid hallucinations, "going into other worlds" or "seeing God" while anaesthetised, and these unwanted psychological side effects have reduced the use of ketamine in human medicine.

The first time I tried ketamine, everything seemed to become clearer. I was able to see the infinite bigger picture in the messy world that I was exposed to daily. I was self-medicating to keep the 'black dog' at bay, and not go down the usual depression route of taking prescribed legal drugs, which most of my friends had used at one time or another. I never joined the club of antidepressant pill-poppers, but turned elsewhere to find the answers.

It was the perfect drug for me at the time but, like most chemicals, ketamine fucks you up in the end and can cause serious bladder problems. I have a friend who has lost the septum in his nose through consistent use. Ecstasy, another drug I had taken, ends up reducing serotonin levels and defeating the reason for the trip. The comedown always lasts longer after prolonged use, and that couple of hours feeling loved up at weekends can leave you suffering with a bad hangover for days afterwards. The first trip is always the best and you can never experience this again.

I started experimenting with drugs later than most, when I had been with Theodore, but it was Tony who got blamed. Don't I have a mind of my own? Why would I let anyone force me to do anything I didn't want to do? It would be surprising to do an honest straw poll with young people today. I'm sure you would find that most do experiment with drugs. Most people grow out of it eventually, but I think it's important to make an informed choice, and I chose to try most things once. Drugs enable you to tap into the resources of the mind, to explore other things about yourself and the world we live in. Let's face it, most of the classic songs were written while under the influence. Even the clean-cut Beatles had a substantial dabble.

Although chemical drugs can do you great harm, and I've seen it first hand, I still maintain that any non-toxic plants given to us by God, which grow naturally and abundantly on this planet, cause no harm. Anything giving us great insight, knowledge and healing should be wholly embraced. However, cannabis has been forced into a potentially harmful hybrid by keeping it underground and illegal. How can God's plants be so evil when they are proven to have such healing properties, providing natural pain relief that is especially effective for MS sufferers? Please Lord, make cannabis lawful, so that we can use it responsibly.

Did you know that not one death has been caused by cannabis use? Alcohol and tobacco kill millions of people worldwide every year, yet they are legal drugs. It doesn't make sense to me. Does it to you? But it's all about money again, and that old chestnut, suppressing the masses, as they've done for centuries with beer and tobacco. Do a bit of research yourself as to why hemp/cannabis was made illegal. It just wasn't in the best interest of those in power, and so they prevented people from using it. Seems like a pattern emerging.

At least magic mushrooms are mostly left to grow unrestricted, and were legal to buy in all the smoking joints in Amsterdam. When Theodore and I were still in the throes of love and a long-distance, courting couple, we visited this beautiful city. We had bought the mushrooms earlier in the day and consumed half when we got back to our guesthouse. Whilst their effect on me had been to make me fall into a deep slumber, Theodore had been pacing round the room having his trip alone. When I awoke he told me about his trip and, before going for our usual beer before dinner, we gobbled some more, as I felt I'd missed out.

I didn't realise that the mushrooms had taken effect until after I'd berated Theodore when he couldn't work out the euros to pay for our beer. Annoyed, I said, "Oh, for goodness sake: I'll do it." At that moment, I knew what he was talking about, because those coins were not making sense to me, either. I'd almost forgotten how to count. Either that, or numbers had finally got the better of me. I think we just left all our change and hoped for the best and then scuttled out of the bar into Dam Square, knowing that we had to get back to the hotel, which was located by the river in the red light district, pronto. Those who have visited the city know that all roads lead to Dam Square, and so we got lost several times. When we finally got back to our hotel room and sanctuary, we were in a full-blown trip.

I knew this when I asked Theodore for the time and he looked at his watch saying, honestly, "I don't know!" I got annoyed with him, thinking he was being funny. I grabbed his wrist, with his watch attached, and looked for myself. He was right: I couldn't tell the time either. The numbers on the face made no sense to me at all. I spent the next few hours crying and imploring Theodore to get me some toilet roll from the shared toilet in the hall. It kept freaking him, having to keep leaving the room. He was having a very dark time as he'd double dosed before the afternoon trip had fully worn off. I was unable to help him, knowing that, for at least the next few hours, we only had ourselves to battle; our own demons. I settled down to enjoy the ride, and cried not through sadness, but more like cleansing. When I closed my eyes, I saw a movie reel of what was happening in my head and it has had a very profound effect on me ever since, but I don't think I've ever understood its lesson completely until now.

I was in a very small room with low walls and I could only just fit into the space available. Half the space was taken up by a very dusty cabinet, which had stood forgotten for at least a hundred years. In this cabinet stood a wooden, toy-sized old man, from the Victorian era. He wore an old, well-worn jacket and I knew him to be a drunk; just like you know certain things in dreams. I'm a bit claustrophobic so I found being in that small, tight space a bit challenging, but I remember keeping myself calm and taking long, deep breaths. Like Pinocchio, the wooden man came to life and became human, while remaining as small as a doll. I watched as this old drunk did the same thing he'd done for years: get pissed, then wank himself off. He looked pathetic, as I watched him rub himself furiously, until he finally ejaculated dust. I also knew that he'd got off on me watching him masturbate, which made my skin crawl.

He was usually alone, except for the characters at the other side of this dusty, glass cabinet. He was a sorry soul with very basic human desires, stimulating his base chakra but ignoring the others; a desperate man, leading a disrespectful life.

The wooden man's neighbours were desperate in a different way, for they came from the opposite spectrum of life. They were God-fearing peg women, with pursed lipstick-painted lips, hard faces and headscarves, which dated them to the 1940s. They were on a little, open-topped wooden bus and I knew that they were going over a cliff by the angle of said toy bus, and by the tight grip they all had on the seat in front, to brace themselves for the impact. We all knew they faced a certain death. Despite this knowledge, they remained tight-faced and respectable until the end. They refused, even as they were about to enter the kingdom of heaven, to let go of their judgements and embrace love instead. The teaching of the Bible, "Love thy neighbour as thyself," was only paid lip-service to when necessary.

It is ironic that those characters, who claimed they were close to God, were facing certain death. Yet still they refused to be true to themselves, for fear of other people finding out their own imperfections. We can't expect that by saying a few Hail Marys, we can behave without integrity. But it happens all the time with the most respected church people. The truth lies behind every front door, and the neighbour sees only the show. But we have to remember that we are all human and therefore inherently imperfect. This is a good thing, because everyone always has something to learn, if only we could just learn to let go.

The old man would still go on living free for probably another hundred years until disturbed again by someone on a mushroom trip. At least he wasn't hiding behind anything, and actually being true to himself, however sad we may think his life is. For me it feels better to imagine his story and empathise with his situation, whatever that may be, without judgement, and to offer my help, similar to the good Samaritan. I'd like to think someone would do that for me if I was in a pickle, and they have. The old ladies were beyond my help, but they'd rather have died than ask for it.

Thankfully, after observing the characters in the cabinet for a while, I was able to make my escape from the claustrophobic setting through a wooden trapdoor in the ceiling, which led to the universe. I could see hundreds of stars. As I left I thought, "Gosh, aren't you aware that the universe is so very close?" As you can see, this was a very important trip for me and made a lot of things in my quest much clearer. I can now see the connection between the old ladies and my own father. Dad would never admit he was in the wrong. He refused to see the bigger picture and never tried to have any empathy with my situation. It was just wrong.

Despite my dad and brother's concern for me relating to my drug-taking, they kept their distance and I kept mine. With their concern, and subsequent distancing, they unwittingly compounded the problem, and for a while, we used ketamine more. I was in a dark place: I had just taken a blind leap into the unknown. I was angry with both my dad and brother, but it hurt Tony a lot more. I still went to visit Mum most weeks, but barely spoke to Dad.

I had already started writing this book and it originally began with the introduction below. However, I feel that it fits better here, to show you, in context, how I was feeling as I first put pen to paper. I started to write my memoirs because I had to get everything down in black and white and start afresh. I was compelled to write the truth about my life, so that my father would finally be able to understand the bigger picture and not just see the parts he wanted to see. I was much, more complex than that. But for whatever reason, the book *Becoming Me* had begun its long trek through the unknown, and I had no idea where it was going to take me.

January 2009

As I write this with my mind in tatters, I can now see that light which shines so brightly in the not too distant future; something I have not experienced for a very long time. As I write this, my husband, whom I shall describe at length later, is banging away on his guitar, disturbing my flow!

So why would you want to read an autobiography of a 38-year old woman from Sheffield? I'm a nobody, but a girl who has finally found her freedom from a system that has been programmed into me by my father ever since birth. Who has finally jumped out of that angry sea, with her flimsy surfboard, and is observing this world from the calmer waters of the shore.

Am I mad? Definitely, but I believe that I am not as mad as you lot out there, who continue to buy into a system with no credibility. A system that treats everyone like a number; when you've done your sentence you are farmed out like mining ponies, to wind down before death gets you, possibly before you find inner peace, if indeed you last that long. I was in one of the best pension schemes going, but needed that money to live now, not when I'm a worn-out shell of a human being; that's if there's anything left, anyway.

If this is starting to resonate deep within you then read on. We all have the capacity for unconditional love. We haven't got long to go, so hold on to your hats – the rollercoaster is about to depart...

I thought a little explanation was in order to get you up to speed on where I am now and how I come to write my memoirs at such a young age. I went through my initial metamorphosis when I went travelling and came back 'free' and ready to take on a 'sane' world. I would spend the next few years flapping my wings, until they were stripped of their colour. I was then kept inside a dark box, for their fear was of me escaping. Little did they know that when the box was finally opened, I would be the beautiful thing they had fallen in love with once again.

I'm always reminded of that saying: "If you love something, set it free. If it comes back to you, it's yours. If it doesn't, it never was." Or, if you prefer the possessive version: "If you love somebody, don't ever set them free in the first place." I think this was their plan.

I was finally coaxed out, terrified, scarred and broken, by a toothless fairytale Prince Charming;
the most divinely connected person I had ever met. I was so scared of what I'd become or rather what
was really the truth. I'd been programmed by everyone around me to act a certain way, do the 'right'
thing, join the system and be compliant. My father was one of my biggest programmers.

Just after my birthday, we moved out of Priory Road. Poppy had moved out some few weeks earlier and it just wasn't the same without her. We were invited up to Poppy's old flat by the new people, and sitting in her old kitchen, I remembered all those times spent in her flat. Those memories, made over the years, just melted into the past. It was time to move out.

Tony and I went to look for alternative, cheap accommodation as I was unsure whether I would still be getting a wage the next month. I decided to phone Mert, our ex-landlord, to see if he had any properties, and he did. We arranged to go and see him at the new property in Woodseats, a couple of miles away, and on seeing it, we agreed to take it on straight away. It was a pretty looking, red brick Victorian semi at the end of a quiet suburban street and was cheaper than we were paying Nazeem at Priory Road.

Mert said that he was happy for us to move in once work had been done on the fitted kitchen, which was in the process of being installed. It even had a fireplace, which we presumed still worked, as the remnants of a fire were apparent in the hearth. An open fire had always been on my wishlist for my dream home, as it took me back to my childhood. There was a decent sized garden with an apple tree at the end and the prospect of growing our own vegetables was in our mind's eye. We thought that Neneh could have the large attic room as she could spread out and entertain her friends on sleepovers and parties.

We'd heard from Poppy that Nazeem had been difficult about the bond and one or two other bits, and so we were determined that we would be in control of this situation for a change. I dutifully gave him a month's notice and I stopped my standing order before the last payment had been made. He still had my bond, which I knew he would not pay back. Thankfully, the law has now changed with regards to bonds. The landlord has to pay it into a separate account, and they are bound to pay it back at the end of the tenancy, and not keep it on some spurious charge of damage, which is usually only wear and tear anyway. I had paid him half of the next month's rent in cash and arranged to give him the rest when we exchanged keys.

With help from our friends and a borrowed van, we moved all our stuff into our new home. The final bits were taken to the new house, including Jarvis, and there was just mine and Neneh's bikes to be transported back. I had texted Nazeem that we would need a few hours longer; just enough time for me to leave a note on the fridge door and the keys with the neighbours. I did not want to be around when he read it!

The note as I remember it, as I didn't make a copy, told him a few home truths, including about his repeated bullying from the very moment we met, before he had even purchased the property and which then continued throughout my tenancy. He was to use the rest of the bond money for payment of the final month's rent and for the extra for wear and tear etc. I even left him a tumble drier. Gosh, looking back, it was more than fair, really! Neneh and I cycled to the Vine to meet Tony and our ex-landlord only called once. Tony answered and he told Nazeem not to phone again as we had nothing more to say. He never did call and I think he would have got worse if he had seen me in person; he should have been thankful for the letter. I also ensured that the flat was left immaculate.

At least I was in control this time, and I was no longer going to let this man think he called the tune. We left the keys with friends who knew him, and cycled away from a place I had called my home for over five years, and in which I had experienced great joy and great heartache. With a new home, we cleaned up our act and the ketamine stopped almost immediately, but I was still living in limbo with work and I found it quite difficult leaving the house at all. I had to force myself to take trips out, which generally meant either a coffee at Airy Fairy, a place frequented by like-minded people on a spiritual quest, or the supermarket. Tony and I were having blazing arguments, as we found it difficult to defuse the negative energy. I threatened to leave him on numerous occasions.

In late April, I found out I was pregnant. Ironically, due on Dad's birthday. I had never had a scare nor been pregnant before, but had never been on the pill, either. Ashley, my first husband, had said he wouldn't have taken the pill himself and so he didn't expect me to, either, and so I never used this as my preferred method of contraception. Nor did I like condoms, so the withdrawal technique was always used by my partners. I was aware of my thirteen moon calendar cycle and so knew when it was my most fertile time; either to avoid or take advantage of. Tony was very in sync with me and always knew exactly when I was due on.

I had thought that I just wasn't fertile, especially after Sienna's mum inferred I was "like her" during an uncomfortable period one day. "But you went on to have Sienna, Auntie Billy," I said, as she walked down to the car after taking Neneh on a long walk with the dog. "Yes, but only after a painful operation," she announced as she got into the car and drove off. I was left on the pavement with her negativity attacking my vulnerable energy field, believing that it was indeed not my destiny to be a mother; that I was not fertile.

The conception day was different from any lovemaking we had experienced before. It felt like we'd fallen into each other's bodies, not so much entwined as lovers but morphed into one, the colours being like those a darn good reiki session would produce. That day, Tony and I created something that was so pure and part of the miracle of life. We decided to name the baby either Elliott or Ellie, depending on gender, but we did think it was a boy.

Pregnancy was a completely life-changing experience. As my body started to transform physically, emotionally I was all over the place; my hormones completely unstabilised.

After about eight weeks my baby died in my belly, although I carried him for another month before his undeveloped body was expelled from my own. I knew something had happened one hot, sunny weekend as I lay at the bottom of the garden, catching some rays. I felt odd, as though I had been deserted. After that, my body seemed to change back to its normal state. I thought that it was merely the change onto my next trimester, when I had been told things would be more settled.

Being pregnant put a slightly different perspective on what the future held in terms of my career. I didn't want to go back to that place, but now maternity leave would be an option to buy me some time. Sandra, my UNISON steward, also phoned to say that the communications department was being restructured, and that my job would no longer be available upon my return anyway.

I had an appointment with the occupational health consultant, who would determine whether I was fit to return to work. She said she would advise Leena that I needed some more time off. As I left her office, I must have just started to bleed. Poppy and I met for a coffee and a chat after the appointment, and when I went to the toilet, I found blood. She took me into the Sure Start centre close by, and they said that one of the midwives would contact me shortly. I went home fearing that my baby would no longer reach full term. The midwife phoned me later and told me to go straight to my GP, which I did, with Tony by my side. As we held hands, the uncaring doctor made an emergency appointment at the hospital for a scan the following day.

The baby was too small to show on an external scan, so a probe was sent inside me and the screen showed a very small, perfectly formed baby curled up in my womb. He had been dead for some time and I knew then when it had happened. I decided to have a natural miscarriage at home as I had wanted a home birth anyway. They sent me away with a patient information leaflet and the advice in the post-scan consultation was to take painkillers if necessary. We went home and battened down the hatches, knowing that the next few days would not be pleasant.

Like births, miscarriages are all different, and mine was apparently the worst case scenario. I went through labour pains, not as intense as I now know, but still more severe than anything I had ever experienced before. I scanned the booklet for information about pain, which an Ibuprofen wouldn't touch. The advice was to phone the department but it was 'out of hours' and unfortunately for me, the phone line had not been put through to the 24-hour department. I was left to go through it on my own without the beautiful distraction of a healthy baby to look forward to.

If I had got through on the phone they would have asked me to come into hospital and would have probably given me some strong painkillers, but what I needed was information that this was normal. My waters even broke, which can apparently happen too, but I was angry that I hadn't been warned of possible miscarriage symptoms. Pre-warned, pre-armed springs to mind.

After I had had some time to get over my miscarriage, I sent a long letter to the patient information manager for the hospital trust, in which I outlined my experience and expressed my concerns. She was also a colleague, as I was the patient information lead for our NHS trust. We had spent many meetings together, always trying to encourage patients to give feedback, so I felt I owed it to her. I wrote that the patient information was not adequate and that the post-scan consultation didn't give the full facts.

Although the trust was very understanding about my situation, the only outcome of my complaint was that they merely added an extra phone line to the patient information leaflet. They still refused to give out information about the worst case scenario for women who choose to go through this painful process at home. It was clearly a 'need to know' basis, and I wasn't in the know until it was too late. Since speaking with other women who have been through very uncomfortable miscarriages, which are also much more common than you think, I have learned that my experience is more normal than I was led to believe.

The next few months were tough. I continued to receive information about baby massage, as well as my first scan reminder text, which twisted the knife further. One positive outcome was that I knew I was actually fertile after all.

Shortly afterwards, Tony and I attended a meditation workshop organised by some friends. This is where I was introduced to Archangel Michael for the first time. I have recently been told by my Jehovah's Witness friend that Archangel Michael is the resurrected Jesus. During the guided meditation, I imagined Michael not as a pure do-gooder angel, but as a rather scruffy individual who was propping up the bar with a smile and a pint. An entity you could empathise with, and not one whom you didn't feel worthy of contacting for mundane requests and protection. We were told to call on him for protection by saying three times: "Archangel Michael, oh so bright, seal me with thy tube of light." I certainly feel safer when I call him.

We went straight from the workshop to Redmires, our little camping spot out in the woods. I took some painted glass jars and incense and made a little altar for our dead baby. We both wrote down what we wanted to say to him on a piece of paper and then threw it onto the fire, crying and hugging each other as we said our goodbyes.

Tony wrote:

Even though your time was brief and you chose not to stay,
Even though you broke my heart when you went away,
Even though you taught your mum and me how to be,

I know my child that you will reside where your heart will fly free.

I will love you my child always – Daddy.

We were advised at the workshop to cut the cords and I imagined our little baby lifting higher and higher in a hot air balloon. I used my imaginary sword to cut the final cords, enabling the colourful balloon to drift off out of sight, while Elliott called out, "Let go of me mummy, I'll always be with you, but I need to go now." This was a great help for me, finally being able to let go and move forward.

A friend had also told me a story about a little girl and her mum who had experienced a miscarriage years earlier. Out of the blue, this little three year old said to her mother, "I didn't stay last time because you weren't ready for me." This gave me the strength to move forward.

Odonata, Reduncancy & the Hot Cycle

Our lives begin to end the day we become silent about things that matter.
— **Martin Luther King Jnr**

Whilst I was pregnant I had started to organise a women's event in Roy and Gwen's field in Edale. The miscarriage didn't stop me from continuing my plans. I threw myself into it even more, as I thought it may help to keep me busy after such a difficult time. I also knew I needed to spend some time in our special spot to heal. The ethos of the camp was simple: *"To have fun, respect nature and fellow goddesses at all times, be at one with yourself and nature and laugh a lot!"*

I had a committee of ladies helping me with the planning as they too were keen on organising *'An exclusively female affair'*. This is the flyer I produced for the occasion:

GODDESS OF THE RIVER
'An exclusively female affair!'
Little goddesses are very welcome

Friday 31ˢᵗ July (setup from 3pm) – Sunday 2ⁿᵈ August 2009
Edale, Derbyshire

Allow your feminine side to re-emerge in safe surroundings; forget the outside world for a day or two while you enjoy breathtaking views of the Derbyshire countryside.

Be kind to yourself
Enjoy some healing, have lots of fun
and find the goddess within you.

Find out more about yourself
Explore your Mayan, Chinese and astrological signs.
Read more in our book corner.

Have a knit and a yatter
Enjoy a game with new friends or read a book
with a cuppa and homemade cake by the fire.

Be creative
Bring your creative side. Lose your inhibitions
by having a go at alternative dance or yoga.

Get back to nature
Camp out in the beautiful Derbyshire countryside by the river Noe.
Let your little goddesses run free in a safe environment.

Explore your past
And enter into the true meaning of the harvest supper and learn about its Pagan origins
by celebrating one of the eight annual Pagan sabbats, Lammas, and share a communal
meal with cake, ales and entertainment.

Before arriving on site, I'd already had several people text to say they weren't coming, and that was about half of my committee! When I knew the support I was relying on was not going to be there I took refuge, away from the rest of the group, at the spot where Tony and I had spent our honeymoon, and slumped down in a heap by the river Noe. I felt a huge weight of responsibility and the crushing lack of support by those who had been so keen in the run-up to the event. I cried inconsolably as I spoke to God or anyone else who would listen to me, requesting a sign that I was doing the right thing and had the support, at least, from the universe. Just as I'd lost hope, a beautiful, iridescent green dragonfly landed on me and stayed for a few moments while I kept perfectly still, blessed by its presence. I took this as my sign and after that I let go, and the people who did attend were quality.

Baljit, an old and close friend from work, and her two beautiful daughters camped for the first time, as did Janet, another old work colleague. Baljit helped with the cooking as much as she could with two small girls. Neneh was a little star that weekend and was a great help to proceedings, without having to be asked. She could see that I was under a lot of pressure to make sure everyone was having a good time, was comfortable and fed.

Despite the numbers, we still managed to have a really girly time, building a blazing fire for ourselves without the men interfering, for a change! I must say, Tony was fantastic throughout. After helping put all the structures up and digging a hole for the compost loo, which Lianne helped with too, the boys and one girl headed off in the direction of the start of the Pennine Way. And the ladies were left to their own devices for the weekend. We transformed the compost loo tent into a boudoir with a few female touches and lots of candles. Baljit and Janet were dreading using the facilities, but were delighted by what they saw.

I had asked the guests to bring clothes to exchange and we even managed an impromptu fashion show. Eliza helped me put up loads of bunting round the relaxation area, with beanbags and cushions to sit on under the *gayzebo*. I had baked loads of cakes and we sat by the fire, occasionally putting on another log from our half-tonne pile to keep us warm. Baljit, a Libran and so my polar opposite, got the fire started on the first night with all her cardinal air, as she filled me in on the last eight months of work. It was one of those summer weekends that would be better placed in mid autumn. The fire was necessary to break the chill, and was not just an indulgence.

I had worked with Janet when I was at Orgreave, but she had moved trusts before the merger. Baljit had been a 'brick' at 722 when I used to escape to public health to scream about something or another. The public health department was jam-packed full of great people who all had such passion for their jobs. I worked with many of them closely over the years. They were frontline workers who made a difference to the health of the city, unlike some of the other pen-pushing departments. I was asked to do publicity on most occasions so I needed little or no excuse to visit their section and be vacant from my seat for a while. They still managed to keep smiles on their faces as the no talking rule, which permeated the rest of the floor, didn't seem to apply to this department. Public health staff were under the no-nonsense but empathic Dr W, and it showed. Baljit said morale was even rock bottom in public health now.

On the Saturday night, we held a Lammas celebration; the first harvest festival of the year. Leigha and Wendy were stars, making the marquee we'd hired from a friend cosy and snug by using all the cushions and throws I had brought to decorate. They set the altar and Eliza and I performed the Lammas ceremony together; her representing the yin and me the yang, as males were strictly forbidden on this occasion. Cakes and ale were enjoyed by all that night, and I awoke with a thick head!

Despite the inclement summer afternoon, it didn't stop some of our party from stripping off as nature intended, to cleanse themselves in the very cold water of the river

Noe. This was noted by a group of guys in the campsite opposite and, as in some primal courting ritual, they sent messages across the river to the younger ones in the party via Neneh, who acted as the go-between in exchange for sweets.

We had a tent, full of books, which was where we read one other's tarot cards on the second afternoon. One card I pulled was 'Ask for help', and everyone agreed I should do this more. I did take this on board, and at the breakdown of the event did ask a couple of people for help, but they were not forthcoming with it. So what did this tell me? Should I, shouldn't I?

By the end of the weekend I was knackered, but we'd had a fab time. Women's energy is so healing and I think we all came away rejuvenated by our time without men, putting ourselves first for a change. I will definitely put on another women's event in the future though, as we created such a healing space. Next time I'll get the money up front so I know I'm not going to be out of pocket if people don't turn up!

Shortly after the event, I attended a meeting at work to discuss my future. I had already spoken to Sandra, my union steward, about the possibility of redundancy. This meeting was convened to discuss taking that forward. In the proposed new structure, there was only one band 6 position. I made the decision not to apply for it, as I didn't want to go up again for the job I had already failed to get at interview. It was unlikely that they would consider me for the position anyway, after so many months off. I agreed to sign back to work in order to start the redundancy process. It was unlikely that another job would come up as 'suitable alternative employment' during those six months, and after that, they would have to make me redundant.

I had recently bumped into Sienna, my sister's best friend at school, and my other big sister, at the Nether Edge farmer's market when she was visiting her parents. It was great to see her again, as I'd already heard through Trace that she'd left her job at British Airways, sold her house and bought a rundown property in Portugal to set up a yoga retreat with her boyfriend, Kratos. She looked so glowing as she spoke about her new life of self-sufficiency, her many animals and her growing yoga retreat. She had been practising yoga for many years and this was her dream. It appealed to me greatly and she told me I would love it. Although Sienna is not my biological sister, we always felt like real siblings and more on the same alternative wavelength than my own flesh and blood.

She came over for dinner before she went back. She urged us to go over for a visit as soon as possible. So, in need of some time off, and to get away after the anxiety of the last few months, we booked flights to Lisbon for two weeks in late August.

Neneh went to stay with her mum in Goole. We took Jarvis to Berry Hill for Mum and Dad to look after for the time we were away. I made Dad promise to not let him out for at least a week until he had got used to his new surroundings. I left crying, as anyone would; leaving my baby with grandparents for the first time. Possibly subconsciously knowing what was to come.

We spent a night in Lisbon, then headed north on a bus to the small town of Arios, about three and a half hours away. We arrived at about 9.30pm and were greeted by Sienna and Kratos, who were obviously glad to see us, as we were the first of their friends to visit since they had set up the retreat. We drank take-out beer from the local friendly bar in the park, while acclimatising to our new surroundings and taking in the peaceful, laidback atmosphere of the place. We then got in the pickup, which took us further into the mountains, where they lived. When we arrived, the whole place was lit by candles and it looked magical, but we wouldn't see the full extent of its beauty until the following day.

Quinta Christelle is set on a mountainside overlooking a valley, and the land is made up of terraces cut into this mountainside. The breathtaking view stretches for miles, with only a few properties visible on the opposite side of the valley, their nearest neighbour being a climb up the hill away. Karin, a Kiwi who lived in France, was on the retreat the week before we arrived. Unfortunately, or fortunately for us, her trusty camping car was being repaired in the garage in town and so she was staying an extra week. It was Sienna and Kratos's week off, so we had some time to relax until the paying guests arrived. On our first day, they headed off to the vet's with their puppy for his first injections and to buy some provisions; a three-hour round trip. They were accompanied by Karin and Allouette, her brown and white terrier who she travels everywhere with.

Tony and I were left alone to take in the tranquillity of this beautiful place and let the outside world melt away. We spent the day doing some tidying and then both picked up a pad and pencil and started to draw, which was incredibly relaxing. We were starving, and so I rustled us something up using the freshly laid eggs on the counter, as the cupboards were otherwise quite bare. As it got later and later and they hadn't returned, we started to get rather worried. Kratos had said the night before that the brakes on the pickup were dodgy. As the light faded, we turned Jimmy the donkey out into his field, fed the cats and their other dog Lizzy and secured the chickens and the goats. It was 9pm before Kratos returned, followed by Sienna and Karin with the animals and the friend who had dropped them off. They had had an accident and the car was a writeoff, but thankfully all of them were fine.

Relaxing in Portugal

The next day, Sienna and Kratos went off to the mechanic's in town in their other car to sort out the pickup, and then came back and took us all down to the river. We spent the day covered in the rejuvenating mud of the river bank, which was rich in mica, drinking rosé wine and enjoying the picnic Sienna had prepared. It was great catching up with my sissy and my niece's godmother, our paths having been interlinked throughout our lives. We'd followed each other's lives closely through my sister Trace, and now it was time to really catch up properly and do some reminiscing.

It was great getting to know Karin, who was such a kind lady. She had a wonderful mother energy, both Sienna and I agreed. My diary reported, "Karin is 50 years old, 6ft 3in and gorgeous and I love her!"

The next day we did our chores; mainly helping Sienna and Karin in the kitchen. They are both great cooks, and I learned a lot about macrobiotic cookery from them. It was purely a vegetarian diet, made from locally grown produce bought in the local town. Everything they served was superb and I didn't miss meat once. They had a small vegetable patch and herb garden, which was not big enough to sustain, but they planned to extend it the following year. Tony was put in charge of Jimmy for the fortnight. He loved that donkey, despite him being as stubborn as a mule. It was always a battle to get him down to the field in the cooler evenings, to turn him out for a bit of exercise when the flies weren't continuously plaguing him. Tony resorted to riding him in the end: he was a very big donkey.

My favourite was their little black kitten, who was called Annie Hall and who had a wonky tail. Their other two cats were Arthur, a tabby, who gave cuddles like Jarvis, and Hugh, so-named because of the hue of his grey coat, and who generally kept himself to himself. She had brought them over from the UK on pet passports and they had settled in straight away, which was understandable considering their new home!

The chickens were headed up by their rooster, Stanley, who was rather vocal from five o'clock in the morning, cock-a-doodle-dooing to urge on the morning so that he and his ladies, three in total, could make a dash for the compost loo deposits. It was hilarious to watch, but made eating their eggs somewhat hard to stomach! The goats, Yin and Yang, a brother and sister team, were always getting into trouble, especially when one of them ate Kratos's newly planted trees. That day, we saw a dark side to him that we didn't like.

During the first week, Sienna and Kratos's closest neighbours up the hill invited us to dinner before the annual local village *festa*, which takes place in every village in Portugal at this time of year. Pedro and Dulce were so welcoming, and had put on an incredible Portuguese feast for us and another English couple who lived close by. Pam and Richard had originally found the properties in a search they had made of the area. They had all come out to Portugal together to work on the construction of the yoga retreat, Pam being a yoga teacher herself.

They had had a fallout, at which time plans to set up the retreat together fell apart. It was quite awkward, as Sienna and Kratos didn't engage with them at all during the meal.

Despite this, Tony, Karin and I made conversation with them, Pam's mum and sister and their charming children, who by now were both fluent in Portuguese, as they attended the local school.

After a lovely meal, we walked en masse to the village square up the hill where the festival was taking place. The PA system would have been much better placed at Wembley stadium, and blasted out Portuguese music all through the night so the whole valley could hear. By the end of the night 'the English' had been accepted and I danced with some of the locals, conversing in body language and smiles. We felt welcomed by all, especially when an old lady, the matriarch of the village, stood behind us and put a hand on our bench as if to protect us, smiling throughout the whole evening. The best bit of the night was the 'bad taste' tombola, and Sienna, Tony and I won lots of very naff ornaments donated by the locals. Kratos was rather miffed that he didn't win anything.

I really love the Portuguese people; they have a very dry sense of humour, very similar to the British as they too like to 'take the piss' out of each other. They do stand out as having a different sense of humour from many other European nations. I think a lot of nations can often take themselves far too seriously.

It was a wonderful night, but after so many cheap local beers, on our way back to our tent, Tony fell down one of the terraces, but was anaesthetised enough not to hurt himself. He had just said, "If you were a real Pagan you'd be able to feel your way in the dark!" and that was his cue to fall. Instant karma, and obviously he's never lived it down!

The paying guests arrived the following day, and they were a lovely group of people from London, Portugal and Denmark. I only just managed to get through the day with such a thick head, and so crashed early. The following day was the start of practice, and Sienna's first class. She was a fabulous teacher; attentive and helpful, and I really enjoyed it. Sienna taught dynamic yoga, while Kratos took the Astanga class in the afternoon, which was much more physical, and very exhausting if you are not used to it. I had been introduced to the sun salutations in my Penny Smith yoga video but his class was much more advanced.

I had done some yoga back in the UK when Claire, my old schoolfriend and I, had enrolled on a ten week Hatha yoga course, when I was still with Theodore. I really liked the teacher but it was the other students who had put me off in the end. Claire lasted longer than me but agreed that the other students were horrid. In such a spiritual practice of moving meditation you would have thought you'd also attract spiritual people. Wrong! In my class, it seemed as if it was all an act and that it was just the done thing to join a yoga class. You never got an acknowledgement from the person on the mat next to you, and smiling was certainly not practised. I was put off after that.

The day started with practice at 8am, and we observed morning silence until after breakfast at about 10am. Until the evening practice at 6.15pm we didn't really stop: clearing up after breakfast, a quick break and then back on with food preparation for lunch, clearing away and then an afternoon break of a couple of hours until it was time to prepare the food for the evening meal. As friends, we weren't paying but were the helpers that week. Because we were living in a tent, it was far too hot to have an afternoon siesta like everyone else did in their cool rooms, with mosquito nets to keep the darn flies at bay. The flies plagued us throughout the whole day and then the mosquitoes took over as the sun set.

Most mornings before Sienna's class, little Annie Hall, the black kitten with the wonky tail, would cause some hilarity. She would climb up the stairs, pausing for a moment whilst considering which was the most comfortable place to settle for her post-breakfast nap. We, as good students, were doing our best to clear our minds with meditation in preparation for our morning dynamic yoga class. We couldn't help but titter, disturbing our flow, as we spied her entering the yoga space, all of us wondering where she would go. She always made a beeline for one of the guests, Mark from London, who didn't so much as flicker an eyelid as Annie Hall took her place in his cosy lap. The rest of us tried to stifle laughter as Sienna ascended the stairs in time for practice, but Mark remained perfectly Zen the whole time!

Mark initially came to the retreat from his high-powered job in London, intending to stay a week, but as the stress visibly melted from his face, he decided to stay for another. He knew he needed it and it was a good call for him. One of the guest helpers in week two was Kate, who cried to Tony and I in the kitchen one day. All stress left her person, setting her free. After that, she bloomed and glowed and baked the most glorious cakes. Kate is beautiful in face and heart and has mastered all those invaluable life skills: cooking, baking, singing, painting and empathy, at the tender age of nineteen. You could hate her for being so great, but you just want to love her, she's so sweet. She has the voice of an angel, too.

As the second week progressed, every part of me started to ache. But with the continued stretching and the delicious and incredibly healthy macrobiotic cooking, I started to feel the difference after our short time there. There had been talk of us moving over permanently and helping them out on the retreat. They said they were prepared to provide us with a base and even pay us for working there. Our new future seemed mapped out and we set a goal to move over there the following year.

Whilst I was there I had a dream in which I was looking over the edge of a canyon from a cave in the mountainside. I could see the turquoise water shining in the lake below, just a dot in the distance. I was so high up. I knew if I jumped that would be it, but I knew I wasn't ready to jump yet. Tony said that it was the tarot card fool and that I needed to have confidence and complete conviction that I would be safe if I stepped off the edge. But really I should just take a deep breath and jump! A bit like a bungee jump, but without the bungee.

By the latter part of the week I had pushed my body in Astanga far too much and so Kratos finally let me off his class. One night I went straight to bed after practice, without any dinner. I thought my head was going to explode because I had pushed my poor excuse of a body to its limits. Tony gave me a full massage and some reiki and all I could see was Jesus's face smiling at me. The next day, I took some time for me, even when I knew there were vegetables to prepare, and sat on the terrace reflecting on the week. I had been through a lot lately and needed some time off in the afternoon sun to repair, as this was supposed to be a holiday too.

A week later, on our day off, Kratos took Tony and I to buy beers at Adelina's, their nearest shop, which was about 5 km away. It's like walking back into the 1950s, with limited dusty stock in the shop that time forgot, but always a fridge full of ice-cold beers. We sat on the steps, observing old ladies carrying oversized baskets on their heads, in what was otherwise a sleepy little village; a far cry away from Saturday afternoons spent in Sheffield. We knew that this was the life we wanted: a simple, uncomplicated life with no pressures, and we sat on those steps talking about the move. On our last night, which also fell on our second anniversary of being together, Sienna took us over to an abandoned property close which had incredible potential.

The property was derelict, like many in that area, from when the young people had left to go and work in the cities after the revolution in the 1970s. The old people died and the young people didn't come back. This house was no exception, and, although some furniture had been removed, clothes still hung from hangers and crockery and pans and packaging cluttered the sides in the kitchen, dating the exodus decades before. We saw an oversized wooden rosary hanging in the living room. Although the wooden floors were in a very bad state of repair, with holes appearing as decay took hold, Tony risked it to rescue the cross. We said that we would bring it back to the house the following year, cementing our plans to return.

We were sad to leave such a beautiful spot, with such healing potential, but we came back to the UK with great hopes for our future life in Portugal.

When we arrived back in the UK, we were keen to pick up Jarvis straight away. Dad informed me over the phone that Jarvis was no longer at Berry Hill; he had fled through the open conservatory door on the day after we took him. We had still been in the country but my father had decided not to let me know, even though we'd have had more chance of finding him such a short time after his escape. I knew I should never have left him there. I had entrusted my father with the most precious thing I had, and he had let me down. Two weeks down the line he was nowhere to be seen. We put up posters around the village and handed out 'Looking for Jarvis' flyers to most houses in the area and in the local pub. We even borrowed a cat trap from the Derbyshire cats' protection league. We managed to catch loads of cats, including one who was black and white, but not Jarvis. A black and white cat resembling the one in the photo had been spotted by our neighbour on a few occasions. When we rushed over there in the car, it was like watching out for Nessie, and my hopes were dashed every time.

I was devastated by my loss; Jarvis had been my companion for over five years and was my baby. Childless women of my age do tend to wash our pets with unconditional love, as you would with a child, and it's always reciprocated. He was like a living teddy bear, much warmer than Jeremy Peapod, and always up for a cuddle during my darkest moments. But I now had to be realistic about my chances of finding him and start the bereavement process. I had heard stories of cats finding their way home over huge distances and I always hoped that Jarvis would too. I only hope that he found some little old lady who took him in and loved him as much as I did, if that was possible. The one reassuring thing was that he was a fantastic hunter, having been a street cat, and the environment he had escaped to, namely the countryside, was full of delightful treats.

Whilst I was off sick I started working at Jeanette's shop, just a few days a week to give me something to do and get out of the house. The X Shop was best described as Bagpuss's shop; an old curiosity shop where you could always find what you were looking for, whether a special button for a few pence, a vintage dress or coat, a cute knitted animal or a hat or scarf made by Jeanette herself. She got me back into knitting, which I'd not done since I was a kid. We spent hours in her shop, putting the world to rights while making another bobble hat or cute animal to sell. Jeanette also provided me with lots of loving support throughout my miscarriage.

Following the success of the camp I decided to set up a women's cooperative and organised a meeting with several friends who showed an interest. To begin with, it was successful and the inaugural meeting at Jeanette's X Shop was attended by about fifteen women. We called ourselves Odonata, inspired by the dragonfly that had landed on me down by the river Noe. This was the publicity we sent out:

Odonata is an order of insects, encompassing dragonflies and damselflies. They are ancient creatures often found in fossil form. The emblem of Japan, they are said to represent playfulness and victory in war, but throughout cultures dragonflies are symbolic of renewal, positive force, hope, change and love.

Thus inspired by such an emblem, a group of women of like minds joined forces and the Odonata cooperative was formed in September 2009. Are you a damsel (fly) in distress and needing support from an exclusively female cast of fashion designers, craft workers, artists, bookkeepers, administrators, communications and PR professionals, businesswomen and performance artists? Do you have an idea for a business or event but need help to realise your dream? Well, Odonata is brimming full of women prepared to exchange their skills and offer that support. Are you an 'Odonata Babe' or are you still dreaming?

Contact Kay/Jeanette/Poppy

KAY ROSE-HATTRICK

Our first event was going to be a charity fashion show, with proceeds going to a homeless charity. We had several meetings, with genuine interest in Odonata and what it could do for us women, in so many ways, but we couldn't get the venue we'd hoped for and after that we lost momentum and so disbanded naturally.

I applied to go on a Vipassana meditation course. Friends had been on it and found great inner strength as a result. For ten days, you don't talk or communicate with anyone other than the course leaders, and spend most of the time meditating. What I needed was some time for me and my inner thoughts and reflection. This is why Buddhism has also resonated well within me. Since reading *Siddhartha*, as Nikolai and Christian had suggested in Vietnam, I had been on a quest for deeper inner understanding. Buddhism is not a religion, it's a way of life; looking deep within ourselves for the answers, not towards the heavens as other 'religions' do. To follow a Buddhist way of life, booze was strictly forbidden, and I felt unworthy of calling myself a true follower as I enjoyed a few beers.

However, I was rejected by them because of reiki. They said:

On your form you mention that you have practised an energy-based healing technique, namely reiki. Since our experience has shown us that this practice is in conflict with the technique of Vipassana, we can provisionally accept you for only one course. However, you must undertake to completely suspend the practice for the entire course period.

I responded with:

Dear registration team,

I am unable to comply with your request and I would therefore ask that I be taken off the list, but thank you for your reply. As a reiki practitioner I live my life with energy exchange and feel that if this would conflict with the Vipassana technique, it would conflict with me. I would not even be able to walk in the grounds and observe nature, as energy exchange happens with the trees and birds too, and I feel I would miss out on essential self-healing, which is what I most need at the moment. It is clear that this course is not appropriate, at present, for my own personal journey.

Kindest regards

Kay Rose-Hattrick

Tony, who was still following his Sufi way, went to visit his sheikh in North Cyprus for his week-long spiritual cleansing; something he had done a few times before. The Sufi leader in Sheffield arranges trips over there and anyone is welcome to go, the main expense being the air fare. You can apparently live very cheaply in the Dergah (sheikh's home), which is opened up for those seeking spiritual growth. They attend lots of prayers and take part in the preparing of the communal meal. As with other spiritual groups, eating together is very important. Sufism is Islamic mysticism, and although they could be described as devout Muslims, they are distinctive in nurturing theirs and others' spiritual dimension. You may have heard of the Whirling Dervishes, who turn as they dance: they are Sufis.

However, the trip had a negative effect on our relationship, as he had become totally pious on his return, expecting me to jump into line with his Sufi beliefs, as if he'd been brainwashed. We were having massive rows, which one night, culminated in me leaving him. I wrote 'The Hot Cycle' at Jeanette and her partner Craig's, who took me in for the week.

The Hot Cycle
26th November 2009

I left home with my rucksack on my back, eyes streaming, but with the knowledge that I had to go. The old adage: "If you love something, set it free" running through my mind. What lies ahead I just don't know but I couldn't, or rather wouldn't, put up with the constant verbal attacks any more. When you start to believe that you are the very worst person, without love in your heart, and a bully, and can only picture how you are going to end this wretched life, you've hit rock bottom. Something had to give and that was to free myself from the suppression once and for all, for the greater good of me and my family.

Tony let me go this time and released me into the great unknown. Since coming back from Cyprus and visiting his sheikh, he has rediscovered his calling. What I can't understand is that he seems to have less joy and is not only beating himself up for not being this pious, self disciplined disciple, but blames me for not allowing this change to permeate our lives together. I have my own path and I'm afraid I'M NOT READY TO FOLLOW HIS SUFI WAY. I don't feel I can be myself any more but am required to mould my life beliefs and practices around his. Sheikh says a woman should stay at home and look after her husband and children, which is fine. But I'm a western feminist and always have been. How can I change my deep-seated beliefs of equality?

It's been a tough journey, coupled with the loss of my child, a mental breakdown, loss of Jarvis and ultimate breakdown of family, and it has left me somewhat scarred and certainly black and blue from the turn of events. The Tony lectures haven't helped heal me, but made me feel even more unworthy of keeping this life. Neneh continues to frustrate me and it has hurt me, continually disciplining her for not listening. I've never felt cruel, but feel I need to prepare her fast for what will be. An uncertain future lies before us and we do not fit in to this 'normal' world.

I have always been judged as a mother, but as Tony says,"You'll never know what it's like to be a mother unless you are one yourself." What else do they want from me? My total submission to my role as a wife and stepmother? But what about me? Do I have a choice in all this? I'm obviously not doing it right otherwise the lectures would cease. I don't know what my future holds now. The great unknown. I'm just numb now, and need the space to clear my head without his incessant rants. I never saw this as my life. I feel as though I'm constantly knocking my head against a brick wall.

I have been given the space to be really free, to make some decisions and re-address my life. Jeanette and Craig have made this possible for me and I'll not forget their kindness. I turned up on their doorstep forlorn, lost and very upset. They took me in and looked after me in my great hour of need. As I write this, I don't know what today brings, but the space to contemplate my life and the way it has gone. I'm not a bad person, but a very scared and confused little girl, whose father has deserted her and who is completely on her own. I love Tony and Neneh, and it hurts so much not being with them, but if I go back, is that the right thing for me and them? Will it just go back to what it was like before after only a few days, or will my absence make us all realise we do need each other and have got to really work hard in cementing our foundation for the future?

Time will tell. Yesterday I was just a shell, but as the day progressed I realised how much I missed him. That rock was no longer at my side, I was estranged from my protector and it was all just down to me. I'm not afraid of being alone; I'm almost grateful that I'm not negatively affecting anyone's life at the moment. A chance to start afresh with a clean slate. I can't see me not going back, but how will this all work itself out?

Like a hot cycle; cleansing the impurities and getting rid of the ingrained stains of the past two years. I always knew that we would have to part for this process to take place, for us to truly realise our part together in this play called life. This is only one scene of one act and the outcome will only be revealed when the curtain finally drops and the audience applauds! I hope to God/Goddess/Allah that it's a happy ending and that my little life is not in vain. And that the final scene will not end on a beach in Runswick Bay, wrapped in a snuggly comfort blanket with a bottle of hard liquor and several packets of extra power pain relief by my side.

Surely the audience would demand to be uplifted, and walk out of the auditorium with hope for the future of the characters, and with joy in their hearts for a better life themselves, with all the hope that brings?

I went back after about a week, fully charged and ready to face the challenges of life head on, and we were able to move forward. I had missed Tony and he me, but it could also have been that I was sharing the settee (my bed) with three dogs!

Just before Christmas, Sam from human resources called me about a temporary communications job for Sheffield PCT, a separate organisation from Pan's. They didn't have any money to pay for another communications person, but I was surplus to requirements at Darnall and paid help until I was made redundant. I sent this email to Leena, my boss, shortly after finding out I was to return. We had recently got a cat for Mum and Amy, my niece, as their last one had died. We had kept her brother, Oscar, a black tom, to fill the hole that Jarvis had left in our family, not that we could ever replace him.

7ᵗʰ December 2009

Dear Leena

I'm fine thanks, taken up knitting big time now and have knitted three hats in the space of two days! It's quite addictive. I am helping out in a friend's craft shop to get me out and prep'd up to an imminent return, as well as learning new skills, namely knitting and crafts, which have been incredibly therapeutic.

I'm also writing my memoirs, which keeps my writing skills sharp and is a great way of letting go of the stuff that doesn't serve me any more. I do miss you all and wish you and the team a very happy Christmas and for you, a very happy birthday too.

We also have a new kitten, called Oscar, who has so much life and makes knitting very difficult when he is 'on one'. Thankfully, he tires himself out rather quickly and knitting can commence again!

It would be good to meet up; I miss you very much and have learned so much from you, and I'll always thank you for saving me from that woman. I have had so much time to reflect on the past year and I'm so much further on my journey now. I was a broken woman and it's taken me a year to heal and re-programme. I want to finish the memoirs by March – they're called Becoming Me.

Take good care of you, and Leena, thanks for being the best manager I've ever had. I mean that, mate.

Love and light
Kay x x x

Tony, Neneh and I had a great Christmas; just the three of us as, as once more, we were not invited to my parents' again for Christmas Day. I started work in the new year. For the next three months, I joined the ranks of working, 'professional' women again, with a bright light at the end of the tunnel this time.

KAY ROSE-HATTRICK

ℜhs – Hillsborough & Turning 40

The first forty years of life give us the text:
The next thirty supply the commentary.
– Arthur Schopenhauer

After a whole year of finding myself again I had to forfeit my 'freedom' to go back to the NHS. This time, however, I was assigned to Tara, who was PR and marketing manager for provider services, based at the Hillsborough Barracks. This was a job I had thought about going for myself, but I'd decided against it considering my appalling track record when it came to interviews. Since I'd been away, the two organisations (the commissioners: NHS Sheffield, and provider services: Sheffield PCT, had split to arm's length status, meaning there was an even weaker connection between them than there had been before. People working for Sheffield PCT were generally happier than those from the 'dark side', as NHS Sheffield had been termed. And a happy workforce is a more productive workforce. It's simple psychology!

I was met at reception by Deborah, someone I had known for some time, who escorted me gently and kindly to where I was to spend the next three months, as I was understandably nervous. She introduced me to the people in the office, and everyone was overwhelmingly welcoming, especially Emma, who would take me under her wing and pick me up when I was down in the months to come. I knew Emma, but not very well; only enough to say "hi" to and pass the time of day with. During my first week back, the snow fell heavily and I gave her a lift back to her house several times. It was then that we bonded and as she opened up, so did I.

I had been off for a whole year, and the usual policy is to gently reintroduce a person back into work. Even after just three months, Celeste had insisted I start with two days the first week, then three etc. It was not until week four that I had hit the full five. It's a complete shock otherwise, especially as I'd been off with stress. Tara had told human resources that she needed me there full time, as she was going off on holiday the following week. She insisted that I had to be fully up to speed by then. I was streaming with a cold on the first day back and she grudgingly let me go home about half an hour early. The following day, the heavy snowfall intervened. Although I'd slid over a few roundabouts already that morning, trying the ridiculous, I eventually phoned in, admitting defeat. I don't think Tara was terribly chuffed, but said I could take it as holiday. Tony and Neneh spent the day making an igloo, while I took down the Christmas tree and nursed my cold with hot Ribenas. Thankfully, I had accrued a lot of holidays while I'd been off and they let me take them. So I tried to do some shorter weeks during those three months.

Tara worked so differently from me; she was another Virgo, like Celeste. She was new to the NHS and had a much more arm's length approach than I did. I knew pretty much everyone, and a hands-on approach was definitely my style. I was tasked with developing an intranet (internal website) for the trust, which was to be separate from the NHS Sheffield site, which was currently being managed by Alice, my old work buddy. It was great working with her again. Our skills complemented each other's perfectly, and we got things done. She was glad I had been given the task of separating the two, as it meant that her job of updating the Sheffield PCT site would finally be handed over, relieving her already heavy workload. Or so we thought.

As in true Aries fashion, I jumped headlong into it with lots of enthusiasm. I contacted all my old colleagues and discussed new intranet plans with them, while catching up on a year of news. Everyone was genuinely pleased to see me back, and let me know often. No one had been told what had happened to me. One day I was there, and the next I was not. Even my 'out of office' reply was still on my email a year later, covering up the real reason why I had not been at my desk. It seemed that I was not alone with my work-related stress, and many other colleagues had felt the pressure too, succumbing to a period of sickness during my absence. A few had also escaped from 722, which was still rigorously controlled by Pan et al.

Simon was at the helm of our ship and he had a completely different management technique. He washed his pots in the kitchen, chatting as he did so, and was genuinely concerned for the welfare of his staff. He would do the rounds and just pop in to see how we were all getting on. This, of course, was a breath of fresh air and a complete contrast to what I had been used to at 722. Even some of the directors there referred to it as the 'dark side' too. Going to West Court was like going home to that beautiful, but dying NHS family, long since disbanded in Darnall.

It's my second week back and still here to tell the tale, not run screaming from the building, with
bulging eyes and heart madly pumping to excess. In fact, it's been fun really, and everyone has
been especially nice and welcoming. It's a far cry from 722, that's for sure; like the old days when
the NHS was a family and you were looked after by uncles and aunts, sisters and brothers when
you needed some TLC. Simon, the MD, came in first thing Monday, personally wishing everyone a
happy new year. I wonder how different it is for those poor buggers still working in commissioning?

My office was great, and we had such a laugh, especially when Tara was out of the office, as she didn't like distractions. Tara was a nice girl and we had a laugh, but her aloof attitude had not won her many friends along the way. I didn't always agree with what she said and we did clash at times. She was, however, really encouraging about our move to Portugal. She instilled confidence in me, realising that we were doing the right thing, and actually jumping, as my dream had suggested. I was a good help to her, and eased her already hectic brief, which she had to cover singlehandedly with no one to delegate to. I also provided a much-needed sounding board to bounce ideas off.

As the weeks progressed, so did the intranet site, although there were times when I was up against many barriers. It was to be an interactive site with regular features, which I had not burdened Tara with, but I'd assigned willing volunteers to do the monthly updates instead. Our features included a slot from Kevin from our office. He was in charge of the 'What's on?' weekly section and was going to do a film review every month. He loved it, and was given the OK by his manager, hoping it would give a bit of light relief after a heavy working week. There would be 'stop press' news, including changes to the structure of the organisation, something that was in the forefront of everyone's mind. No longer having to wait for the dull *Team Brief* for information, which was often hugely out of date, and which I seemed to have inherited again!

Together, Alice and I had created pages for every service and department in the PCT, and I encouraged staff to populate them. They were to be used exclusively by staff, but some departments were more eager to provide the information I needed than others were. The new intranet site was especially welcomed by the tuberculosis team, who for some time had been asking for a page that they could update regularly about the illness and to direct the referral process. Other departments were also supportive of the change, as there was very little cross-department information available.

Finally, between us and with the help of the staff, we developed a site that wasn't just modern and interactive but fun and very inclusive. Alice made it look fantastic and we had insisted on photos from everyone, which gave it a very friendly feel. Despite this, I felt my creativity being sucked out of me, as Tara's attitude to staff continued to be a concern.

The girls in the office also got me on Facebook for the first time. For a long time I had felt like a 'Facebook widow', as Tony had been part of the club. Neneh then set me up with a profile page and I was off; usually spending an hour at night trying to work out how to use it, initially communicating with the people I worked with. I gradually increased my friends list, and through my old school friend Zoë, who posted a primary class photo, I was able to engage with friends whom I had not seen since I was sixteen. Facebook is an incredible tool with which to rekindle old friendships, and I was hooked, like most new recruits to Mark Zuckerberg's well-connected social network.

It was when I was spending more time on Facebook than talking to my family that I realised this was more addictive than I had anticipated. I saw that hours and hours of people's time was spent posting the ridiculous, like "I'm off for a hot chocolate – then bed," which just wasn't interesting. What excited me about the concept was sharing information that was of course not picked up by the mainstream media, about injustice and freedom issues, posted by my more radical friends. It's so easy now to share anything with anyone. Facebook is a tool for circulating information widely to the masses. Conversely, many people who have joined up have subsequently signed their information away. Did I hear that Mark had just celebrated his billionth Facebooker recently? The CIA must be chuffed with him, as Facebook is famously used by them to spy on people. More access to people's accounts means more of the population of the world is open to Big Brother's all-seeing eye.

I am very careful when I put anything live as I've read that posts have caused offence, arguments and even deaths in the past. Social networking has become so very important in the world of communication these days, and is extremely necessary in the attempt to do the unthinkable: self-publish!

In early March, Thomas (RIP) died. Tam, as he was known to his friends, was a regular at the Vine. He was a tall, dark and very handsome Scot with the most piercing blue eyes and soft lilting voice. It's no wonder that most girls fell for his charms; he'd had so much practice over the years and, according to his cousin at his funeral, he'd always been a ladies' man. He had flirted with me heavily when I was single and I had let down my guard, only to be rejected. He knew what he was doing and he knew he could get any woman he wanted with his charm, and then play with her mind for fun, it seemed.

The last time I saw him well, I was in a steady relationship with Tony and had reproached him for his behaviour the year before. I had been vulnerable and he knew it. I'd had a proper go at him, and afterwards we both kept our distance. I first learned he'd got lung cancer when I was pregnant. Tam was concerned for the foetus, with so much radiation around after his treatment, and so he wouldn't let me go near him, so Tony visited alone. The next time I saw him, a shadow of his former self, was at a mutual friend's funeral. Ralph Harrison (RIP) was found in his flat one day by his parents. He'd had a fall, but it was not clear how he actually died. I liked Ralph; a very talented man with so many dreams for his life left unfinished by his prolonged depression and untimely end. He'd always turn up at my parties drunk, not always invited. It wasn't really the same without Ralph ranting on about something.

Tam had lost so much weight and was more gentle and humble than he'd ever been. He had known he was dying and was reflecting on his life with a great deal of urgency, not really knowing how much longer he had left. We had spoken quietly in the waiting room, as it was too cold outside for his now vulnerable body to endure. I had shared his cup of coffee from the machine as we waited for Ralph's body to arrive. Death puts everything into perspective and it was even more evident with the dying man in front of me. We hugged each other and all previous anguish was forgotten. I knew his funeral would be the next one I attended, and sure enough, not long after, Tam passed on.

Tam was buried in the middle of City Road cemetery and the service, held in the beautifully carved church, was led by a gorgeous female (she glowed) vicar from County Kerry, Ireland, whose accent calmed and healed too.

She'd never met Tam, but through his aunts and cousin who had come from Scotland to arrange the funeral, she had made it her business to find out about him to a point that you believed she had actually met him. During the service, Tam was talking to her from beyond our world, which she jokingly made reference to throughout! Yes, she was a Christian, but she was a true Pagan, reiki master and energy healer, oozing goodness and unconditional love. She said that death does not unravel the ties you had with that person; on the contrary, the times you spent with that person made you what you are, and so will continue to blossom.

I believe death is not the end; it merely carries you to another dimension. Depending on whether you have learned your lessons or not, you will either be warranted a place back on this planet or enlightenment will take you to a higher dimension. Well, Ralph had definitely waited until Tam was taken to accompany him on the other side. They both caused havoc until after Tam's funeral, generally with my radio and the poignant songs they played! Tam's wake took place in the Vine, where he had spent much of his time. His friends were there in full force and he was remembered with much love and affection that day.

At work, Emma kept me sane. Throughout the day she drank copious amounts of orange pop and artificially sweetened fizzy diet drinks, laden with aspartame. Knowing the damaging effects of this substance I alerted her to how bad it was.

Aspartame accounts for 75% of side effects complaints reported to the US Food and Drug Administration (FDA). According to research, these side effects include headaches/migraines, dizziness, seizures, nausea, weight gain and depression, to name but a few. But don't take my word for it: do the research yourself! Interestingly, it is manufactured by the multinational giant Monsanto, who also produced Agent Orange.

This didn't stop her drinking the diet drinks though, as the government and food agencies continue to claim it is harmless, so we even give them to our kids.

Work continued, and I was cheered up by emails from Tony, which the girls thought were lovely too.

A poem by Tony – 8th February 2010

Dearest Kay,

I love you 'cos you're nice. I love you 'cos you're cute. I love you 'cos you're as mad as me and crazy as a fruit. I love you 'cos you're wild and free. I love you 'cos you're funny. I love you 'cos your boiled eggs are nearly always runny. I love you 'cos you're mine to love. I love you 'cos you're true. I love you 'cos you're a sexy girl and I really fancy you. I love you 'cos you're naughty. I love you 'cos you're free. But most of all I love you 'cos your heart belongs to me

Have a nice day, baby x x x

Deborah sent this poem, which was doing the rounds in the internal system before I left, and it was so true.

Life is too short to wake up with regrets.
Love the people who treat you right.
Forget about the ones who don't.
Believe everything happens for a reason.
If you get a second chance, grab it with both hands.
If it changes your life, let it.
Nobody said life would be easy.
They just promised it would be worth it.

This time back at work wasn't all love and light. There were days when, before going into West Court in the morning, I'd take a last look at the sun to warm my face and sometimes just burst into tears, reflecting back to those awful Don Valley House days. In February I wrote, "I'm not inspired any more; this place is enough to suck every bit of creativity out of you." It wasn't just me; it seemed that everyone around me was feeling it too. There were more structural changes being made and people were now in genuine fear of losing their jobs; something that had been unheard of at this scale in the NHS before. We kept ourselves going by taking it in turns to get goodies from Morrisons downstairs, and I watched my weight soar again through too much cake and a sedentary job.

It took me a while to build up the confidence to return to 722, but I did so about a month after I got back. I had been asked to attend a meeting about patient information, which had previously been within my remit. I walked into the building and I was immediately overwhelmed by people coming over and greeting me with such love, saying that they had missed me. It started with the fabulous security guards as I first entered the building. I could see the genuine joy in their eyes to see me back, before they complained about what the organisation had done now! Leena, who was chairing the meeting, and my colleague whom I had approached after my miscarriage, were both very supportive. I understood she couldn't have done any more than she did.

After the meeting, I went into the kitchen to chat to Leena and other colleagues I hadn't seen for a year. Pan was also in the staff area, and we caught each other's eyes. I held his confidently and unwaveringly without so much as a smile, with a look that I hope told him exactly what I thought about him, without any grimace. His face flickered an embarrassed smile and then he looked away. I was no longer afraid. I had come back fighting and he was no longer in control of me. Just before I left, Sam from HR said to me, "You can't change the world from inside the NHS, you know." No, but I could have a darn good go from outside it!

Plans were still well underway for our imminent move to Portugal, to escape from this unsatisfying life, and this kept the bright light on the horizon from fading. Sienna and Kratos had been over a couple of times, visiting her parents, and dinners at our house were filled with plans for our future at the retreat. We sat round a blazing fire in the garden, despite the cold night air, and talked about our move.

They encouraged us to train in massage so that we could earn some extra money from their guests and provide a more holistic healing experience. Tony told them that he would make sure that we got over there, even if he had to "rob a bank!" A turn of phrase, and of course not meant literally, but remember it for later. They even bought a beautiful, hand-painted table from a charity shop close by, asking us to keep it for them until we could bring it over to Portugal when we came. They said it would look great on their terrace.

My intranet project was coming to an end, and Alice and I were ready to press that live button at any time, just as soon as we got that nod from above, ensuring that our work had not been in vain. What we didn't know then was that they really had no intention to make it live at all; it was just a tick-box exercise to fall in line with another government directive to improve communications in the split organisations. When I first heard that the PCT was bidding to provide the healthcare for a prison outside Sheffield, I was appalled. This seemed ridiculous to me, but that was the way things had become in this new competitive market.

The PCT had already been required to submit formal bids to continue running their own services in Sheffield, and thankfully, had been successful on most (but not all) occasions. Each bid brought great expense to the PCT, along with the worry that failure to win could potentially mean job losses and disruption to the service. The plans to abolish PCTs altogether, which have now come to light, must have been discussed at top level at that time, and would have had a direct influence over this. It was no longer privatisation by stealth: it was now publicly, and blatantly, entering through the front door.

The fact that the new intranet was the perfect communication tool to inform staff of these changes was obviously ignored, and I'm told it never went live. But I suppose you can't unite and fight if left in ignorance. It had kept me occupied for three months, while I made false promises to staff that they were important and were being valued. But there was nothing more I could do.

I arranged my leaving do for the 19th March and would be leaving the NHS altogether on 24th March, the day before my 40th birthday. It seemed that there was no problem with my redundancy and that I was finally going to escape, despite three months of nagging worry.

I had my leaving do at Trippets wine bar in Sheffield. As the hostess, I had to be there first to greet the early bird guests. A work colleague dropped me off in town after work and, as I walked to the entrance of the pub, I saw an older guy having a smoke while talking on his mobile phone. My thoughts were, "At least it's open," and as I moved towards him he greeted me in a long-lost friend kind of way. On reflection, his line, "Don't I know you?" may have been his attempt at chatting me up. He did indeed whisk me off to a bar stool, surrounded by his friends, who were all fifty plus, and a glass of dry, white wine was placed next to me. He continued to look after me and buy more glasses of wine the entire time I was in his company, and beyond. It became clear that his intention was not to 'chat me up', but to engage with me as an equal.

His friends were also very inclusive. As it was my leaving do and I was coming up to my 40th, the conversation got on to age and then work. My host was in his 60s; he was still an attractive man and certainly didn't act the way that people in their 60s generally act. I guess if we agree that age is just a number, then we should all behave the same way as we did when we first found our true selves, before we were re-programmed by society and our peers to act a certain way so as to fit in.

We also started chatting about work, and one of the party told me about his employer, BT. He said that BT had such a high suicide rate the year before, 2009 (12, the average being four or five), that they had to start a new employee relations programme. This was to counteract the one that had tried to performance manage employees out of their jobs in order to cut the high headcount, and thus reduce their higher suicide rate! I had been performance managed out of my own job for being trouble, and like some of BT's employees, suicide had crossed my own mind.

Kerry and Alice were the first to arrive and JB, the gentleman, brought over drinks for them too. He then wished us a lovely evening and, as I was no longer alone, he left stage right. We all agreed that there were not many JBs left in this world and that he was one of those earth angels put there to protect where necessary. After that, a steady stream of friends and work colleagues started to arrive and I was caught up in a warm feeling of being loved. Some people who said they would come didn't, and some people who I didn't expect to see did. The maudlin feelings came later, soaked in alcohol, and my letting go of the organisation only came completely some time later.

It was a really good night, and a great sendoff, but the problem was that I felt that I couldn't go back for my final three days after that. On the Saturday morning I made the decision that I had severed the ties, and that going back would not be beneficial to my headspace. I'd done most of what I had set out to do. Why should I give that final push of energy to an organisation that didn't listen anyway, and which certainly didn't value my skills? I guess a lot had to do with my boss of three months, who was not a people person, and who didn't want to invest any energy into the workforce or make them feel valued.

My whole energy changed in making that decision, and for a while I was light again. I spoke to several friends about foregoing the three days of my contract I had to work by self-certifying. Something stopped me though. By Sunday teatime, I was in a real state again and slipped down the stairs, causing the biggest bruise known to mankind. Maybe it was a sign, or just that I hadn't been really careful enough descending the staircase?

If I had spoken with Emma that day I wouldn't have gone back; I would have just run scared again from a system that was clearly no good for me, as I think she would have agreed I had nothing to prove. On Sunday evening, I made the decision to go back and see it through for my greater good, and to show that they had indeed not won. I wanted to go out with my head held high and a smile that beamed from ear to ear. I also remembered something that one of the lovely HR managers had said to me in my exit interview: "Kay, you can sign off sick, but they will have won." After making this decision, my mood turned back into deep anxiety, as they would control me for longer. I also thought that I would have to say something to my boss, as I really didn't like her 'let them eat cake!' attitude to internal communications. I must say, human resources were fantastic throughout, and the director, Quentin Horrocks, was always approachable for a moan about work issues.

For the next couple of days, I tidied up all loose ends, finished what I could and handed over future work and development ideas to others, so that they didn't continuously fill my head. I said goodbye to the people who had looked after me and wrote a card to all my lovely office colleagues who had made my last few months working for the NHS palatable and a lot of fun. My last day was good, and I didn't cry once. Considering I had cried a lot during those three months, I knew I was now free and tears had no place in my new world.

Kevin from the office dropped me off home that night, with all my pressies and cards and memories and I knew I had to let go properly now. It took me a few days to stop thinking about work and how we could improve communications, reminding myself that it was no longer my problem as I was surplus to requirements and redundant.

The day of my 40th dawned, and it was the best birthday of my life so far. Tony gave me a beautiful diamond ring and Neneh gave me some angel earrings. The diamond was because I had told him years earlier that Holly Golightly had said in *Breakfast at Tiffany's*, one of my favourite films of all time, that diamonds before one was forty were a little tacky! He'd held me to this and although it was very small, the cleaver casting made it look bigger and made it shunkle (Sheffield term for sparkle) more!

The Vine was my chosen venue for the party, because of its central location. After shopping and waiting for the meat to cook for the sandwiches, we rushed down there to set the place up for a party. One friend, Simon, who hadn't got enough money to buy me anything, gave me the present of his time and helped me make sandwiches. Perfect timing, as the first guests began to arrive, including my ex-work colleagues from the Orgreave days, Brenda and Julie. Julie was also off sick from the NHS with work-related stress. She didn't fit in either, and her work life was made very difficult by her manager. Her laugh had always been infectious. It was like the Mexican wave across the office, and we'd all join in, unsure why was she was laughing anyway.

The manager she worked for as a PA didn't even have the guts to face her in person to address some of the issues she had with her. The deed was done by the office manager but the long list for her persecution was totally unfounded. Enough was enough for poor Julie and she couldn't go on. She went on to hug trees and get the twinkle back in her eyes at last. She realised she was too good for that place after scrabbling back from a very dark hole, as I had.

It was a lovely night; again people turned up who I wasn't expecting, and some people, who I was expecting, didn't. It didn't matter, as it was the people who did make the effort that counted. Tony entertained us with his guitar, accompanied by his musician friends John and Matt, and the buffet went down well. My 40th birthday had passed without me shedding any tears.

The adventure was about to start and my life was about to begin again. Well, they do say that life begins at 40!

KAY ROSE-HATTRICK

Massage & Police Brutality 21

Innocence is no longer valued by the authorities.
It is their behaviour that is now criminal.
– Tony Rose-Hattrick

y head was all over the place due to our imminent move and leaving work. Although Neneh is not my biological child, I still put her first from day one, and sometimes I felt very tied down with the responsibility; certainly more so than her own mother did at that time. I guess I sort of resented it sometimes because she wasn't my own, and it was a constant battle between 'nurture' and 'nature', and I had no way of influencing the latter. I had read the Philip Larkin poem 'Dockery and Son' for 'A' level, and his words have continued to ring in my ears over the years. In Larkin's mind, children were not an addition, but a dilution, and this is how I was feeling at the time.

She pulled the wool over my eyes and behaved like butter wouldn't melt until one day when her friends were round for a sleepover. At Neneh's request, I'd bought them appropriate food for the occasion, namely pizzas and crap! One of her friends, whom I'd never met before, announced, "Neneh said we could get anything out of you." I turned and looked straight at Neneh, who was bright red; her eyes betrayed everything. She knew she'd been caught, and the game with me was finally over. I had been giving her the benefit of the doubt for months now, even though I knew deep down that she was blatantly lying about stuff. Her chink that day showed me how manipulative she could really be and that our relationship of trust was well and truly over. My mum never allowed me to have many of my friends stay over when I had been a kid, because she claimed it would have been too much work. I had missed out on fabulous midnight feasts, an important part of a child's development, and I didn't want Neneh to as well, despite the extra clearing up afterwards!

During the Easter holidays, Neneh went to spend two weeks with her mum in Goole and I was happy to have the space. Like any child, she demanded attention, but I'm told she did more than most. She talked continuously, greedily filling any silent gaps, just like both her parents do! She was thirteen, and since moving from junior school things had deteriorated pretty rapidly in terms of attitude. I know they all go through it, turning into Kevin from *The Harry Enfield Show* over night. They are no longer the big fish in a small pond, but a very small fish in a huge lake, and have to adapt rapidly to their new surroundings. This is when they become cocky and think they know best, until you are hitting your head against the proverbial brick wall. Then you find things like, "We're only doing it for your best," or "One day, you'll know for yourself" echoing from your voicebox at their pure defiance, just as it had from your parents' voiceboxes. The difference was that I had only brought her up for three years; before then I didn't even know her, and she shared none of my DNA.

When we dropped Neneh off at the train station I was relieved that I had some time with no one to think about but myself; my mind, tired of processing my recent redundancy, just wanted stillness. We went for a fish supper, then a pint at the Sheaf View before going over to Martin and Anita's, our good friends who were witnesses at our handfasting, for a visit. After food, that pint, then Anita's hug, I knew I was going to be OK and my head wasn't going to explode!

Later that week, we also went camping to our special place in the woods, where Elliott's memorial still stood. We both needed the solitude desperately; to be in an open space with only nature as our neighbour. Dead trees provided us with more than enough firewood to keep us warm and cook our food. The trees brought to life once again by generating energy for the fire. I love that symbiosis when working with nature.

A great love of mine is cooking, and especially on an open fire, when I can be quite experimental and use wild food wherever possible. Nettle stew/soup is quite delicious; a bit like spinach, and once it's been cooked it doesn't sting any more. Jack by the hedge, found abundantly in the hedgerows, is also really tasty, especially with the addition of wild garlic. Next time you're out camping in the countryside, try them as an alternative to your usual shop-bought veg. Out in the open I become less anxious about hygiene and don't really care if some ash, grass or dirt drops into my stew! I am totally liberated when I'm out with nature, because I feel alive. I'm not meant to be in suburbia, where everyone lives on top of each other, although in this ever-more isolating society, we do manage to keep ourselves to ourselves.

We both had a very relaxing time and packed up camp after a couple of days to head back to Sheffield via the Sheaf View pub for a pint and a gentle re-entry back to city life. They say that Sheffield was built on seven hills, like Rome, and many other places it seems, although it is not as famous or romantic. But what constitutes a hill, and when can a gentle incline be defined as one? That said, Sheffield is indeed very hilly and over half of the city's entire area is green space. Its two million trees give it a higher ratio of trees to people than in any other European city.

After our camping trip, we were able to see things more clearly again. Certainly after such a hectic and emotional couple of weeks, it had been good to feel safe in the woods, away from society and what that represents. Neneh's stay with her mum also gave Tony and me some space to re-group and to work out what we wanted to achieve.

During this time, we enrolled on massage courses so that we had a qualification to take with us to Portugal. I went to Covent Garden to do an Indian head massage course: that is something I'd always wanted to do. I guess it's because personally, I absolutely love Indian head massage and it relaxes me in an instant. I can also use my reiki as part of the treatment.

Tony went to St John's Wood to do full-body, seated massage. When we met up afterwards, at the statue of Eros in Piccadilly Circus, he was buzzing. He was giddy about being in London again. He had lived there for about five years, and we had been there at a similar time. He'd also had a lot of female attention during the day, being the only man on the course, and was on a high! My course tutor had warned us to be careful about drinking after our day of detox. There had been lots of massage, as we had all practised our newly acquired skills on one other during the day. Despite this, we went for a few drinks and a meal before getting back on the train to Sheffield.

As we got off the train, we had a mild quarrel, and I walked ahead, not wanting to talk to Tony because he was being annoying! What happened next is told in the following witness statement I sent to South Yorkshire Police.

> On Saturday 10th April, at approximately 11.11pm, Tony and I were walking from the train station. We had had a mild altercation and he was shouting at me to hold on. At this point, we saw a police car, which had pulled up at the lights by the Leadmill nightclub. I said to Tony, "Now the police are looking!" and so Tony put his thumb up to them to show them that everything was OK and we were just having a mild argument and that there was no need for their involvement. At that moment, the police car pulled over and I thought, "Well, you can deal with this one now, as you were the one who got them involved." So I stood back to let him sort it out and explain that everything was cool. I was clearly not distressed; just a bit annoyed with the whole thing.
>
> The next thing I saw was Tony being pulled to the floor, calling out "I've not done anything wrong; please... you're hurting me!" as they stuck their handcuffs on. I was distracted by a female officer who told me her name was Lilly, and who asked me about his sobriety. I said that he was a

bit giddy but that he hadn't had lots to drink. We had both just been on massage courses that day in London, and were in very positive moods. However, the amount of massage we had received had ensured that the bottle of wine we had shared over a meal before getting on the train had affected Tony more than it normally would have done, especially as he wasn't used to drinking.

At this point, I looked over to where they now had Tony face down on the floor, with a taser gun pushed into his neck. One of the officers was saying that if Tony didn't shut up and stop protesting his innocence, he would zap him with 40,000 volts. I was shocked, thinking I had missed something, because I couldn't actually believe this was happening. I didn't intervene, as I was almost transfixed to the spot through disbelief. At this moment, our friends, who just happened to be walking past, came over and asked what was happening, as they could see Tony on the floor surrounded by police officers. I said that I was unsure because it had happened so suddenly from nothing. At that point, a riot van arrived on the scene and I knew then that this was unbelievably excessive for such a minor incident that should have been sorted by simple two-way communication.

Tony was then forcibly led into the back of the riot van and went off in front of my eyes; it was quite surreal. I was left on the side of the road, thankfully with my friends, to try and process what had just taken place.

I have been working in communications for the NHS in Sheffield for nearly a decade now and therefore know about the necessity for open channels of communication, and to be listened to in the first instance so that the other party can make a judgement based on facts. The breakdown in communication was apparent in the situation with Tony. He was a little bit tipsy, but clearly not violent and certainly, with a little bit of understanding by the officers involved, this incident could have so easily been resolved.

Our treatment by the police that night left me in shock, and unable to really comprehend what had happened, until talking it over with Tony when he arrived back from the police station at about 2.30am. The duty officer had called me earlier, saying that he would be home in four or five hours, but he arrived back within only about an hour and a half of the phone call.

Tony was visibly in shock when he returned and began to tell me what had happened after leaving me. Tony had not raised his voice, except to plead his innocence, and as all this happened in such a short space of time (literally minutes) there had been no opportunity for the police officer to listen to what Tony had to say and just have a chat. Tony was calm, but obviously the police officers were not, as they started to intimidate him and antagonise him, rather than send us on our way home with an "as long as everything's OK with you."

As more officers arrived on the scene, including the riot van with hordes of police officers in the back, the newcomers must have assessed the situation as being much more serious than it actually was and the energy between officers was understandably more charged. I understand that there had been some football violence earlier and that the police response units had been on high alert. But it was clear that we were no football hooligans, as I had stressed to Lilly and another officer who had threatened to administer the taser. We had just been on massage courses and were on our way home.

When I asked one of the officers whether he had used the taser he said no, he had only wanted to frighten him. But why, when Tony was causing no threat to me or anyone else around? The only people around other than the many police officers were our friends. If they'd gone a few yards down the street they would have come across many people, much more inebriated than Tony, coming out of the pubs. But why were they not targeted, but my partner, who only wanted to alert the police to the fact that we were OK, was?

I feel totally let down by the police force as a result of this incident and, although I have had dealings with both good and bad police officers in the past, I am certain that the behaviour I witnessed that night should not be tolerated. And certainly not be allowed to continue on our Sheffield streets. I was under the impression that the police are there to protect and serve, not to antagonise and bully; it is certainly not how peace officers would behave.

It feels very much like targeting individuals. If they do stick up for their rights, then they are abused. It seems to me just another way of generating income for the state by targeting innocent citizens. How can these men be judge and jury and issue an £80 penalty notice for a drunk and disorderly charge, when that person is innocent and just going about his personal business? If he was indeed so drunk, then why let him out of the cells so early?

I hope you will address the issues raised in this statement, so that these incidents will cease. In the NHS we have a very high level of client care, and as a press officer for many years now, I know only too well that such negative incidents are bad publicity for the police force itself. It is a shame that South Yorkshire Police do not seem to achieve the same high standard of customer service as other public sector organisations in the city.

I don't feel safe in this city any more. That is not as a result of crime levels, but I feel as if I am not protected by the police, and actually need protection from them now.

Tony had quite a few cuts and bruises as a result of the evening's events. He told me that when they arrived at the police station, the officers cruelly pushed him down the corridor to the charge desk so that he bounced into the walls, as he was still restrained in cuffs. When he asked them why he'd been arrested they had said, "for being an arsehole". They refused to give him a breathalyser test to prove that he was not over the limit, but the charge sergeant let him go, obviously realising that it was an unlawful arrest very soon after he arrived. He was still issued with a penalty notice for being drunk and disorderly.

This example of dysfunctional and inconsistent behaviour by the police was not the first that I had encountered.

About eighteen months earlier, I had been pulled over by two male coppers for having a broken brake light. They'd flashed their lights and made me pull over, get out of the car and sit in the back of their vehicle. They then started to flirt with me outrageously, and let me off for the brake light and for not having my driving licence on me, which was also still in my maiden name and registered at my parents' address! He had said that

that was another £30 fine, as well as the one for the brake light. I'd got out of paying either because I played the 'so sorry officer; I'm a bit silly, but you're great' card and just essentially massaged their egos. I knew it was going to work and it did. If it had been Tony or any other bloke, they would have probably taken them to task and issued fines.

You already know about the other incident, when I 'danced into the knife'.

I think the best police story I have though is when I was driving along the Parkway, a dual carriageway in and out of Sheffield. I was smoking a cigarette and looked in both mirrors to see if anyone was coming. The carriageway was completely free behind me, and as I checked in the wing mirror, that too was clear. I never usually threw my ends out of the window, but it made more sense from a safety point of view to chuck it out of the window, rather than negotiate the ashtray at speed. Lord only knows where he came from, but typically, just as I'd lobbed my tab end out of the window, a police car drew level with me, cruising at 50 mph, the driver winding down the window. I was obviously shocked, but he started berating me for my actions, and then threatened me with a fine while travelling at that speed. I shouted back, "I'll never do it again, officer!" He then sped off, and I missed my turning! It was only when I regained my composure that I realised how completely irresponsible he was. Surely pulling me over would have been the preferred and safer option?

I must stress that there are still some *peace officers* working out there, thankfully. These are often in the guise of the community bobbies, who are not considered real police officers but do the most important job of any policeman. They are employed to work closely with communities, building up trust, not just issuing penalty notices in order to generate more income. I spent some time with some police community support officers (PCSOs) when I was on my UNISON steward's course, and they all said that they were 'looked down' on by the other coppers. Their job is so important, and mirrors the old style of bobbying of times past, when they still talked to the youth as if they were human, when a clip round the earlobe was the power in force, and tasers were still only seen in science fiction films.

After the experiences I've had with the police it is my opinion that they have become real aggressors; taunting people to react to situations, as if they're on commission from the government to collect as much money from the public as possible. Fines are issued too easily by men and women who, in their black and white uniforms, can play judge and jury every day on any whim they have: if your face doesn't fit you're doomed!

As I walked away with my friends on that empty street, after all the police cars and the riot van had driven away, I kept saying repeatedly, "It's all meant to be." I knew why this had to happen to Tony and me on that day; it was to further our development on the path to the truth. I had to remember to look for the positives in everything, as what you think you do want is not necessarily what you actually need.

Something shifted between Tony and me that night and it was certainly needed. I stopped rebelling against him and rebelled instead against the persecutors; we started working in unison and not against each other. We became much closer on a physical level too. Tony also wrote a long letter of complaint to South Yorkshire Police, and I sent my witness statement.

That whole week had been a time of re-bonding. When Neneh came back on the Friday, I was in much more of a healed space and able to address the feelings I'd had before she left, and work with her in developing our relationship. On the Sunday, it was market day on Sharrow Vale Road, where Jeanette's X Shop was located. She let Neneh have a table outside her shop to sell the wares that she had been busy baking that weekend.

Market day went really well and she made over £40, which more than covered all the ingredients for the cakes she had made, and so she made quite a bit of money. I was really proud of her. Neneh's a great baker and I have always encouraged her love of baking, just as my mother had in me. Tony and I love cooking and taught her important skills, which have resulted in her being a fantastic cook from a very early age. She is now at catering college, pursuing her dream to be a chef, something which Tony and I are immensely proud of.

Jeanette was face painting that day and so had a stream of parents and their children waiting eagerly to be painted. She's very good at face painting and is great with the kids. I watched from the door of her shop, which I was minding that day, and my heart was melted by the faces of the wee ones as they were being painted.

I got so broody as I watched the children let Jeanette do whatever she wanted, their mouths dropping open as the brush gently tickled their face, and a kind of trance set in. I don't think their parents had ever seen them sit so still and be so compliant before. They all looked fabulous afterwards, and I loved the moment when Jeanette showed them their reflection and their faces lit up with glee. There was only one boy, who wanted to be a pirate, who looked really disappointed! Jeanette made quite a bit from the face painting; there had been no set price but parents were asked to throw some coins into a pot for payment. She donated all her earnings to charity, and her shop also made a nice profit.

I started practising my Indian head massages on anyone who would have one and the queue steadily formed, including my dad. I took a sneaky peek at his face when I had done his scalp and his mouth was wide open, jaw totally relaxed. Of course he said he'd never have another one, but that's what I'd come to expect of him. Mum told me every few minutes that she loved her massage, as her Alzheimer's made her forget most things straight after she had said them. The memory tablets were clearly not working.

Our move was imminent though. We still had lots of preparation to do before we could be on our way. My main priority was to find Oscar a new home before we left. My bridesmaid, Pea, had started a relationship with Lance, who also lived in Vincent Road.

They were keen to start a home together, and alone, as they were sharing the house with two other blokes. It was agreed that they should therefore move into the property we would be vacating. I was happy to let my bond carry over to them, so they didn't have the initial expense of that to find, as well as the first month's rent. I said that they could pay off the £500 over time and that there was "no real rush at the moment." The main thing was that Oscar would be looked after by people who would love him and cause him minimal disruption.

We had been in regular contact with Sienna and Kratos, and she had encouraged us to go out in June, so as to be able to help them for the whole season. But we were realistic and knew that this break from our old lives would take longer than first expected. The postman had also brought my P45 and final wage slip, which containing my redundancy payment. I knew I was home and dry, and that it had gone too far for Pan, or anyone else, to jeopardise this. I sat quietly by the window overlooking the garden, with the cat curled up on the window ledge, and thought that finally, our plans could start to be realised. We now had the funds to start realising our dream. "Bye-bye Sheffield – Hello Portugal!"

Ɛpilogue:

Ƀecoming Free – The Diary of a Noebody

"Spirituality is the act of becoming more normal
and eventually disappearing completely."
– **Stuart Wilde**

'm sure everyone at some time has had to deal with utility companies; usually when you move house, but we were moving out of the 'system' completely, which seemed to complicate matters. BT had messed up and disconnected us, even though I had extended our contract. We had given up our TV and vision box nearly two months earlier and I had specifically told them that our move date had changed, so we would require internet access to be extended. "No problem, madam," I was told. Yeah, right!

I was now writing a diary that chronicles our adventure, so bear with me as I move over to the diarised style, which you'll find in book two: *Becoming Free.*

11ᵗʰ May 2010: Reconnection day, or so I thought!

They just won't let me! HELP! I can't bear it any longer! Get me outta here, NOW! Calm down, take three deep breaths and relax. It's BT again. I've just got through to a woman with the softest sounding voice I have ever heard. It was like getting through to the mother of BT, who would make everything OK. I only got to say hello to her before the line went dead! I've now got to phone back and go through it all again!

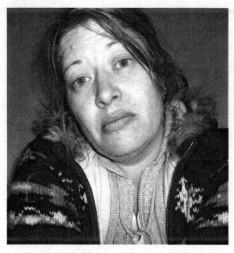
Selfie after BT

Wish me luck...

I've just been put through to an advisor in southern India, who though delightful, when recounting my frustrating story got it all wrong. I was almost in tears; well, actually, there were tears in my eyes. I said to him, "I've been working in communications and complaints in the NHS for almost a decade. If we did this to people, it would be plastered all over the papers. Get what I mean?" Not that it made one bit of difference of course, as how should he know of the NHS and its worldwide reputation!

After that, I said I really needed to speak to someone in head office in the UK and cried out to their overseas office, "I'm really sorry, but this needs to be taken further now. Can you give me the number?" I think I'm now holding for them. I had to put the phone down after 24 minutes as the darn holding music wasn't on, which was a sure sign I had been cut off again.

I phoned back on the number he had given me that was supposedly for the UK, and went through to southern India again, so once again, I had to explain, with even more frustration this time, that I wanted to be put through to a manager in the UK. Thankfully, he put me through to Nicola, who after hearing my story told me that the man in India had put me through to her even though she'd protested it was the wrong department!

Nicola listened, which is what I wanted. To know that she truly understood every word I was saying was a great relief. Everyone just wants to be listened to after all. She couldn't help me personally though, but knew someone who could, and that's all I needed to know. The light was on the horizon and I would finally speak to someone who could sort out this unholy mess once and for all. She put me on hold without the music, at my request, and then came back, thanking me for being patient and saying, "Here's the number you want." Why had it taken so long, leading to me getting worked up into such a state, just for someone just to listen and know what to do? I have just taken a self-portrait to show my acute anguish and frustration. You can literally see that the very essence of me has been sucked out of my physical being!

After this supposedly simple task, the phone has died a death. Well, it had been used continuously to make calls to BT for the past three and a half hours. But I'm all fired up now, and it's killing me! I think I should go and have a hot bath and try to figure out where this is going. It's all happening for a reason, which is certainly to write about another crumbling British institution and to illuminate the truth. It seems strange that I met that guy in the pub on my leaving do, who told me about performance management and suicide rates being linked within BT.

Right, I'm off to relax and have a bath.

23rd May 2010

Well, I've finally picked up my book again, and this time it's on my new netbook, that I've called Billy. I bought it with my redundancy money, and it's a necessary piece of kit for writing this book. The battery lasts about seven hours on a netbook, compared with less than an hour for my old trusty laptop, and so I will need it on the road, when electricity is precious. I'm just trying to get used to typing on it, and it's not that easy as the keyboard is so small. It's time to hand over the other computer to Tony as he hasn't got one. My book's now on Billy's hard drive, as well as on a memory stick for backup.

As I sit here writing this, there is a cool breeze moving through the open door and enveloping me in its welcome embrace; so much so I've moved to the step where it started its journey through the house. I can now go anywhere with my portable netbook, and the step is my preferred place to write these days, especially since the good weather arrived. It's been a scorcher this weekend, which has resulted in half the population getting sunburned, probably. I'd have done the same, but the party we went to on Saturday afternoon, Pea's 21st in fact, had only one seat in the full sun, and Tony nabbed that one!

Raphey had put on a party for Pea at his house. He pushed the boat out for her and treated her like a princess all day. He had even bought loads of fireworks for a spectacular birthday display at sundown. Raphey does love his fireworks. He's behind our move all the way, as he knows this place is suffocating me now. I just need to be free of it and lead the simple life I was meant to. Pea and Lance are really looking forward to moving as they're a couple and want to set up by themselves now.

I'd just like to get you up to speed with how *Becoming Me* is getting on. Since receiving my redundancy money for my eight years' of completed service with the NHS, I am now able to start actioning our plans. Because the amount was tax-free, it was roughly the same amount I was receiving per year in take-home pay. I was paying close to £10k in tax. It could certainly have supported a small family on benefits, but would more likely enable a hefty pay increase for our politicians, or ammunition for the war that no one wants, apart from our government.

We have to act fast as this home will be no longer ours when Pea and Lance move in. They are moving into Neneh's attic room and she will be sleeping in the spare room until we set off. Neneh seems happy enough with it and she even spoke excitedly about the move to our friend Haidee at the Peace in the Park festival. It's a new experience that will alter her life forever, and she seems willing to embrace the new changes. Her old school, Abbeydale Grange, is closing, so all her friends will be scattered across the area in the next school year. There would be disruptive change afoot for her anyway. She certainly knows her dad and I can't stay here any more.

We've been looking for a left-hand drive on the internet for a while and there weren't many, but one caught our eye, and we called to see if it was still available. Tony and I drove down to Essex last week to look at the LDV Convoy with a squat nose, and immediately saw the potential she had to provide us with a mobile home.

Inside Leeloo

She was previously used to transport tyres, so is rather grubby, but with a lick of paint, some adhesive glass I've just ordered from Betta Buys, a few throws and scatter cushions, I will make her into a home! We have decided to call her/him Leeloo, after the androgynous alien in *The Fifth Element*. Her registration number is also an anagram of GOD, a sign perhaps that we will be protected on our mission!

Thankfully, Terry from Essex drove Leeloo up to her/his new temporary home yesterday and handed over the keys. It was a poignant moment, as it was the catalyst to move our plans forward, and of course, a photo was taken. Thank goodness we didn't have to drive it from down south, as we're both a bit nervous because of her size, and the fact that the driver sits on the 'wrong' side. We will, however, be very grateful of that once on the continent, I'm sure. Terry was going to pick up another van in Leeds, so Tony dropped him off at the station. I'd actually already had a premonition about the delivery, and it fitted our plans perfectly. He wanted cash, and it was rather exciting going to the bank to watch £3,500 being counted out. We had fun with the paper, but later, when I recalled all the blood, sweat and tears I had to shed to acquire that pile, I got quite emotional.

Tony's on one now, and has just disturbed me on my step for the second time, saying that he's 'working', but what am I doing, if not working? Granted, he's working for our future, but then so am I. Writing a book, although not physically challenging, takes a lot of discipline and makes your head ache, as is the case with any muscle that hasn't been challenged for a while. I've been lacking motivation lately so I can't slack off now.

30th May 2010

We've both just had letters as a result of our complaints. Mine was from BT, eventually, and Tony's was from the inspector in charge of complaints. That makes five letters from South Yorkshire Police to one letter from BT, and I had written three letters of complaint to BT that week. Tony had written only one, so the police win hands down.

After my dissatisfaction with BT a few weeks ago it had got even more frustrating. We finally got to the bottom of the problem and realised why, after having discussed one thing with an advisor, our connection was cut off anyway. The answer was that they were using two different systems; some advisors were using the new system and some were still using the old one, and never the twain shall meet. Agggrrrhhh! Incompetent and overpaid IT consultants! The advisor I finally spoke to, after writing my third letter of complaint in a week, realised what the problem was straight away. He would reconnect me as soon as he could. Instead of a complaint letter, I wrote a letter outlining why this advisor should be nominated for a staff award. I copied it to the advisor himself, his manager, the complaints department and human resources, and congratulated BT on 'excellent' customer service for a change. Why, oh why, didn't I get him in the first place?

I had included an invoice with the complaints letters, charging BT my hourly rate based on my final salary, as I was unable to get on the internet and get on with my book, and more importantly organise the move. Finally, a letter back from their complaints department, saying:

> Blah blah blah… *sorry for the inconvenience*, blah blah blah… *sorry for the delay in writing*, blah
> blah blah… *sorry to hear that you incurred financial loss due to the problems you have experienced*
> *with your service. I can only imagine how upsetting this must have been for you and I am extremely*
> *sorry for this. Whilst I appreciate you work from home, I am unable to consider your business*

expenses as you only have a residential line with BT. If you are running any business activities from your line then your account should be registered as a business account. If you would like to change your account to a business tariff, please contact our business start-up team on...

They got out of that one pretty quickly!

Am I disappointed with my response from them? Yes, rather! I'm thinking all those hours of frustrating phone calls, having to repeat my story over and over again to faceless advisors in southern India and across the UK. Finally, after three letters, they answer with: "Sorry, but you've not got a leg to stand on, and there won't be any point in taking this further, as you've been a very naughty girl in using your line for business!" It took a lot of energy out of me so should I stop this now?

I am so tempted to write a letter to the chairman of BT, to see if that holds any weight. My old chairman would have to respond straight away, but here we'are talking about the difference between the private and public sector. Who knows, if I do get the energy from the sun banks to do something, then it will happen.

I've just done some research on the internet, as connection has finally been made again, and I've found out that the chief executive of BT, Ian Livingstone, is due to get a pay rise of over £1 million, while the workers are planning to strike for a 5% increase. The payout is based on financial targets, customer satisfaction and environmental and social factors. About 40,000 BT managers will also receive bonuses as a result of BT's improved performance last year. Well, how can that be, considering the large BT complaint forums I've checked out online, as well as from my own experience? I'd say they weren't analysing their data properly as they had three letters of complaint from me alone, and no one could say I was a satisfied customer!

Tony's letter from South Yorkshire Police was inviting him to a meeting with the inspector in charge of complaints, to talk about his concerns face to face. What a difference between the complaints procedure in the private and public sectors!

31st May 2010

Shit! What am I doing? I'm making such a life change, and I'm scared shitless! What if it goes wrong? What if we have to come back? What if...? Stop it! I have to stay positive. Everything that has happened has led to this; we can't back out now. What is the alternative? To stay here, apply for another job in the corporate world, which I wouldn't get anyway, or to follow my dream to be free? I'm not free here. It's clear from trying to get out of the 'system' that the challenges have been abundant, and I know it's not over yet. I've got to deal with banks, insurance, passports, deed polls, schools, creating a new home.

I have suffered from mild agoraphobia for over a year; not with open spaces, but when there are lots of people around. I *need* open spaces to function, but the city stifles me, and sometimes scares me, to the point of making me anxious, and I avoid this at all costs. I have learned that the only way is to confront my anxieties, and the best therapy will be to travel hundreds of miles across Europe in a van!

I feel much better than I did: fighting my agoraphobia demon with another demon. I had to go back to the NHS to show myself and the NHS that I had the fight, and that I hadn't been broken, and more importantly, to say a proper goodbye to my family that I had accumulated during my time there. But the whole experience has made me even wearier! At least I'm no longer in limbo, and I can finally move forward and really live my life for a change, and not just damn exist in this suffocating society.

I'm sick of being judged and frowned upon; mainly by my own father and brother, but also by others in society who continue to keep focusing the blame on others; distracting us from their own imperfect lives. Like the painted 1940s peg doll ladies in my mushroom trip, they look down on the way I have chosen to experience life. But I am by no means that Pinocchio tramp, with only base emotions, because I found the *universe* that was *so* close to both of them. They just couldn't, or wouldn't, see it themselves.

I know this is the biggest challenge in my life so far, and I have to fly outside the box again, and put myself at the mercy of the universe. Who knows what's going to happen, but I feel able to breathe once again. Who will read a book about my life if it's not a rollercoaster ride? Would you? Do you think I'm mad? Look at me, who am I talking to? My readers? Oh… do I have readers? Mmmm, maybe one day! I've just got to jump; there's nothing else for it. Buddha tells us to embrace the here and now, after all.

Actually, I'm really excited by the adventure ahead, but also shit scared, although I feel better for writing it all down. The power of writing is incredible. I seem to work through most of my issues this way now. This book is by no means complete, but then the future hasn't been written yet; or has it? I know I have a long journey ahead of me, but that road will never end. But the *Yellow Brick Road* has to start somewhere, and it couldn't be any clearer where it begins. Glinda is right next to me, as are the Munchkins! So bring it on!

1st June 2010

Today was supposed to be our leaving date, but plans are made to be changed according to the flow of the universe, and of course incompetents like BT messing up. At least with the internet up and running again, we were able to sort out the paperwork for Neneh's home schooling. We've got to take her out of school before the end of term. All being well, she will attend the local Portuguese school after the summer holidays, with Sienna's English neighbour's kids. I've still got to change our names by deed poll and apply for passports in our new name so that we will all officially be the Rose-Hattricks.

Pea, Lance and Treacle moved in on Friday. It was a bit like *The Great Escape*, the escapee being the cat, who was clearly not happy with events. I was scratched many times until I could calm him, while Pea looked on in hysterics. They told us that they had been the ones looking after Treacle for the past year, ever since Matt, his official owner, had moved up from the south with him. Pea felt that she and Lance could look after him better than Matt could, and so made the decision to steal him. There was not much we could say, as it was ultimately their decision, and they had taken over the tenancy agreement. But I didn't want him to come, for Oscar's sake, and I certainly didn't think it was fair on Matt.

A news report has just alerted me to the anniversary of the 'Battle of the Beanfield', which I had learned about after listening to the song of the same name by the Levellers. It's more poignant now, as we will also be travellers, living in a van. How will people treat us?

On 1st June 1985, approximately 140 caravans, vans and ambulances etc belonging to a convoy of 'new age travellers' (so essentially people's homes) were destroyed by the police. They were on their way to a free festival near Stonehenge, but were stopped by police roadblocks and forced into a bean field. What took place next has mainly been forgotten, or was not brought to the public's attention at the time. You can see the extent of the police brutality for yourself on YouTube, as an ITN journalist who braved the 'battlefield' reported that the police were just wildly hitting everyone, including women with their babies, and smashing their vehicles.

The footage was never used by ITN and a much more biased report, in favour of the police, was broadcast instead.

Over 400 people were arrested that day and almost all charges were eventually dropped. There was never an inquiry, and although some of the travellers did take the authorities to court and won, this only covered the court costs. It didn't cover their homes and livelihoods, which had been destroyed on that fateful day. These travellers were simply being harassed by the authorities for being free and not conforming to the usual way of living in this society.

8th June 2010

Jamal and Graham came round to help Tony start kitting out the van. We'd bought insulation and new wood for the walls, so it was time to start the reconstruction of an ex-tyre van into our new home. I took Oscar for his final injection and burst into tears when I changed his owner's name to Pea's. I then spent the next few hours sorting out the deed poll certificates.

Changing your name is easier than you think, and only costs £20. What they send you is an interesting legal document, which asks you to 'renounce, relinquish and abandon' your former name. Fair enough, but the deed also declares:

> In witness whereof I have hereunto subscribed my former and adopted names of Kay Elizabeth Leen and Kay Elizabeth Rose-Hattrick and simultaneously in witness whereof I have hereunto set my hand the day and year first hereinbefore written.

What? You need legal training to understand exactly. The rest of us simple folk remain ignorant, relying on the lawyers to translate the legalese; a language only they understand, at great expense to the masses. Thankfully, I only had to pay administrative charges for both my divorces, as on both occasions, Luke had translated the forms for me and had told me what to write. This saved me the solicitor's usually extortionate fees.

Oh God, please let this stop and let me climb into a hole before my head explodes! If I listen to another explanation about fixtures, fittings, inverters, insulation or toilets, I will have to smother them. It's not that I don't care about Leeloo, our new home. But I have never been able to get my head round physics and power voltage and how much energy is needed to charge certain electrical items. It baffles me. I need to see it in action before I understand what they mean.

Graham says that I can take a couple of lamps and the printer. I have no idea where these things are going to go, though. No longer do I see our mobile home as the inside of the Tardis, or an articulated lorry with room for a chandelier, sofa, chairs and a dining table. It's so small that I can't imagine having everything I need in such a minute space. Well, they seem convinced. So I guess I'll just have to have faith!

Tony's just taken Graham home and it's so quiet; no talk about vans and travel and moving and reminders that, in under two weeks' time, my home will be on the road.

Ahhhrrrggghhhrrr... there it goes... my head's just exploded!

9th June 2010

I threw up three times today, and just wanted to crawl back under the duvet. I was unsure whether the weather (rain all day) had an effect on my mood, or whether it merely reflected it. Both, I'd say. Everyone I had spoken to had felt the effects of days of rain, after beautiful sunshine. England is such a beautiful, lush country but it needs a lot of rain to create such a green and pleasant land. I think most people suffer from Seasonal Adjustment

Disorder (SAD); the weather has a profound effect on my mood for sure, especially when I'm stressed to hell already!

Lance, but mainly Pea, have made it quite clear that this is their home now, and when Tony answered the phone yesterday with, "Welcome to the madhouse!", Pea made it clear: "It's our house, now." I am still paying for the utilities until we leave, and they have our bond. She's really pissed off with me at the moment, as Treacle's gone missing. I let him out, thinking he was Oscar, and it wasn't. Well, they're both black cats, and I was knackered. He's done a runner now and I feel bad. But it's happened, so we can only hope he'll either go back to Vincent Road, or come back here in his own time.

I know they want us out and it was very unsettling when Pea bought some brown paint and started painting over my lovely green walls. They've already redecorated the bathroom. Can't she wait a couple of weeks until we go? I just don't think she realises how difficult this is for us all. I know it's their house now, but a bit of empathy would have been good. But what can I say; we've made the decision to leave.

They are welcome to keep some of my furniture and pictures etc, but I hope I've made it clear that I want them back when we're settled. This includes Sienna and Kratos's dining table and chairs. As they walked round the house, choosing what they wanted to keep, it reminded me of Mick's visit years earlier, only without the humour. She's moved straight into my fully kitted kitchen, which has taken me years to build, as I can only fit a limited amount into Leeloo. I've said the rest is hers, including all of my crockery, pans and kitchen utensils. I'm finding it really difficult letting go of my possessions, but at least I'm fulfilling one part of the Buddhist teachings by giving up my 'attachments'. The rest of my really precious belongings, including most of the pictures Pea and Lance didn't want, are going to be stored in Kerry's attic room.

Today I went to see Emma, my good friend from work, and her gorgeous little girl, Imogen. Emma was pregnant at the same time as me, and it's taken me a while to meet her daughter. I have found it very difficult to be around babies, including my own niece, who are similar in age to the age Elliott would have been. Despite my fears, it was great to see them both, and what a bundle of joy Imogen is. Emma is a fabulous mother, showing the maternal side to her nature that lay dormant until the birth of her first child.

10th June 2010

Tony went to see the inspector today, as a result of his complaint. It was the second time he'd been to see him. Last time, he wanted to hear Tony's side of the story before he approached the police officers in question. They'd obviously got slapped wrists as a result of the complaint. In their defence, they had said that Tony was strong, and that trying to restrain him had been difficult.

My husband is a teacher of the ancient Russian martial art of Systema, which was developed by Russian warriors in the tenth century and then more recently by the Spetsnaz, the Russian special forces. He used energy work and small movements, not brute strength, to slip out of attempts to restrain him, while repeatedly demanding, "Why are you arresting me? I've done nothing wrong!" He was resisting an unlawful arrest as "being an arsehole" wouldn't have stood up in court, surely? Does a man trained in such a discipline just succumb to the demands of these men for no legitimate reason? They also hadn't bet on Tony making a written complaint, probably arrogantly thinking he couldn't even write!

The inspector told Tony he would no longer be liable for the fine. The only problem was that he had already paid the penalty notice for the drunk and disorderly charge. We were leaving Sheffield and didn't want a court case hanging over us. Although the police officers were sorry, or rather, were made to say sorry, they still cost us £80 and once again reinforced my NON-belief in the South Yorkshire police force.

15th June 2010

The pressure is really on us to leave, but we had a phone call from Kratos that caused us some concern. When I answered, he asked to speak to Tony directly, and for the next 20 minutes, there was only one side to the conversation. By the time Tony came off the phone, he was quite white and said that they didn't want us there now until at least August. I never got to speak to Sienna about why this was, but we have no alternative but to continue with our plans to move.

Neneh's friend came round after school and we were talking about move plans. Neneh made a comment about staying in Sheffield and not wanting to leave her buddy. I said, "How can I write a bestseller by sitting on my backside in Woodseats?" They both responded, "We'd buy it!"

18th June 2010

Today is just frantic, as you can imagine, as it's finally arrived: our leaving day. I've just got a moment to myself in between running around in a mad panic, making sure that everything's done in time for our official departure to Edale later on. It's Mum's birthday today, but I'm afraid I won't be able to wish her happy birthday face to face. There are still passport forms to take to the post office and the van's not even finished yet, so I can't start to pack. We've ended up throwing all our stuff into our old bedroom, to process over the next few weeks, as Pea and Lance say we can come back. Funnily enough, the only thing left under the bed, when we did a check, was a copy of *The Fifth Element*!

They just want to get rid of us now and I'm so desperate to go. It's become all the more difficult, watching our former home become someone else's, in front of our very eyes. It's difficult enough moving a three bedroomed house into a van, as it clearly doesn't fit. We've only had two weeks, because of the pressure to leave this house, to convert an old tyre van into a liveable space and find storage space for tools, books, clothes and other things that we would need to live. Needless to say, it's been incredibly stressful and I'm still throwing up every morning through anxiety; my mind threatening to explode at any time. Tony and I are constantly battling and snapping at each other, but understandably so, due to the pressure we are under.

We are now officially living on the road, with just a van to call our home, for the next month, until we arrive at our base in Portugal. It's an uncertain future that lies ahead but also exciting, as I'm keen to be on the road again and free of this system. We have no choice but to go to our special spot in Edale for the next few weeks. There at least, we know we'll be able to take a deep breath and process all the junk we have both insisted on keeping, but which ultimately no longer serves us. Neneh will be visiting her mother during this time to say her farewells, as it could be a while before they see each other again.

I've got to go now and check whether Tony's finished. Whether I can start packing, as we've only got a few more hours until we leave, and I've still got to drop the passports off. I'm hoping Neneh is packing as we speak. I'd better go and check and so will sign off here.

Well? Wish me luck!

The 'Big up' List

This is dedicated to the following people, as without their help and support, this book would have never got to this stage:

Tony Rose-Hattrick (for his passion, support and love, and who always believed in my abilities)

Freya Gabriella Rose-Hattrick (for being gorgeous and being the true catalyst for becoming me)

Eliza Bouttell (for babysitting, being the first person to read this book and also being a second edit reader)

Claire Birch (reader: first and second edit, and for our much-needed rendezvous at the Broady)

Lisa Hattersley (cover shots): http://hattersleyportraits.prosite.com

Paul Jackson (designer/critic/friend): www.othila.com

Amy Benson (website)

James and Nicola Davies (promotions and video): www.avaproductions.co.uk

Sam, Hannah & Jill (readers for some chapters in first edit)

Graham (for printing second draft)

Alex 3 (for printer cartridges and paper)

Tracey, Sarah, Alison, Tamara, Tom, Emma, Steve, Jamal and Raphey (second edit readers)

Jodie Podie (marketing)

Julia Muir (marketing)

Steve Allen (T-shirt design, music and promotions)

Dr Robeatnik ('No Escape')

Michael Lightweaver (*The Galactic Fairytale*): www.mtnlightsanctuary.com

Brian Parkinson (useful links to self-publishing)

Bernadette and Musonda (for providing weekly spiritual support and chocolate biscuits)

All the ladies at nursery (for their support and understanding through a difficult time, and for lots of shoulders to cry on)

All those at my school reunion (for their belief in me, especially Karen Brownson!)

All my friends and family (for their continued and enthusiastic support)

Anyone who wants to get involved in the cause

and finally

Gordon Hattersley (who said he didn't want to be on my BIG UP list, but who is on it anyway, as he did support this project, albeit grudgingly!) May he now rest in peace.

BOOK 2

THE DIARY OF A NOEBODY

19th June 2010 – 19th June 2011

In *Becoming Free*, the fairytale continues as we are invited to follow Kay's adventures across Europe and feel the emotion in real time, just as she experiences it, as we read her diary. We meet the characters she encounters along the way, all leading an alternative lifestyle, outside the normal social order. And for a while, she too is part of this. But what brought her back to the UK so soon, to re-enter the society she had fled only six months earlier, and from which she had been so desperate to escape?

A week before Christmas, she finds herself back, in sub-zero temperatures, to a homecoming not fit for a fairytale. Back in the rat race she had left behind, stripped of all material possessions and with no home or job to fall back on. But with the compassion of friends and the kindness of strangers, she started to rebuild her life. Then God dealt her a blow that would change her life forever. And out of the fear came hope. The fairytale had to end happily ever after, now!

For more information visit **www.becomingme.co.uk**.

Lightning Source UK Ltd.
Milton Keynes UK
UKOW04f1457230914

239028UK00007B/371/P